VICTIMS OR VILLAINS?
SOCIAL SECURITY BENEFITS
IN UNEMPLOYMENT

JOAN C. BROWN

Joseph Rowntree Memorial Trust

This JRMT publication is distributed by the Policy Studies Institute, 100 Park Village East, London NW1 3SR (01-387 2171).

Booktrade Sales Representation: Pinter Publishers Ltd.

Bookshop orders to: Marston Book Services Ltd, PO Box 87, Oxford, OX4 1LB.

Direct mail and individual order from: PSI Booksales, 100 Park Village East, London, NW1 3SR

Published by
The Joseph Rowntree Memorial Trust,
Beverley House
Shipton Road
York YO3 6SQ

Tel: (0904) 629241

ISBN 1 872470 00 9

Laserset by Policy Studies Institute

Printed in Great Britain by BPCC Wheaton's Ltd, Exeter

Contents

List of tables

Introduction

This study is concerned with benefits during unemployment. At first sight the provision made is common to all unemployed people. In fact, there have always been differences made between those with social insurance rights and those without. Different rules have applied to young people and to women. Moreover, the impact of the benefit system is different, not only in relation to short term and long term unemployment, but for particular groups, notably the older unemployed and disabled people. And there are further complications. Unemployment benefits are part of the social security system and must relate to the rules and norms of that system. But they must also relate to the wages paid in the labour market and to the requirements of the employment services.

Throughout the century there has been a tension between policies which see unemployed people principally as victims of economic forces beyond their control and those which see them as villains, ready to live in idleness on the benefits provided by the State. As victims, they need policies which offer adequate support for themselves and their families, so as to protect them, to a greater or lesser extent, from the consequences of unemployment. For villains, and those who might develop such tendencies if no pressure was applied, the benefit levels and the operating rules must be designed in ways which deter voluntary unemployment, induce active job search and root out fraud.

The study explores the way these questions have been dealt with during this century. It looks at the issues which should have been discussed in the 1984/85 Social Security Review, and the failure of that review to tackle them. It examines the spate of new legislation and practice introduced since the review and the current state of policy.

In the final chapter it questions the suitability of that policy for the labour market of the future and makes proposals for change.

This study was originally researched and written in 1986, while I was employed as a Senior Research Fellow at the Policy Studies Institute. During 1989, it was revised and additional research was undertaken in order to update it. Indeed, so much had occurred in the policy field since 1986 that it became necessary to rewrite the last two chapters completely.

Both the original work and the revision and updating was made possible through the financial assistance of the Joseph Rowntree Memorial Trust, and this support has been deeply appreciated. Thanks must also go to the many organisations which responded to my request for material, especially at the time of the Social Security Review. My gratitude also goes to the staff of the library of the Policy Studies Institute, who gave invaluable help at both stages of this study.

1 Victims or villains?
Establishing the ground rules

Official policy on the unemployed in the nineteenth century was harsh. Individuals and families were responsible for their own support and if they had no income, they must work. This duty to work to support oneself or one's family extended, not only to single women and able bodied men, but to children of quite tender years, to married women where necessary, to widows with and without children, to other lone mothers with children, to disabled people who were not totally incapacitated and to the elderly still capable of work. If they were unemployed and destitute, they might turn to the Poor Law, but they should not expect sympathetic treatment. It would be assumed that work was available to those willing to work, and that to offer any degree of comfort to those not working would be to encourage idleness.

The Poor Law, as a policy, aimed to be disliked by the unemployed, and to offer a standard of living lower than could be achieved in the least well paid employment. The principle of less eligibility was laid down in 1834 by the Poor Law Commissioners who said:

> The first and most essential of all conditions is that the situation of the individual relieved should not be made really or apparently so eligible as the situation of the independent labourer of the lowest class.

For the unemployed, this principle was implemented through insistence that relief be given only in the workhouse, or through the application of a work test – commonly stone breaking or other heavy labour – before relief was given outside the workhouse, and through low rates of payment whether in cash or kind. The object was to deter dependence on the Poor Law.

Because the Poor Law was administered locally, this stark policy was not uniformly applied. Moreover, there was some recognition (both nationally and locally) that not all the unemployed were out of work through their own fault. Nor were they all naturally idle. However, such recognition would still be tinged with caution. In 1837, for example the Poor Law Commissioners acknowledged that a period of distress, due to bad trade conditions, had left large numbers out of work through no fault of their own. But, they urged adherence to the rules, saying:

> The distress which actually ensues is always accompanied by a demonstration of a large amount of fictitious distress, and the idle and the fraudulent are forward to avail themselves of the sympathy which is then called forth. It is, therefore, of the highest importance that the operative classes should be taught lessons of frugality and forethought at those times when they are able to earn more than is actually necessary for their immediate support, and that they should then save up the surplus to meet emergencies like the present.[1]

The Local Government Board (the successor to the Poor Law Commissioners) showed a similar caution in 1886. Noting the 'exceptional distress amongst the working classes' which extended to 'large numbers of persons usually in regular employment', it commented:

> The spirit of independence which leads so many of the working classes to make great personal sacrifices rather than incur the stigma of pauperism, is one which deserves the greatest sympathy and respect, and which it is the duty and interest of the community to maintain by all the means at its disposal... It is not desirable that the working classes should be familiarised with poor law relief, and if once the honourable sentiment that now leads them to avoid it is broken down, it is probable that recourse will be had to this provision on the slightest occasion.[2]

The later nineteenth and early twentieth centuries saw a gradual narrowing of the categories of people expected to work for their own support. Labour legislation, over time, made the employment of young children illegal, while educational provision drew more and more children into the schools. Education was made compulsory to the age of 12 years in 1880 and to 14 years in 1921. Old Age Pensions were first introduced in 1908 for those 70 years and over and from 1925 for those 65 years and over, though not all the elderly qualified for such pensions. Widows had to wait until 1925 before they received a pension, but the duty to work, where they had dependent children, was not usually enforced after 1914 and, after 1925, the pension was payable without the necessity of proving inability to work. Other lone parents (separated wives for example) remained subject to the Poor Law but commonly were not required to work while the children were under school leaving age.

The situation of the disabled remained uncertain. The introduction of National Health Insurance in 1911 meant that, provided they had paid the requisite contributions, those wholly incapacitated for work would receive an allowance, which might in turn be supplemented by the Poor Law. The same would apply to those receiving Workmen's Compensation (introduced in 1897 and extended in 1906), where they were wholly unable to work. The partially disabled, however, continued to be classified and treated as unemployed if they could not find work.

The introduction of Unemployment Insurance

Accounts of the period given by historians of social security attribute both the shift away from the Poor Law, as it related to the aged, the sick and disabled and widows, and the accompanying modification of attitudes to the unemployed, to many factors. The reports on poverty by Booth and Rowntree in the late nineteenth and early twentieth centuries, the development of socialist theories, the growth of working class movements and the development of new economic theory are typically listed.[3] The last, which included studies of the cyclical nature of trade crises and consequent unemployment, was important in challenging the view that unemployment was the outcome of personal weakness or of deliberate idleness.

These new theories of unemployment, in which the normally hardworking poor were seen as victims of economic forces rather than as loafers and spongers on Poor Law relief, opened the way for a change in official policies. However, while it is reasonable to assume that the influences outlined above led to the decision to try out a modest scheme of Unemployment Insurance for the victims of trade depressions, it was the old view of the unemployed as potential 'villains' which substantially shaped the scheme. Moreover, experimental as the scheme legislated in 1911 was, it proved to be long lasting both in its general approach and in the rules under which it operated. It is, thus, important to the understanding of all subsequent schemes. The discussion which follows will be concerned only with the structure of provision for the unemployed in general. Later chapters will consider the position of specific groups such as married women, young people and others.

The political and civil service planners of Unemployment Insurance could not draw on much in the way of experience in other such schemes. While there had been social insurance schemes to deal with sickness and disability in other countries, most notably in Germany since the 1880s, there had been no national schemes for the unemployed and the few local schemes had had rather unhappy experiences.[4] Trade Unions in the UK did operate successful benefit schemes, but mainly for skilled workers in fairly stable employment.[5] The decision taken, therefore, was to introduce a limited scheme of compulsory insurance in a selected group of trades. These were trades such as shipbuilding, engineering and construction, which normally offered good employment, but in which the employees were subject to temporary and fairly predictable periods of unemployment. Declining trades where long term unemployment might occur were excluded, as were industries where casual work was the norm. The industries to be covered were ones in which male workers predominated.

The number of workers to be covered was around 2.25 million manual workers – a small proportion of the labour force which was then around 18 million.[6] According to the later (1927) Blanesburgh Report on Unemployment Insurance, the principle which underlay the scheme 'was that the insured trades should help to maintain, through times of depression and under-employment, the reserves of labour which they required in seasons of good employment'.[7] The scheme was financed through weekly contributions from employee and employer, with a subvention from the State.

It was natural in an experimental scheme to seek to build in safeguards to ensure its financial viability. The benefit period offered was short – a maximum of 15 weeks in an 'insurance year' (i.e. July to July). This was expected to be sufficient for the type of trades covered and during the period in which the 1911 scheme was in operation, proved to be so.[8] Benefit was earned through contributions. A minimum of 26 weeks contributions had to be paid in order to qualify and no worker could claim more than 1 week of benefit for each 5 weeks of contributions. In addition, no cover was given for the first week of unemployment (the waiting days). Thus, both proof of regularity of employment and self help (though contributions and self support for the first week) were built in. A further safeguard was the requirement to register for work at the newly established Labour Exchanges (introduced by an Act of 1909), to show availability for and willingness to work.

At the time the National Insurance Bill was being prepared, there was considerable argument on whether these provisions were sufficient. One point on which the politicians and civil servants involved were agreed and that was that the benefit should be set low, so as to 'imply a sensible and even severe difference between being in work or out of work'.[9] This was presented as a means of maintaining the incentive to work, but it also reflected the 'less eligibility' tradition which was still operating (under that name) in the Poor Law. There was some discussion of wage related benefits – which to an extent were available under Workmen's Compensation – but this idea was not pursued.[10] It was argued that the better paid worker – who would suffer a severe drop in income – would have savings to draw on, or might be covered by Trade Union benefits.

Winston Churchill, who as President of the Board of Trade was the Minister involved, considered this package sufficient to ensure a viable scheme. The principal civil servant, Llewellyn Smith, wanted more. He argued that the scheme must be protected against the wastrel. Workers who lost their jobs through their own misconduct – laziness, drunkenness or carelessness – should be ineligible for benefit. An insurance scheme which aimed to cover cyclical unemployment should not also cover unemployment due to the personal defects of the individual. Churchill, on the other hand, argued that if a worker had paid his contributions, he should receive benefit regardless of the cause of his dismissal. He said, 'I do not like mixing up moralities and mathematics'.[11] The fund should be protected by insurance rules, not the personal judgements of administrators. He pointed out that:

> A disposition to over-indulge in alcohol, a hot temper, a bad manner, a capricious employer, a financially unsound employer, a new process of manufacture, a contraction in trade, are all alike factors in the risk. Our concern is with the evil, not with the causes, with the fact of unemployment, not with the character of the unemployed. In my judgement, if a man has paid to the fund

> for six months he should have his benefit in all circumstances, including dismissal for personal fault even of the gravest character.[12]

The limited period of benefit, Churchill thought, its low rate and the requirement for prior contributions ought to be safeguard enough. What the benefit would do was to mitigate the often disproportionate penalty for personal failings, not remove it altogether. What finally emerged in the Bill was a compromise. Benefit would be withheld from those who lost their employment through 'misconduct' or left to 'without just cause', but only for six weeks. The key safeguards – the penalty for unsatisfactory behaviour and the low level of benefit – represented the view of the unemployed held by the Poor Law, i.e. that given an inch, the worker would take a mile. No doubt there were idle poor – just as there were idle rich – but the penalty clause for 'misconduct' or leaving 'without good cause' was open to administrative interpretation based on employer's reports, and was likely to catch many more than the true idler. The decision to set a low rate of benefit, moreover, would affect 'good' and 'bad' alike. It assumed that the average worker needed the sting of poverty to induce him to work, and that even the normally industrious could not be trusted to seek to return to work as quickly as possible.

It was, perhaps, a little ironic that the Board of Trade who held this view, was at the same time piloting through a Bill to protect workers in the sweated trades which, according to a House of Lords enquiry (in 1890), were characterised by:

> ... a rate of wages inadequate to the necessities of the workers or disproportionate to the work done; excessive hours of labour; the insanitary state of the houses in which it is carried on. These evils can hardly be exaggerated. The earnings of the lowest classes of workers are barely sufficient to sustain existence. The hours of labour are such as to make the lives of the workers periods of almost ceaseless toil, hard and often unhealthy.[13]

It was not the picture of a naturally idle labour force.

The level of the benefit did not prove a serious problem to unemployed people while the 1911 scheme was in operation. Employment opportunities for those in the covered trades were good, and the coming of war in 1914 enhanced them still further. Those who benefited from the scheme (which from 1916 included workers in war industries) were usually able to avoid the necessity of applying to the

Poor Law,[14] which continued to maintain the rest of the unemployed on the old principles.

Unemployment provisions in the 1920s

The low rate of unemployment in the insured trades from 1911 to 1920, the provision for one week of waiting days, the short benefit period and the low benefit paid, all combined to ensure a handsome surplus in the insurance fund and to induce a confidence in unemployment insurance as a method of provision.   Problems in the immediate post-war period, concerning the resettlement of the armed forces into civilian employment and the industrial readjustment for civilian workers, due to the winding down of war-related industries, were dealt with outside the 1911 scheme.   Provision was made in the shape of non-contributory 'out of work donations' leaving the insurance fund still in surplus and, thus, a financial 'success'.   These were, however, temporary arrangements and, conscious of the political difficulty of restricting unemployment insurance to a minority of the labour force after so many others had received aid during the post-war period, the government in 1920 extended the insurance scheme.   It was now to cover all manual workers (excluding agricultural and domestic workers) and non-manual workers earning less than £250 p.a.

The new Act was to face far different conditions from its predecessor.   There followed a period of high unemployment and, what was more important, of much lengthier periods out of work for many.   From 1920 to 1935, successive governments engaged in a series of expedients to avoid throwing large numbers of unemployed on the Poor Law.   The details need not be elaborated here[15], but the issues discussed in this period by two inquiries are of interest.

The first of these was the Unemployment Insurance Committee which reported in 1927 (The Blanesburgh Report).   The sharp increase in unemployment since 1920 had been accompanied by many accusations of fraudulent claims.   The Committee first found it necessary to consider how far these were true.   If a system of unemployment insurance was open to widespread abuse, it might be necessary to recommend discontinuing it altogether or, at the least, to impose additional rules to control abuse.   Having examined the evidence, the Committee concluded that even given the many recent difficulties, the insurance scheme, as administered by the Ministry of Labour, was able 'while dealing fairly with the genuine claimant'[16] to guard against abuse. Indeed, it found that the level of abuse recorded was 'almost negligible'[17]. The evidence of the Secretary of the influential Charity Organisation Society added further interest. He said he had believed that abuses were serious, but on enquiry was unable to find them. He said of his evidence:

> When this material was read to our people... they were much disappointed at the general character of almost all of it. They had hoped that many more examples would be forthcoming illustrating the criticisms passed upon the present working of the unemployment insurance by almost everybody who discusses the subject. This shows the value of bringing these criticisms to the test of demanding examples, and more than one of our secretaries said they quite expected to find from our case papers numerous samples of abuses, but when they came to look they found very few. This does not of course prove that their previous impression was not a sound one, on the other hand, it may quite well prove that unfavourable instances impress themselves upon the memory, while the proper and smooth working of a scheme passes almost unnoticed[18].

It was a pointed commentary on the value of anecdotal evidence about social security abuse. The Committee thought it had 'great force'.

Having established to its satisfaction that unemployment insurance was workable, and that, indeed, it must 'now be regarded as a permanent feature of our code of social legislation'[19], the Committee went on to discuss the role the scheme should play.

The 1920 Act, like its predecessor, offered only 15 weeks benefit and aimed only to tide over the worker for what was expected to be a brief period out of work, preceded and followed by regular employment. All other needs would be met by the Poor Law. The huge increase in unemployment which followed, and which overwhelmed the resources of locally financed Poor Law, created the need for a more substantial role for national provision. The Blanesburgh Committee, therefore, sought to identify the proper boundaries of an insurance scheme. It began by saying:

> And first, it must be clearly understood that the purpose of any unemployment insurance scheme is to provide an insurance against unemployment on certain conditions, that is to say, with certain limitations. It is not a scheme automatically to give assistance to every insured person who is out of work. It does not provide an out of work donation. The distinction is vital. It flows from it that a beneficiary under an insurance scheme must be

willing and still able to work, that he must still remain in the field of employment; that he must, in a real sense, be genuinely unemployed only from circumstances and in no way by choice. No other person can properly be a beneficiary under an insurance scheme. A scheme to provide benefit in the event of unemployment would impose no such conditions[20].

Having excluded those not still in the field of employment, the question then was how far unemployment insurance could cover all those defined as genuinely unemployed. One school of thought argued that the scheme should be run on strict actuarial lines with benefits directly related to individual contributions. All other unemployed people should fall outside the insurance scheme and be the responsibility of the community at large. The other school held that provision in the insurance scheme should be made for all genuinely unemployed people and no matter how long they were unemployed.

The Blanesburgh Committee chose a path between these two extremes. Practice since 1920 had given contributors the expectation of more favourable treatment that would be available under strict actuarial principles, but a contributory insurance scheme which covered long term unemployment would impose a severe burden on workers and on industry.

The Committee proposed that benefit should be available for 26 weeks to anyone who had paid 30 contributions in the previous two years. The Committee assumed that it would normally be possible to find at least 15 weeks work in any one year and that this evidence of labour market attachment should be enough to give entitlement to benefit without means test. On the basis of estimates of future unemployment supplied to the Committee, it took the view that its proposals would cover all or at least the great bulk of unemployed people, for as long as they needed benefit. The minority not covered would be subject to Poor Law provisions in the normal way[21].

Unfortunately the unemployment estimates proved to be awry. The government was forced once more into temporary measures, and, in doing so, strengthened the national role in supporting the unemployed. In particular, it extended the benefit period for those who had qualified for Unemployment Insurance, through nationally financed subventions to the local Poor Law Authorities - called Public Assistance after 1929. These paid what was called 'transitional benefit' to those who had run out of insurance rights.

In 1930, a Royal Commission on Unemployment Insurance was established and it once more addressed the issue of the appropriate role of an insurance scheme. Like the Blanesburgh Committee, the Royal Commission affirmed the usefulness of a scheme of insurance for unemployment. It defined such a scheme as one in which the major cost was borne by the potential beneficiaries and their employees and in which the fund provided by their contributions, with a subvention from the State, would operate in balance taking one year with another[22].

The insurance scheme, as originally conceived in 1911, was intended to be 'no more than a partial expression of the collective responsibility of the community for relieving want arising from unemployment'[23]. Unemployment Insurance was to be seen as a 'first line of defence' against unemployment, but, financed as it was by mutual insurance (employers and employees) within industry, it could not be expected to deal with all types of unemployment or to provide benefit of indefinite duration. If, in order to do this, the State subvention became, not the minor, but the major proportion of the funding, then the scheme would lose its character of mutual insurance. It would become 'simply an agency for the distribution of State money to particular categories of unemployed workers'[24]. Therefore, if it was desired to maintain an insurance scheme, and one which was financially viable, limits would have to be placed on its operation.

The insurance scheme, then, would meet the needs of workers who were unemployed for periods of limited duration. These were expected to be the majority of all those who became unemployed. However, it would not be reasonable to expect the remainder to be dependent on Public Assistance, which was still regarded by working people with considerable distaste. Some alternative means 'suited to modern needs and acceptable to the public conscience'[25], must be found. During a depression and when major industrial reconstruction was taking place, workers who had a history of regular work were displaced. Those who, as a result, were unemployed for a long period might be no less anxious to work than those whose unemployment was of short duration. A specific scheme for assisting the longer term unemployed was therefore necessary, financed and supervised by national government, but administered locally. Because indefinite benefits paid regardless of need would be very costly, it would be necessary to relate benefits to needs, i.e. they would have to be means tested. Those who could support themselves would be left to do so.

The Royal Commission was not, however, at one on this subject. A Minority Report took a different view. It questioned the whole concept of an insurance scheme, theoretically based on actuarial principles, when the risk being 'insured' i.e. unemployment, was so unpredictable. One way or another, the State had to provide for the unemployed worker, whether by a smaller or larger subvention to the insurance scheme, or through additional expenditure outside the scheme. The State, in effect was called upon to decide 'how many of the unemployed it is to maintain within the Scheme and how many outside it'[26].

The Minority Report also questioned the simple division of the unemployed into two classes - the short term unemployed drawing benefit at a flat rate, as of right, and the long term unemployed compelled to seek relief on the basis of need[27]. Unemployment, especially in a period of depression was more complex than this. Large numbers of the unemployed fell between the two classifications. Their unemployment was intermittent and, as a result, at times they had insurance rights and at other times they did not, so that they moved between employment and unemployment and between insurance and relief payments. Nor could they be easily divided up by the 'type' of unemployment. The report added:

> We cannot distinguish between normal unemployment and the abnormal unemployment of today, because, in normal times, sudden changes in industry may cause abnormal unemployment on the part of a certain section of the workers. All that can be said is that it is important to frame a scheme which will meet both the needs of more favourable times when unemployment is low and the needs of abnormal periods like the present[28].

Moreover, the argument (which formed part of the Majority case), that the payment of an indefinite benefit by right would demoralise the worker and tempt him to depend on benefit rather than to work was unacceptable to the Minority group. What was operating here was 'a return to the out worn principle of deterrence'[29]. It was being assumed that virtues of self help, thrift and forethought would be stimulated in the unemployed worker if he knew that his right to benefit was limited. At the same time, those dependent on relief were to be deliberately placed in a less advantageous position. 'Their status is to be lowered. They are to be made to feel that they no longer have any rights, and that if they need assistance they will be a charge on the community'[30].

The Minority Report proposed that the State should take over responsibility for the payment of unemployment benefit, covering all forms of employment and paying benefit, without limit in its duration, to the genuinely unemployed.   Contributions would continue to provide part of the finance, but would not determine the length of benefit payments: 'If an unemployed worker had once established his place within the Scheme, and if he continued to fulfil the conditions laid down, there should be no arbitrary conclusion to his receipt benefit' conclusion to his receipt of benefit'[31]. The conditions would include willingness to work and availability for work, the undertaking of re-training where appropriate, and the readiness to move to another area for work if necessary.

The details of the proposed Minority scheme, spelt out in the report, need not be elaborated.   It was not adopted.   It was the Majority view which prevailed.

Three categories of unemployed

The legislation which followed in due course, divided the unemployed not into two, but three categories; those who had paid the requisite contributions and were entitled to Unemployment Insurance; those who were capable of and available for work but had run out of insurance entitlement or had been unable to acquire rights; and those who were considered to be, for all practical purposes, no longer in the labour market.   The 1934 Unemployment Act established the Unemployment Insurance Statutory Committee (UISC) which was to advise on the running of the insurance scheme and the Unemployment Assistance Board (UAB) to deal with those who had no insurance rights, but were still regarded as being within the labour market. The residue of the unemployed fell to the Public Assistance authorities.

Unemployment Insurance

When Unemployment Insurance was established in 1911, it was not thought necessary to build up a large fund against future claims, of the type then established for National Health Insurance.   Instead Unemployment Insurance would operate, more or less, on a pay as you go basis. Since it was then believed that levels of unemployment could be predicted, planning could be based on the level of contributions required from those in work which could meet the current benefits for those out of work, and leave enough in reserve to cover short term fluctuations in unemployment levels. Should there be a temporary inability to meet claims, the Fund could ask the Treasury to advance money as a loan, to be repaid out of later contributions once the short term problem was over. Should the Fund remain in deficit, then either benefits would have to be lowered or contributions raised[32].

The new plan, operating from 1935, was based on the same principles, though with some practical differences. The accumulated debt to the Treasury, which by 1934 had reached more than £105 million, was separated off. This was to be repaid, with interest, from the Unemployment Fund, at a rate of £5 million per year, so that the debt would be cleared by 1971. If there was a surplus in the fund in any year, more could be paid off the debt but there was no requirement to do so. For current commitments, in the words of Sir William Beveridge the chairman of the Unemployment Insurance Statutory Committee (UISC), unemployment insurance was to be 'financially self-contained and self-adjusting'[33]. New borrowing from the Treasury was to be repayable within two years. Summing up the position, Beveridge said in a report on the scheme, 'Under the Act of 1934 the insurance scheme is thrown entirely on its own resources; must pay off the old debt and must pay its way in future'[34].

The effect of this was that those currently in employment, and their employers, with a proportional State subvention, were not only paying for the current unemployed, but were paying off debts in relation to past unemployed people, dating back to 1920. That the Fund was successful in achieving financial viability was due to three factors. Credit must be given for good management by the UISC. A second factor was the fall in unemployment. In early 1933, just under 3 million were registered as unemployed in the UK, and there were still 2.4 million when the UISC began to operate. Thereafter the numbers fell fairly steadily reaching 1.2 million in mid-1939[35]. However, almost as important was the fact that the insurance fund aimed only to cover around 48 per cent of the unemployed. On this basis, it decided in 1935, it could balance its books, taking the good years with the bad, and assuming an unemployment rate of 18.1 per cent[36]. When the unemployment rate went down, the UISC adjusted its calculations but maintained the goal of covering around half of the unemployed.

Under the UISC, benefit could be paid for 26 weeks provided that 30 contributions had been paid in the previous two years. A person who could show a good past employment record over the previous 5 years could, on the basis of his contributions, draw additional days benefit up to 30 weeks in all. Once the maximum benefit period had expired, benefits could only be re-earned by a period of employment. Otherwise it was necessary to apply for means tested assistance from the Unemployment Assistance Board.

The fall in unemployment after 1935 fairly rapidly produced a surplus in the insurance fund. This was used to speed up the repayment of the debt so that it was actually paid off by 1941. Other uses were to increase the rate of benefit, to improve dependency additions and to reduce the waiting days from 6 to 3 days. At the same time, agricultural labourers were, for the first time, brought into unemployment insurance though for a lower contribution and a lesser benefit. Some other marginal groups were also brought in. All of this improved the position of those who qualified for benefit. The only extension in the benefit period occurred in 1939 when all qualified claimants became eligible for a maximum of 30 weeks benefit. The long term unemployed remained outside the scheme.

By October 1942 (in the middle of the second world war), the fund showed a surplus of £145 million. Unemployment then stood at 122,000[37]. At the benefit rates in payment it would have been possible to consider a further extension to the benefit period. Instead it was decided to build up the fund against expected post-war disruption in the labour market.

Unemployment Assistance

The Unemployment Assistance Board (UAB) was established in 1935 as a national agency operating through local office. It took over the unemployed without insurance entitlement in two stages. In the first stage, those unemployed who were 18 years and over and on transitional benefit became the Board's responsibility. These had a fairly clear labour force attachment in that, relatively recently, they had been entitled to Unemployment Insurance on the basis of their contributions. In the second stage (from 1937) the net was widened to include the unemployed aged 16 to 64 years who had worked in employment covered by other contributory schemes (old age pensions, for example) and people who would have worked in such employment, were it not for the depression. The unemployed individual must also be capable of and available for work[38].

The eligibility requirements covered the major proportion of all the unemployed not receiving Unemployment Insurance. The scale of benefits paid, though lower in some respects than the insurance benefit, was higher in others in that the UAB gave additions for rent and for special needs and made higher allowances for children. There was, however, an important difference. Unemployment Insurance was paid at a flat rate by right of contributions. Unemployment Assistance was subject until 1941 to the Household Means Test and thereafter to a simplified test. The former took into account the income of other members of the household and of liable relatives. The effect was to exclude any household with means above the line laid down by the Board or to reduce the benefit paid.

Although the recipients of Unemployment Assistance might value the fact that they were no longer classified as paupers on Public Assistance, their relations with the UAB were frequently unhappy. They were spared the imposition of a 'genuinely seeking work rule' which had applied from 1921, and which had required them to satisfy a Local Employment Committee, under cross-questioning, of their eagerness in the search for work. This had been abandoned as unnecessary in 1930, and buried in what Beveridge called 'a dishonoured grave'[39]. But the operation of the Household Means Test was greatly disliked, even detested, especially for the way in which it placed an unemployed head of household in dependence on other members of the household. An increase in the wage of a 14 year old son or daughter, for example, would lead to a reduction in the father's benefit[40].

Public Assistance

When, in 1937, the UAB cast its net more widely some 140,000 of the unemployed were being supported by local Public Assistance[41]. The latter authorities were naturally eager to transfer as many as possible of these to the UAB, and from local to national expenditure. Some cases were quite straightforward, while others went to an appeal procedure to settle the matter. At the end of this process, some 44,000 persons, classified by Public Assistance as able bodied unemployed, were rejected by the UAB on the grounds that they were so unlikely to work again as to be effectively out of the labour market.

At the beginning of 1937, of the registered unemployed in Great Britain, 50 per cent were receiving Unemployment Insurance, 35 per cent Unemployment Assistance and 15 per cent either received no benefit or were supported by Public Assistance[42]. As the rate of unemployment fell, the numbers receiving benefit from all these

17

sources declined. Moreover, as more jobs became available, the length of time out of work tended to be shorter and more of the unemployed could qualify for insurance benefit. Thus by the end of 1938 (the last annual report of the UAB) some 60.4 per cent were supported by insurance, 32.2 per cent by Unemployment Assistance, and 7.4 per cent were on Public Assistance or without benefit[43]. Of the Unemployment Assistance group, 45 per cent had been out of work for 12 months or more and 16 per cent for a least 6 months but under 12 months[44]. The remainder included those without insurance rights even though they were short term unemployed. Thus the UAB became the principle safety net for the unemployed, with emphasis on the longer term unemployed.

The outbreak of war in 1939 completed the process of returning the country to full employment. By 1940, the unemployment role of the UAB had diminished so much that it was renamed the Assistance Board, and given a number of additional functions which required a national rather than a local approach. In 1941 it also took on the task of paying supplementary old age pensions. In the process it acquired a new respectability which was to have an influence on later events.

References

1. Quoted in Maurice Bruce (ed), *The Rise of the Welfare State*, Weidenfeld and Nicolson, London, 1973, pp.56-7.
2. Ibid, p.134
3. See, for example, A.I. Ogus, 'Great Britain', in Peter A. Kohler and Hans F. Zacher (eds), *The Evolution of Social Insurance 1881-1981*, Frances Pinter, London, 1982, pp156-73.
4. Bentley B. Gilbert, *The Evolution of National Insurance in Great Britain.* Michael Joseph, London, 2967, pp.265-6.
5. Ogus, op.cit. p.186 and Gilbert, op.cit., p.265.
6. Department of Employment, *British Labour Statistics Historical Abstract 1886-1968*, HMSO, London, 1974, p.195.
7. *Report of the Unemployment Insurance Committee*, (the Blanesburgh Report), Vol.1, HMSO, London, 1927, p.9.
8. Gilbert, op.cit., pp.284-5. Most workers were back in work within a few weeks.
9. Winston Churchill, quoted in Jose Harris, *William Beveridge: a biography*, Clarendon Press, Oxford, 1977, p.171.
10. Ibid, p.172.
11. Quoted in Gilbert, op.cit., p.272.

2. Ibid.
3. Fifth Report of the House of Lords Select Committee on the sweating system, quoted in E.H. Phelps Brown, *The Growth of British Industrial Relations*, Macmillan, London, 1965, p.197.
4. The Blanesburgh Report, op.cit., p.10.
5. There are a number of detailed accounts of this period available. See, for example, Bentley B. Gilbert, *British Social Policy 1914-1939*, Batsford,London,1970 and Alan Deacon,*In Search of the Scrounger*, Bell and Sons, London, 1976.
6. The Blanesburgh Report, op.cit., p.20.
7. Ibid., p.21.
8. Ibid., pp.21-2.
9. Ibid., p.28.
20. Ibid., pp.43-5.
21. Ibid., pp.43-5.
22. *Royal Commission on Unemployment Insurance:Final Report*, HMSO, London, 1932, pp.114-15.
23. Ibid., p.115.
24. Ibid., p.116.
25. Ibid., p.118.
26. Ibid., p.385.
27. Ibid., p.389.
28. Ibid., p.393.
29. Ibid., p.399.
30. Ibid.
31. Ibid., p.405.
32. See Gilbert, *Evolution of National Insurance*, op.cit., pp.280-2 for a more detailed explanation.
33. Sir William Beveridge, *The Unemployment Insurance Statutory Committee*,Political Pamphlet No.1, London School of Economics, 1937, p.28.
34. Ibid.,p.29.
35. *British Labour Statistics Historical Abstract*, op.cit., pp.309-10.
36. Beveridge, op.cit., p.31.
37. Clara Rackham, 'Unemployment Insurance', in William Robson(ed), *Social Security*, Fabian Society/George Allen and Unwin,London, 1943, p.123 and *British Labour Statistics*, op.cit., p.311.

38. Unemployment Assistance Board, *Annual Report 1935*, Cmd 5177, HMSO, London, 1936, p.75.

39. Alan Deacon, 'Concession and Coercion:the Politics of Unemployment Insurance in the Twenties', in Asa Briggs and John Saville(eds), *Essays in Labour History,1918-1939*, Croom Helm, London, 1977, pp.9-35.

40. See, for example, the account in Michael Foot, *Aneurin Bevan 1897-1945*, Paladin, London, 1975, pp.257 and 328-30.

41. Unemployment Assistance Board, *Annual Report 1937*, Cmd 5752, HMSO, London, 1938, pp.27-9.

42. Ibid. The proportions in Northern Ireland were different. See Paddy Devlin, *Yes We Have No Bananas: Outdoor Relief in Belfast 1920-39*, Blackstaff Press, Belfast, 1981.

43. Unemployment Assistance Board, *Annual Report 1938*, Cmd 6021, HMSO, London 1939, p.181.

44. Ibid., p.65.

2 The Beveridge Report and the postwar reforms

In 1941, the government appointed Sir William Beveridge to head an inquiry into Social Insurance and Allied Services. The report of the inquiry was published in 1942 and formed the basis of decisions on post war legislation.[1]

The evidence to the Beveridge inquiry
The evidence submitted to the Beveridge inquiry was prepared in a period of low unemployment. However, there was an awareness that this was due to the demands of war and an uneasiness about the future, once the war was over. Some organisations laid stress on the importance of planning for full employment. The National Council of Women of Great Britain, for example, called for:

> A planned economy which will eliminate mass unemployment. The re-organisation of industry is properly outside the scope of this inquiry, but it is a sine qua non of social and economic security. It is felt that this point cannot be over emphasised; any social security plans for the future must, if they are to succeed at all, be based on a state of society in which there is possibility of work for all, and at an adequate wage.[2]

The proposals of Political and Economic Planning (PEP) were also based on the assumption of 'economic planning for something approximating to full employment'.[3]

An important factor influencing the shape of the recommendations made, was the knowledge of the successful 'rehabilitation' of Unemployment Insurance following its reorganisation under the UISC after 1935. Proposals for a contribution based insurance scheme for unemployment were common to all those who gave evidence on this point and little or no doubt was expressed about the ability of this type of provision to operate efficiently. Indeed, some wanted to extend its coverage to include all working under contract of service. The Liberal Parliamentary Party also wanted to bring in groups such as shopkeepers, farmers, nurses and others not under contract of service.[4] Others sought the greater inclusion of part time workers – the Fabian Society, for example.[5]

The questions then were, how long insurance cover should last, what should happen to the long term unemployed and on what conditions and at what level should benefit be paid. On the issue of the duration of benefit, the division of opinion was not entirely predictable. The TUC, the Liberal Parliamentary Party and the Fabian Society favoured a benefit of indefinite duration,[6] while the National Labour Organisation, PEP and the National Council of Women proposed a six month duration for the insurance benefit, followed by means tested assistance payments[7]

For the Fabian Society, an 'insurance-cum-assistance type of scheme' was outmoded. Its own proposals, it said were aimed:

> at providing sufficient maintenance for those who temporarily or permanently lose their earning power – that is the simple service which a community owes to its members.[8]

But the citizen had a 'profound reciprocal obligation' to co-operate fully in the restoration of his earning power. Full cash maintenance would be provided by society but 'only to the extent to which its members are willing to accept their corresponding social obligations'.[9]

The Fabians, therefore, sought a flat rate benefit of indefinite duration, at a level adequate to cover reasonable needs and without a means test. In addition the actual rent of the individual would be paid. 'This would give the worker real security against the economic effect of these contingencies. He would know that his rent was covered and he would have enough to live on. He would also have the assurance that the resources of society would be directed to the restoration of his earning power'.[10] Sanctions (unspecified) would have to be applied to the 'slacker' who refused to co-operate with placement or retraining services.

The National Labour Organisation, on the other hand, wanted to see the Insurance Fund operated as a 'sound insurance scheme'. It appeared to assume that this required a limited duration of benefit and the maintenance of an Assistance scheme. Payment of benefit should be conditional on attendance at a Ministry of Labour training centre and on being 'capable of undertaking and willing to undertake suitable work, and of taking reasonable steps to obtain employment'. Failing this a six weeks suspension from benefit would be imposed.[11]

Generally there was a desire to provide at least a subsistence level of insurance benefit, which would not require means tested supplementation. The National Labour Organisation suggested that the present scale of benefit was only adequate 'on the assumption that wage-earners are able to make substantial savings while at work'.[12] This was not the case. Nevertheless, it had to be recognised that the level of benefit would have to be set in relation to the level of contribution which would be publicly acceptable. For others giving evidence, the object of limiting the benefit level was to maintain a margin between benefit and wages. The British Employers' Confederation emphasised this and so did the Shipping Federation and the Liverpool Steam Ship Owners' Association.[13] The aim would be to provide the individual with a strong incentive to return to work as soon as he can, and at the same time discourage the dependence of the work shy and encourage thrift and self-reliance.

Proposals for training for the unemployed were quite common – either as a means of dealing with the 'work shy' or more positively to combat the demoralisation of long periods out of work and to help the individual to find employment. The TUC also proposed a scheme of transfer allowances (for lodgings, removals, etc.) to make it possible for people to move when an industry closed down,[14] and the National Council of Women wanted to see the use of Assistance payments, over and above maintenance 'for any form of assistance which might be considered to have a constructive aim'.[15]

The views of Beveridge

Beveridge had a long history of involvement in the issue of unemployment and the development of social insurance dating back to the early years of the century[16] and more recently as chairman of the Unemployment Insurance Statutory Committee (UISC). His biographer (Jose Harris) suggests that it was his period at the UISC which convinced him of the popularity of the contributory principle among working people and taught him to understand the impact of unemployment on individuals and families.[17]

Beveridge's proposal was for a scheme of social insurance against all forms of interruption and destruction of earning power and for certain special expenditure. The principal cash payments, including those for unemployment, would be without means test and would be 'paid from a Social Insurance Fund built up by contributions from the insured persons, from their employers, if any, and from the State'.[18] It would be compulsory for all employed as well as self-employed persons to pay contributions to the Fund. Beveridge argued that:

> benefit in return for contributions, rather than free allowances from the State is what the people of Britain desire. This desire is shown both by the established popularity of compulsory insurance, and by the phenomenal growth of voluntary insurance ... It is shown in another way by the strength of popular objection to any kind of means test.[19]

The reaction against means testing was not surprising – it was part of the legacy of the bitter depression years and the detestation of the Household Means Test, even though this had been modified in 1941. What was perhaps unexpected, in light of the way Beveridge had run the UISC, was the proposal that, not only for old age and sickness or disability, but also for unemployment, benefits should be paid 'as long as the need lasts'.[20]

The proposal stemmed directly from Beveridge's view of social insurance. There were, he said, important distinctions between social insurance and voluntary insurance. The latter had to adjust premiums to risks, 'since without this individuals would not of their own free will insure'. This adjustment was not essential in a compulsory State scheme. Further, in voluntary insurance, a fund had to be built up so that contributions paid in early life provided for the increasing risks of later life. Reserves had to be accumulated against individual liabilities. The State, on the other hand:

> with its power of compelling successive generations of citizens to become insured and its power of taxation is not under the necessity of accumulating reserves for actuarial risks.[21]

It might choose to adjust premiums to risks or to build up reserves, but that was a matter of policy, not of necessity. Moreover, the new scheme would be based, not on the cover of selected groups as in the past – manual workers and low paid non-manual workers – and on permitting those with low risks to opt out. Instead all social risks would be pooled. Industries with low unemployment risks would share equally with those having high unemployment risks, acknowledging that the volume of unemployment in a particular industry was not to any effective extent within its control. 'All industries depend on one another and those which are fortunate in being regular should share the cost of unemployment in those which are less regular'. Equally each individual 'should stand in on the same terms; none should claim to pay less because he is healthier or has more regular employment'. 'Social Insurance' would imply both 'that it is compulsory and that men stand together with their fellows'.[22]

At the same time, it was important that it was recognised that the benefits paid would come from a fund to which the recipients had contributed and to which they might be required to make larger contributions if the fund proved inadequate. If part of the cost of unemployment was borne separately by the State, in order to keep contribution rates down, it would have two adverse effects. The insured person might feel that income from idleness, however caused, could come from a bottomless purse, and government might feel that, by paying dole, it could avoid the major responsibility of seeing that unemployment was reduced to a minimum. He went on:

> The place for direct expenditure and organisation by the State is in maintaining the employment of labour and other productive resources of the country ... not in patching an incomplete scheme of insurance.[23]

There were some provisos attached to these proposals. The self-employed would not be covered for the risk of unemployment since there was no way of ascertaining whether or not the individual was working. However, for this group, a training benefit, subject to the condition that training took place, and paid for a limited period at the same time rate as Unemployment Benefit, could be made available.[24]

Training was also a feature of the proposals for the longer term unemployed. The new benefit was to continue indefinitely, and without reduction or means testing as long as unemployment lasted. But this did present some dangers:

> Most men who have once gained the habit of work would rather work – in ways to which they are used – than be idle ... But getting work ... may involve a change of habits, doing something that is unfamiliar or leaving one's friends or making a painful effort of some other kind. The danger of providing benefits which are both adequate in amount and indefinite in duration, is that men as

creatures who adapt themselves to circumstances, may settle down to them.[25]

It was necessary, therefore, to enforce the citizen's obligation to seek and accept all reasonable opportunities to work and to cooperate in measures 'designed to save him from habituation to idleness'. Those who were in receipt of unemployment benefit could not be allowed to hold out indefinitely for work of the type they were used to or in their present place of residence, if there was work which they could do, at the standard wage for that work. In addition those unemployed for a certain period:

> should be required, as a condition of continued benefit to attend a work or training centre, such attendance being designed as a means of preventing habituation to idleness and as a means of improving capacity for earnings.[26]

This would also serve as a 'way of unmasking the relatively few persons ... who have perhaps some concealed means of earning which they are combining with the appearance of unemployment' – but this was 'an altogether minor reason for the proposal'.

The period after which attendance at a centre would be required could vary from person to person and be longer when unemployment was high than in times of good employment. On average, six months might be a suitable period to pay benefit without conditions. Failure to comply with conditions would attract a penalty.

The third proviso – and this was presented as one of the assumptions on which the whole social security plan was based – was that governments would seek to maintain employment and prevent mass unemployment. This did not imply the abolition of all unemployment – indeed the plan was framed on the basis of 8.8 per cent unemployment – but 'it should be possible to make unemployment of any individual for more than 26 weeks continuously a rare thing in normal times'.[27]

The ending of mass and prolonged unemployment was essential for a number of reasons. The imposition of a training condition would be impractical if the unemployed were numbered by the million. The test of unemployment through the offer of work broke down in mass unemployment and would make necessary the elaboration of conditions which should be avoided in a satisfactory scheme. Further, even adequate benefits were no substitute for a reasonable chance of productive employment. Finally, although it was within the power of the community to bear the cost of the plan for social security being put forward, the cost would be heavy and if 'waste' was added, the cost could become unsupportable:

> Unemployment, both through increasing expenditure on benefit and through reducing the income to bear those costs, is the worst form of waste.[28]

Beveridge's proposals for benefits under the scheme varied by age and sex. The treatment of married women and young people will be discussed in subsequent chapters. Here the proposals for adult males and single women will be outlined. The basic principle to be applied was that:

> The rates of benefit or pension provided by social insurance should be such as to secure for all normal cases an income adequate for subsistence.[29]

The benefit would be paid free of means test and therefore could form a base upon which savings or other voluntary provision could build. On the other hand, where there were abnormal needs, a means tested assistance programme – to be called National Assistance – would be available to supplement the benefit. It was intended that this should be an exceptional arrangement, meeting the additional needs of a small minority of the unemployed.

The benefit rate would be set on the basis that it had to cover food, clothing, fuel, light and household sundries at a minimum level for a man and dependent wife, and the report set out some criteria for producing a benefit suitable for the cost of living in 1938 which would then be uprated by the degree of inflation from 1938 to the year it was introduced. There were, however, two other matters which had to be considered.

The first was dependency additions for children. Here the question of the relationship of benefits to wages entered into the discussion and particularly as it concerned low wage earners. A subsistence level adult male benefit was not likely to reach former wage levels or prospective wages, even for the relatively low paid and even where an addition for a dependent wife was given. However, once additions for children were given, especially if there were several children involved, an overlap between benefits and wages could occur. The issue of the treatment of the low paid is a subject in its own right, and will be dealt with in a separate chapter, but here it may be noted that Beveridge argued for the payment of Family Allowances to those in work and out of work alike.[30] These were to be paid at subsistence level for the second and subsequent children in all families and, for the unemployed, an extra allowance at the same rate would be paid for the first child. The assumption was that a man in work could earn enough to support himself, his wife and one child, while those out of work needed subsistence rates for the whole family.

The second item of concern was rent.[31] As seen some of those giving evidence to Beveridge recommended a subsistence benefit plus actual rent. Beveridge acknowledged the sense of this, especially as the Unemployment Assistance Board had met the cost of rent and those who would not in future qualify for an insurance benefit, but would receive means tested National Assistance, could also expect to have their rent paid. The problem for Beveridge was that his plan was based on flat rate contributions which would earn a flat rate benefit, while rent varied from one part of the country to another and from person to person in a way which was not always related to the size of family. Individual assessments would introduce significant administrative complications to the scheme, and regional rates could not allow for the wide differences within regions or between families. On the other hand, rent was not an item on which immediate economies could be made – as they could for clothing for example – and the level of rent was not always within the control of the individual.

The solution adopted was acknowledged to be less than satisfactory. This was to include a flat rate sum in the benefit as an allowance for rent and to rely on the plans for post-war improvement in housing provision to even out rents. In addition, if more choice was made available, it would enable the unemployed to adapt their housing costs to their circumstances.

Underpinning all these arrangements would be a safety net in the form of means tested National Assistance. This, as seen earlier, would deal with abnormal needs, which would include high rent where necessary.

Government and Parliamentary reaction

In 1944 the government published a White Paper setting out its response to the Beveridge Report.[32] It accepted the broad sweep of the Beveridge Plan, that is for a social insurance scheme to cover sickness, widowhood, old age and unemployment. Participation would be compulsory for the whole working population who would pay flat rate contributions and, in return, could claim flat rate benefits.

Beveridge's view that the self-employed would have to be excluded from unemployment benefit – though not from other parts of the social insurance scheme – was also accepted.

On unemployment, the parting of the ways between the Beveridge Report and the government came on the question of the duration of benefit. The White Paper rejected an indefinite benefit for unemployment and offered only a maximum of 30 weeks, subject to the giving of additional days' rights 'where the contributor has a good record of employment in recent years'.[33] Claimants who exhausted their insurance rights could requalify by the payment of further contributions. The reason given for the limited duration was not that the long term unemployed could not be accommodated in the insurance scheme, but that an indefinite benefit was open to abuse. Beveridge's proposal to cover this point – the imposition of a training condition – was rejected. The White Paper said that the government agreed that:

> training schemes are of the utmost importance in preventing unemployment and in securing fluidity of labour, and that claimants unreasonably refusing to undergo a course of training should be disqualified from receiving benefit. They are satisfied, however, that the requirement to undergo training after a certain period of unemployment would not constitute an effective safeguard against possible abuse of benefit.[34]

The recommendation (by Beveridge), of a training allowance was taken up. If an unemployed person, including the self-employed and widows, undertook a course of approved training, an allowance, at a higher rate than unemployment benefit, could be paid. This allowance would be quite separate from Unemployment Benefit. It would be paid, not from the social insurance fund, but by the Ministry of Labour.

The second major difference between the Beveridge plan and the White Paper proposals was in the rates to be paid. From the beginning the government had disliked the idea of subsistence rates and it had indicated its likely rejection of them in the House as early as February 1943.[35] The objections were twofold. First the government regarded the concept of subsistence rates as payments adapted to individual needs and conditions – as had been the practice in Unemployment Assistance. Social insurance rates had to deal in averages and should provide equal benefits for equal contributions. Moreover, to align benefits with subsistence would imply the variation of rates in accordance with the cost of living and even if minor variations were ignored, this was seen as impracticable.

The second objection was more fundamental. The White Paper said:

> Benefits must be paid for, and a high level of benefit must mean a high level of contribution. The Government therefore conclude that the right objective is a rate of benefit which provides a reasonable insurance against want and at the same time takes account of the maximum contribution which the great body of contributors can properly be asked to bear. There still remains the individual's opportunity to achieve for himself in sickness, old age and other conditions of difficulty a standard of comfort and amenity which it is no part of a compulsory scheme of social insurance to provide. And in reserve there must remain a scheme of National Assistance designed to fill the inevitable gaps left by insurance and to supplement it where an examination of individual needs shows that supplement is necessary.[36]

This rejection of subsistence level applied not only to the main adult benefit, but also to the proposed new Family Allowances. Nevertheless, the proposal by Beveridge that only the first child of the unemployed would receive a dependency addition in Unemployment Benefit, while the remainder were supported by the Family Allowance, would be maintained.

The debate in the House of Commons on the proposals for the unemployed in the White Paper, and the subsequent discussion of the legislation to bring the new scheme into effect, returned frequently to the three issues of the role of training, the duration of benefit and the benefit rates. In presenting the White Paper to the House, Sir William Jowitt (the Minister of Social Insurance Designate) put a more acceptable gloss on the rejection of the training condition as a means of enabling an indefinite benefit duration. He suggested that training was so important that it should not be discredited by making it an instrument of control of benefit abuse.[37] This had a certain appeal to the House. James Griffiths, Labour MP for Llanelly who was to be the Minister responsible for introducing the later legislation, said, for example:

> I cordially share the view expressed by more than one speaker that the provision of training to fit a man for other work, when there is no real prospect of getting work in his own occupation, ought to be removed from any idea of a sanction and from the old association of the idea of giving them unemployment benefit and

> putting them on the basis of driving them into these centres.
> Training ought to be offered to a man as an opportunity of starting
> a fresh life, rather than as a penalty for his having been in
> unfortunate circumstances.[38]

However, this did not mean that there was such common agreement on the duration of benefit. Sir William Jowitt pressed the government's view in 1944. He suggested that 'everybody who has studied the matter must realise that it is dangerous to have a benefit which is unlimited in point of time, unless it is strictly controlled by some check'.[39] It was true that the vast majority would prefer work to wages, however generous the benefits, but 'there has always been, and I suppose there always will be, a small minority who are apt to bring discredit on the scheme and earn the resentment of their fellows'.[40] If training was rejected as a sanction, then, to deal with this minority, a limit had to be placed on duration. The period offered would cover the needs of the great majority and National Assistance would be available for the remainder. It was quite true, he added, 'that national assistance is subject to a means test, but, at any rate, it is not the household means test which caused such heart burning in years gone by'.[41]

James Griffiths, on the other hand, objected to the division of the unemployed into two classes 'those who get benefit as a right and those who get it as a kind of charity'.[42] He went on:

> The worse thing we can do to an unemployed man is to heap
> indignity upon indignity, because the loss of work in itself is a bad
> thing. I have seen fine, brave men reduced by continuous, enforced
> unemployment to a state in which they feel they are forgotten,
> unwanted, thrown on the scrap heap, and to say to them at the end
> of 30 weeks 'your benefit stops and you go on assistance' is not
> the way to build the kind of Britain we want. I hope consideration
> will be given to this problem and that the government will
> reconsider these points of the continuity of benefit, and of the
> responsibility of funding employment being placed squarely where
> it ought to be placed – upon the government. We cannot place it
> upon the man.[43]

Unemployment benefit, he concluded, ought to be a right, conditional only upon the acceptance of work when it is provided.

Two years later, as Minister in the new Labour Government, Griffiths presented the National Insurance Bill to the House. Embodied in the Bill was a 30 week limit on the duration of unemployment benefit, together with the same provisions as those in the White Paper for additional days and for the payment of further contributions to attain a restored right of benefit. This change of view on benefit duration was not, apparently, based on the likelihood of abuse. Griffiths' reasons were threefold.

First, the government had adopted a commitment to try to ensure full employment. This, together with the fact that the high employment of the war years had given most workers a potential right to claim additional days, suggested that the period provided would be adequate. Second, the Minister recalled the effect of large scale unemployment on the unemployment fund after 1920. In the new scheme, the National Insurance Fund had to meet the needs, not only of the unemployed, but also the sick, widows and the aged. 'If, by some disaster mass unemployment, lasting for a long time, should come to us',[44] the financial implications would spread far beyond the unemployed.

Third, and following directly from this, the government had concluded that only short term unemployment ought to be borne by the Insurance Fund. 'We believe', the Minister said, 'that the responsibility for long term unemployment should be undertaken by the State as a direct responsibility'.[45] It was not suggested, however, that this would be through means tested provision. Indeed the Minister asserted his desire to avoid means testing the unemployed. Instead, for a period of five years, those living in areas of high unemployment could, on expiry of their benefits rights, apply to a local tribunal for an extension of benefit. If this was granted, the cost would be met directly from the Treasury and not from the Insurance Fund. The period of five years was set in order to allow for post-war industrial reconstruction.

There was little opposition to these proposals. The House, no doubt, was conscious that it was embarking on a huge scheme, the financial consequences of which were not clear in the period of post-war economic uncertainty. It was satisfied with, or willing to be convinced by, the Minister's argument.

The question of benefit rates was naturally raised in the House in the White Paper debate in 1944. Enlarging on the points made in the White Paper, Sir William Jowitt said:

> There has been a good deal of criticism and interest in our refusal to adopt what is called a subsistence level. I emphasise again that our scheme is a scheme of social insurance which involves premiums which we hope all should be able to pay, in return for

which benefit are to be received which we hope will at least take the edge off the mishaps of life. It is not and does not pretend to be a scheme of social security.[46]

Conservative and Liberal Members were inclined to accept this and be reassured that need would be met through supplementation by the National Assistance Board.[47] Griffiths, for Labour, on the other hand, argued that if the insurance scheme was to ensure freedom from want, subsistence scales were essential. He sought to establish a 'principle of a national minimum, laying it down that every person in this country is entitled to a minimum below which no one ought to fall'.[48] If government set out to ensure economic stability, then the prices would not fluctuate greatly and this objection to the subsistence principle need not arise.

When Griffiths introduced the National Insurance Bill in 1946, he referred back to the 1944 debate and suggested it had raised three questions on the issue of a subsistence rate:

First, is it practicable, and, if so, is it desirable to peg the benefits to a definite cost of living, with automatic adjustments up and down; secondly, is it possible to fix a general level of benefits that will adequately cover the variations in personal needs, and, thirdly, is it possible to cover the variations in rent in a scheme based upon flat rate contributions and benefits?[49]

He went on to say that the government felt it would not be possible to have frequent adjustments to the rates, that varying needs could not be met in an insurance scheme and that varying rents could not be covered either. However, it was considered important that the initial rates were at a level 'which can be justified broadly in relation to the present cost of living' and that definite arrangements should be made to review the rates at periodic intervals. The new rates proposed would meet the first condition and provision was made for 5 yearly review by the Minister, which must be reported to the House. He called the new rates 'the beginning of the establishment of the principle of a National Minimum Standard'.[50] In spite of this, it was acknowledged later in the debate that benefit rates were being held lower than would seem desirable, in order to moderate the contribution rates.[51]

The legislation providing for Family Allowances had been passed at the final stage of the last Parliament in 1945. This had implemented the White Paper's proposal not to set subsistence rates for Family Allowances. In spite of this, the decision to pay a child dependency addition to Unemployment Benefit only for the first child was maintained in the 1946 Act. The rates established for the unemployed, therefore, had three weaknesses. They were at a low basic level, they could not meet the cost of rent above the average levels provided for and they could not meet the cost of children. Provided unemployment was brief, and followed a period of good wages, this need not be a serious problem, but in frequent or longer unemployment, difficulties for the recipient could be expected.

In 1948, the National Assistance Bill was placed before the House. In its first clause it, reassuringly, abolished the Poor Law. A new National Assistance Board was to replace both the Assistance Board and local Public Assistance. The shift in responsibility for the unemployed from local to national government, begun in 1911 and continued in 1934 with the creation of the UAB, was now complete. The new Board would be an expansion of the Assistance Board, which had established a reasonably good reputation during the disruptive war years. Its task was described as 'residual'.[52] The main responsibility for supporting those without income would be undertaken through National Insurance, but 'there must always stand behind the existing social services a national scheme to assist people in peculiar and special circumstances'.[53] There would be, the Minister of Health (Aneurin Bevan) added, a number of people not eligible for insurance benefit, including some not eligible for unemployment benefit, and problems of the 'fire, flood and Act of God' variety would have to be dealt with. The Board would also take over duties related to the aged in institutions and to homeless vagrants. The workhouse would be abolished, and for the vagrants, there would be resettlement programmes and assistance to obtain employment.

The House clearly enjoyed the task of ending the Poor Law and abolishing the workhouse. In discussing the Bill, however, the main focus was on how it would improve the well-being of the elderly. Comparatively little attention was given in the debate to two functions which might be of importance to the unemployed. First, the payment of benefits to those whose rights to insurance benefits could not be established (because of inadequate contributions) or whose rights had expired. Second, the supplementation of National Insurance benefits, where these proved insufficient. In both cases the means test would apply. The Ministers who spoke in the debate gave the impression, no doubt in good faith, that the numbers involved would be few.

References
1. *Social Insurance and Allied Services* (the Beveridge Report), Cmd 6404, HMSO, London, 1942.
2. *Social Insurance and Allied Services: Memoranda from Organisations, Appendix G to Report by Sir William Beveridge*, Cmd 6405, HMSO, London, 1942, p.31.
3. Ibid., p.36.
4. Ibid., p.42.
5. Ibid., p.39.
6. Ibid., pp.16, 42 and 38.
7. Ibid., pp.48, 36 and 31.
8. Ibid., p.38.
9. Ibid.
10. Ibid.
11. Ibid., p.48.
12. Ibid.
13. Ibid., pp.9 and 23.
14. Ibid., p.16.
15. Ibid., p.33.
16. Harris, *William Beveridge*, op.cit., Chapter 6.
17. Ibid., pp.359-60.
18. Beveridge Report, op.cit., p.11.
19. Ibid., pp.11-12.
20. Ibid., p.11.
21. Ibid., pp.12-13.
22. Ibid., p.13.
23. Ibid., p.12.
24. Ibid., p.54.
25. Ibid., pp.57-8.
26. Ibid., p.58.
27. Ibid., p.164.
28. Ibid., p.163.
29. Ibid., p.76.
30. Ibid., pp.154-8.
31. Ibid., pp.77-84.
32. *Social Insurance Part I*, Cmd 6550, HMSO, London, 1944.
33. Ibid., p.17.
34. Ibid.
35. *House of Commons Hansard*, 16 February 1943, 1668.

36. *Social Insurance Part I*, op.cit., p.7.
37. *House of Commons Hansard*, 2 November 1944, 990.
38. Ibid., 3 November 1944, 1195-6.
39. Ibid., 2 November 1944, 990.
40. Ibid.
41. Ibid.
42. Ibid., 3 November 1944, 1196.
43. Ibid.
44. Ibid., 6 February 1946, 1744.
45. Ibid.
46. Ibid., 2 November 1944, 984.
47. See, for example, Ibid., 3 November 1944, 1176.
48. Ibid., 1193.
49. Ibid., 6 February 1946, 1740-1.
50. Ibid., 1742.
51. Ibid., 7 February 1946, 1192.
52. Ibid., 24 November 1947, 1604.
53. Ibid.

3 The short term unemployed

The provision of unemployment benefits through social insurance in the UK has been principally designed to deal with the short term unemployment of those normally in regular employment who need to be tided over a period of temporary difficulty.

The type of provision established was based on a number of assumptions. The first was that a man or woman with a good employment record would not experience serious difficulty in finding another job. The second was that such a person would not have any difficulty in building and re-building a good contribution record. The third was that, given there had been regular employment, the person concerned would have some savings or other private provision or, if not, could weather a period on a relatively low benefit in the knowledge that work would soon be available again. The low benefit encouraged and supplemented self help and at the same time provided a spur to job search, a search which was expected to be successful.

Such a scheme naturally functions at its best when unemployment is typically brief and when it does not occur too frequently for any individual. In periods of economic downturn, when jobs are harder to find even for those with a good work record, too short a bridge between one job and another will be insufficient. Steps may then be taken to lengthen the bridge by increasing the maximum number of benefit weeks, though in these circumstances, the low level of benefit presents greater problems. For those who are unemployed more frequently than the scheme has planned for, some provision can be made through the rules under which a period of unemployment is calculated, and the linkages made between one period and the next. But this may be rather random in its outcome because individual circumstances differ so much, and where unemployment occurs too frequently, the provision will cease to be effective.

Outside of the insurance system altogether, are the long term unemployed. However, the definition of long term can be modified. Each time the bridge provided between one job and the next is lengthened, the later the unemployed person is defined as falling into the category of long term unemployed and excluded from insurance provision.

The operation of the scheme to 1965

As Table 3.1 shows, throughout the 1950s and 1960s, the new plan for unemployment benefits operated in a favourable environment. The national rate of unemployment never rose above 2.6 per cent, right through to 1970, and for 12 of those 21 years, it was below 2 per cent. There were regions in the country which were less well placed. The North, Wales and Scotland often had rates of more than 3 per cent and Northern Ireland rarely went below 6 per cent,[1] but even these rates were lower than the 8.8 per cent average unemployment on which Beveridge had developed his plan·

The National Insurance Act of 1946 came into operation in July 1948. It provided a maximum of 180 days (30 weeks) standard Unemployment Benefit for those who met the basic contribution conditions. Someone with a good contribution and benefit record could be granted additional days of benefit, directly related to the number of contributions paid which had not been 'used' for previous periods of benefit. Up to 1952, the maximum benefit period permitted was one year, comprised of benefit plus additional days. However, only 4 per cent of the unemployed claimed the additional days provision.[2]

When these rights ran out the unemployed claimant could apply to a tribunal for extended benefit for up to a further six months at a time. The tribunal had to have regard to the particular circumstances of the individual and the industrial conditions of the area. This right was more extensively used. In July 1951, for example, 20 per cent of beneficiaries received extended benefit, and the tribunals approved over 90 per cent of the applications coming before them.[3]

In 1953, extended benefit was withdrawn on the grounds that it had served its purpose and industry had now settled down to peacetime activity. The provision for additional days was extended at the same time, to a maximum of 492 days or 19 months combined standard

Table 3.1 Number of registered unemployed persons and rate of unemployment, United Kingdom 1950-89

Annual averages

Year	No. (000s)	Rate %	Year	No. (000s)	Rate %
1950	341.1	1.6	1970	612.2	2.6
1951	281.4	1.3	1971	792.1	3.5
1952	462.5	2.2	1972	875.6	3.8
1953	380.0	1.8	1973	618.8	2.7
1954	317.8	1.5	1974	614.9	2.6
1955	264.5	1.2	1975	997.6	4.2
1956	287.1	1.3	1976	1358.8	5.8
1957	347.2	1.6	1977	1483.6	6.2
1958	500.9	2.2	1978	1475.0	6.2
1959	512.1	2.3	1979	1390.5	5.7
1960	392.8	1.7	1980	1664.9	6.8
1961	376.8	1.6	1981	2520.4	10.4
1962	499.9	2.1	1982	2916.0	12.1
1963	612.3	2.6	1983[2]	3104.7	11.6
1964	413.4	1.7	1984	3159.8	11.7
1965	359.7	1.5	1985	3271.0	11.8
1966	390.0	1.6	1986	3289.1	11.8
1967[1]	556.7	2.3	1987	2953.4	10.6
1968	583.3	2.5	1988	2370.4	8.4
1969	576.2	2.4	1989[3]	2074.3	7.4

Sources: Department of Employment and Productivity, *British Labour Statistics Historical Abstract 1886-1968*, HMSO, London, 1971. Department of Employment, *British Labour Statistics Year Book 1976*, HMSO, London, 1978.   *Department of Employment Gazette.*

1.   Figures from 1967 onwards exclude the temporarily stopped. If included in 1967 and 1968, the figures would be 599.1 and 601.3 respectively.
2.   After 1983 only benefit recipients were included in the count and many men over 60 were excluded from the count.
3.   1989 figure for January only.

benefit and additions, dependent on the contribution and benefit record as before, but under more favourable terms. In addition, anyone insured under the old pre-war scheme, was treated as if he had a full record of contributions before July 1948. The immediate effect of the changed rules was to increase the numbers of people getting additional days.[4] Those who did not qualify (or did not qualify for many days) and who would no longer be able to apply for extended benefit, could claim National Assistance (NA).[5]

The rules for benefit established in 1948 have been varied in a number of ways since that time but the broad structure remained intact, until the 1980s. Someone who had left his job of his own accord or had been sacked for misconduct would receive no benefit during the initial six weeks – a period first established in 1911. If he needed assistance he could go to the National Assistance Board (NAB) but would be paid at a reduced rate. For those out of work through no fault of their own, no benefit was paid for the first 3 days. No benefit was paid for an isolated day of unemployment, but 2 or more days in any period of 6 consecutive days excluding Sundays constituted a 'period of interruption of employment'. This could be linked with another similar period separated by no more than 13 weeks. The link could be made also with a period of sickness which prevented work. In the second of the two periods, no waiting days would have to be served.

When the maximum benefit entitlement expired, it would be necessary to work and pay 13 weeks contributions before benefit would be available again. Any unemployment which occurred during this period would qualify for National Assistance, but only on the basis of a means test.

Figures prepared for the National Insurance Advisory Committee for mid December 1951 to mid December 1952 gave a picture of how unemployment benefit operated.[6] Most spells of unemployment were short term. Some 83 per cent of all the unemployed were back in work within 3 weeks, and 98 per cent within 6 months. Only 2 per cent could be classified as long term unemployed under the then prevailing definition.[7] Thus, for the great majority the benefit duration was reasonably appropriate to their circumstances. Table 3.2 shows the number receiving Unemployment Benefit on a day in November each year from 1949 to 1965.

As the table shows, the numbers involved at any one time during the period were quite modest. However, the use of Unemployment Benefit was much more extensive than this. In the early 1950s, for example, between 2.5 and 3.5 million claims were paid each year, and around 1.5 million of these claimed more than once in the benefit year.[8]

The benefits provided were quite low. As a percentage of gross average male manual earnings, Unemployment Benefit for a single

Table 3.2 Number receiving Unemployment Benefit in November 1949-65. Great Britain.

000s

	Male	Female	Total
1949	219	67	286
1950	178	64	242
1951	146.7	79.6	266.3
1952	211.7	116.3	328
1953	145.2	68.7	214
1954	99.5	50.5	150.1
1955	82.4	42.1	124.5
1956	109.0	45.7	184.7
1957	141.9	45.7	187.6
1958	247.4	86.6	334.0
1959	185.6	55.3	240.9
1960	134.9	41.8	176.7
1961	192.1	51.9	244.0
1962	249.0	64.6	313.4
1963	195.4	59.1	254.4
1964	132.1	40.4	172.5
1965	132.7	33.6	166.4

Source: *Annual Reports* of the Ministry of National Insurance and the Ministry of Pensions and National Insurance 1949-52 and 1953-65 respectively, HMSO, London.

man or woman represented 18.2 per cent of average male manual earnings in 1949, fell as low as 15.9 per cent in 1954 and stood at 20.4 per cent in 1965. For a married man with 2 children, who received dependency additions for his wife and children, the figures were 34.7 per cent in 1949, 26.9 per cent in 1954 and 42.6 per cent in 1965.[9]

The variation reflected the policy on uprating of benefits. While wages rose most years, benefits were increased much less regularly.

Even if this periodic loss of value is left aside, the benefit could only be regarded as adequate for subsistence if the unemployment was brief and infrequent, if the unemployed person had some reserves to draw on or if living expenses were very low. Where this did not apply, it would be necessary to apply to the National Assistance Board for supplementation. Table 3.3 shows the percentage these formed of all those on Unemployment Benefit at any one time.

Table 3.3 Proportion of those receiving Unemployment Benefit who received supplementation from National Assistance, December 1949-65. Great Britain

Percentages

1949	11.0	1958	19.1
1950	18.0	1959	17.5
1951	16.0	1960	17.5
1952	20.1	1961	14.4
1953	22.3	1962	17.4
1954	20.5	1963	18.2
1955	16.3	1964	15.3
1956	18.1	1965	13.4
1957	20.6		

Source: As Table 3.2

In addition to those receiving supplementation of Unemployment Benefit, there was another, often larger group for whom National Assistance was the sole benefit support in respect of unemployment. Table 3.4 gives the figures for Great Britain. As can be seen the total numbers began to mount up after 1958, but were still relatively modest in comparison with later years.

The National Assistance Board was bothered by the need to pay benefits to the unemployed for any length of time in a period of full employment and in several of its Annual Reports, presented analyses of the group. In 1961, it examined 66,000 cases on National Assistance alone (after excluding a group with substantial records of sickness or imprisonment as well as unemployment) and found that 19,000 of them had been unemployed for less than six months, while the remainder were relatively long term unemployed – 3,000 unemployed from 6-12 months and 44,000 for a year or more.

The short term group were a mixture of school leavers and immigrants who had not been long enough in employment to qualify for National Insurance, and persons whose unemployment benefits were suspended on the grounds that they left or lost their jobs through their own fault.[10] No reference was made to those too frequently unemployed to maintain insurance benefit rights, though presumably they did figure among this group.

Table 3.4 Number receiving National Assistance, with and without Unemployment Benefit, December 1949-65. Great Britain

000s

	With UB	Without UB	Total
1949	30	36	66
1950	38	39	77
1951	33	33	66
1952	59	43	102
1953	48	46	94
1954	30	50	80
1955	20	41	61
1956	30	43	73
1957	41	55	96
1958	66	85	151
1959	59	96	155
1960	43	85	128
1961	45	86	131
1962	89	113	202
1963	62	123	185
1964	38	93	131
1965	34	78	112

Source: *Annual Reports of the National Assistance Board 1949-65*, HMSO, London

New benefit provision 1965-79

Social security for the unemployed in the period 1965-79 operated in markedly less favourable economic circumstances than in earlier years. As Table 3.1 showed after 1967, annual average unemployment never fell below half a million and by 1975 it was just short of one million. From 1976 to 1979 it hovered between 1.3 and 1.4 million.

Before this unfavourable trend got moving, four benefit changes of some significance were introduced in 1965 and 1966.

The Redundancy Payments Act 1965

Introducing the Redundancy Payments Bill in 1975, the Minister of Labour (Ray Gunter) reminded the House of the undertaking in a White Paper (on the economic situation) of the previous year, to carry out an active policy to make it easier for workers 'to change their jobs in accordance with the needs of technological progress'. He added that the government wanted to 'push forward the modernisation of British

43

industry as fast as possible, and to enlist the co-operation of workers as well as management in this process'.[11]

To this end two measures were to be introduced. Both were designed to facilitate the mobility of labour. The first of these would provide for severance payments for those losing their jobs. The Redundancy Payments Act provided for the establishment of a Redundancy Fund, financed by a levy on all employers as a small addition to their National Insurance contributions. The Fund would meet 60 per cent of the cost of redundancy payments, the balance falling on the individual employer. Thus, the cost would be shared by that part of industry enjoying good times, while the individual employer would be deterred by his share of the cost from making employees redundant without good cause.

Redundancy pay would take the form of a lump sum payable to an employee who had been more than 2 years in the job after the age of 18 years. He or she would receive half a week's pay for years of work with the same employer at the age of 18 to 20 years, 1 week's pay for years between 21 and 40 years of age and 1.5 week's pay for the period worked from 41 years of age. (There were some special provisions for older workers which will be discussed in Chapter 7.) This payment was given as compensaton for loss of security, possible loss of earnings and fringe benefits, and the uncertainty and anxiety of a change of job. These could be experienced even if there was no unemployment involved, or only a brief period, and the payment was justified on these grounds, in addition to a proposed provision of higher unemployment benefits.[12]

The amount of benefit redundant workers received under the Act naturally varied a good deal, since the amount was related to both length of service and pay. For those who qualified, there was a ceiling of 20 years service, made up of half, full and 1.5 weeks wages as appropriate. The receipt of this redundancy pay would not affect the right to Unemployment Benefit. It should also be noted also that the level of payment received would not necessarily bear any relationship to the duration of the ensuing unemployment.

Someone who lost his job after less than 2 years with one employer got nothing. This also applied to a worker who found himself redundant for a second time in less than 2 years. These would continue to rely on Unemployment Benefit in the normal way. The choice of a 2 year qualifying period, it was suggested later, was because it 'would be long enough for the worker to have begun to build up a measure of security in his job and to have proved himself to be a satisfactory employee in the eyes of his employer'.[13] It would also reduce the scope for 'acrimonious disputes' about the cause of dismissal, since redundancy payments were not intended for persons who lost (or left) their jobs for reasons other than the fact that the need for their services no longer existed.

The eligibility period established, however, had the capacity to exclude a significant proportion of the labour force. In 1968, for example, over one third of all women, one quarter of manual men and one fifth of non-manual men had been in their employment for less than 2 years. In some forms of employment, the proportions were much higher, for example 43 per cent of men in construction and 47 per cent of manual women in miscellaneous services.[14]

In the event, studies of the unemployed showed that only a small proportion of them had received redundancy pay and the amounts received were not usually high. A national survey of the unemployed stock in 1973 (i.e. all those out of work at any one time) found that only 7 per cent had received payments under the Redundancy Payments Act.[15] The Manpower Services Commission reported that in May 1980, of those newly registering as unemployed, 63 per cent had not been made redundant, and therefore would not qualify for redundancy pay. A further 19 per cent were under 20 years or for other reasons did not qualify under the 2 years continuous employment rule. Some 7 per cent had received under £500 in redundancy pay, 6 per cent between £500 and £2,000 and 5 per cent more than £5,000. Other studies confirmed a similar pattern.[16]

The Earnings Related Supplement (ERS)

The second of the two measures announced by government was introduced in 1966. This was provision for a supplement to Unemployment (and Sickness) Benefit, payable for a period of 6 months. Like redundancy pay, it was presented as having an important part to play 'in promoting mobility of labour which is very much needed to meet economic and technological change'.[17] To this was added a social reason – the 'drastic fall in income for a man who becomes unemployed' which could cause 'very severe hardship' and 'excessive worries for many families'.[18]

To benefit under the new scheme, it was necessary first to qualify for Unemployment Benefit. Those who were frequently unemployed and had run out of insurance rights would not, therefore, qualify. No payment was made for the first 12 days. This was to exclude very short spells of unemployment and, since the same rules applied to Sickness Benefit, to exclude short illnesses. This decision was made mainly for administrative reasons[19] – short spells gave too much trouble – but it also reduced the numbers who would be eligible.

Until 1975, the benefit paid was one third of earnings between £9 and £30 pw, with a maximum of £7 pw. After 1975 a further 15 per cent of earnings came into play in respect of earnings over £30 pw up to a fixed maximum. By 1980/81, the rates were one third of earnings between £17.50 and £30 pw and 15 per cent of earnings between £30 and £120 pw with a maximum benefit of £17.67. If ERS plus Unemployment Benefit exceeded 85 per cent of gross wages, ERS would be reduced or withdrawn altogether.

One factor affecting the level of ERS was the use, for reasons of administrative simplicity, of the wages from the last full tax year as the basis for calculation. These would be out of date, perhaps notably so in periods of high wage inflation. Moreover, if there had been any periods of sickness or unemployment, the wages on which ERS would be calculated would be lower than normal. This might bring more than the normally low paid into the 85 per cent net. It was estimated in November 1978 that about 10 per cent of recipients were affected by this ceiling.[20] The average payment received was a good deal lower than the maximum. In November 1980 when the maximum was £17.67 pw, the average ERS for men was £9.67 pw and for women £6.41 pw. At this time the single person's Unemployment Benefit stood at £20.65 pw and that for a married man with 2 children at £35.90 pw.[21]

The extension of Unemployment Benefit duration

In the Bill which introduced ERS there was a further measure for the unemployed. Unemployment Benefit was still payable only for 180 days, though additional days could be earned subject to the contribution and benefit record. The Minister (Margaret Herbison) indicated to the House that it was felt that these added days provisions were outdated. She said:

> Unemployment usually arises through social and economic factors over which the individual has little or no control, and it is unfair to pay benefit for a shorter period to the man who has worked in a less stable industry and been harder hit by economic factors.[22]

The additional days arrangements would therefore be dropped (apart from existing rights) and Unemployment Benefit (UB) paid in future for a full 12 months.

From the end of 1966, therefore, an unemployed person received UB only for the first 12 days (less the waiting days), UB plus ERS, if eligible, for the next 6 months and thereafter UB only for 5 months. The proportion of men on Unemployment Benefit receiving ERS at any one time was around the 40 per cent mark.[23] For the remainder, only UB was available from National Insurance. In 1971, changes were made to the provision for the sick. Sickness Benefit, previously of indefinite duration, was cut back to a six month period and a new long term benefit, Invalidity Benefit was introduced. From 1973 this was paid at a higher rate than Sickness Benefit. This higher rate after 6 months on benefit was not, however, applied to the unemployed, the whole of whose 12 month benefit continued to be set at what was now, in National Insurance terms, a short term rate. Short term had, in effect, been redefined as up to 12 months unemployment, not 6 months as before.

The Supplementary Benefits scheme

The fourth change in benefit arrangements, also made in 1966, was the conversion of National Assistance to Supplementary Benefits (SB). For the short term unemployed, the change was not particularly significant since most of the old rules were reapplied in the new scheme. Those receiving Unemployment Benefit would now remain longer on UB and thus postpone the time when they had to claim full support rather than supplementation from SB, but their income would not greatly alter. Those receiving UB and ERS might now find themselves above the eligibility level for SB but some did still qualify for additional assistance.

Table 3.5 shows the numbers who received Unemployment Benefit in November each year from 1965-79. The sharp increase from 1965 to 1966 reflects the longer duration of UB introduced in late 1966. For the rest of the period the growth in numbers is a consequence of the increased rate of unemployment shown in Table 3.1 and its longer duration. Table 3.6 shows the proportion of Unemployment Benefit recipients who received supplementation from SB. Again the higher figures reflect both the longer duration of UB, the greater numbers of the unemployed and the longer average periods out of work.

Table 3.5 Number receiving Unemployment Benefit, November 1965-79. Great Britain

000s

	Male	Female	Total
1965	133	33	166
1966	231	45	276
1967	268	50	318
1968	255	39	294
1969	242	38	279
1970	260	43	302
1971	393	66	459
1972	293	59	352
1973	166	31	197
1974	234	41	275
1975	426	99	545
1976(a)	468	120	587
1977	416	145	347
1978	347	146	492
1979	317	150	467

Source: *Social Security Statistics*

(a) Figures for May and November not available because of industrial action.

Table 3.6 Proportion of those receiving Unemployment Benefit who received supplementation from Supplementary Benefits, December 1965-71 and November 1972-79. Great Britain

Percentages

1965	13.4	1973	21.4
1966	15.3	1974	26.5
1967	23.0	1975	22.7
1968	20.2	1976	na
1969	22.5	1977	21.6
1970	19.5	1978	18.3
1972	24.0		

Source: *Social Security Statistics*

Table 3.7 shows those receiving SB, with and without Unemployment Benefit. None of these tables show the full tally of the unemployed. In November 1979, for example, the total numbers were 816,000 men and 336,000 women – over 1 million in all. Of these, around 18 per cent of both sexes were not drawing benefit[24] sometimes because they were awaiting acceptance of their claims, and in other cases because they were suspended from benefit.

Table 3.7 Number receiving Supplementary Benefit, with and without Unemployment Benefit, November 1965-79. Great Britain

000s

	With UB	Without UB	Total
1965	34	78	112
1966	77	102	179
1967	86	138	224
1968	73	147	220
1969	71	157	228
1970	73	166	239
1971	129	258	387
1972	87	305	392
1973	48	201	249
1974	73	228	301
1975	135	400	541
1976	na	na	654
1977	128	543	671
1978	93	505	598
1979	70	486	566

Source: *Social Security Statistics*

The policy debate in the 1970s
During the 1970s, there was considerable controversy about the benefits paid to the short term unemployed. As seen earlier, the introduction of redundancy pay and ERS was intended to promote the mobility of labour. However, it was now claimed that ERS, in particular, was acting to increase the numbers unemployed because it reduced work incentives by offering too high a level of wage replacement during unemployment. This was characterised as 'insurance-induced unemployment'. Maki and Spindler, for example, in 1975 suggested that an increase in the ratio of benefits to ordinary

work income could lead to an increased consumption of leisure. 'This may take place by employed workers initiating their own unemployment for some period of time or by unemployed workers extending their period of unemployment'.[25] On the econometric model they used, they calculated that the introduction of ERS had increased male unemployment rates by 33 per cent in the period 1967-72.

In the highly technical debate which followed over the next few years, much of which related to the non-ERS variables which ought to be included in the model, these stark conclusions were modified. The idea that men and women were induced to become unemployed because of the existence of ERS was rejected. Nickell, for example, writing in 1979 used figures of the monthly flow into unemployment to show that the numbers had hardly varied from year to year since 1967 in spite of the massive rise in unemployment since that date.[26] The stock of unemployed, on the other hand, had increased and there was, therefore, a question of whether ERS acted to prolong the duration of unemployment by reducing job search activity or making the unemployed more choosy about the jobs they accepted. His conclusion was that there was an ERS effect of about 10 per cent increased unemployment rate.

Other writers questioned whether the econometric models were unduly based on a theoretical level of ERS rather than the actual amounts received or not received. Once this was taken into account, the ERS effect faded still further.[27] Moreover, when the question was individualised in surveys of unemployed people receiving benefit, more doubts were raised. In 1977/8 a team of officials from the Department of Health and Social Security (DHSS) was reviewing the Supplementary Benefits scheme. In the course of this, they examined a number of the studies referred to above as well as others on the same subject, and studies of unemployed beneficiaries. They also made their own calculations of benefit to wage ratios.

They began by reporting: 'We found no evidence that any significant number of men were giving up their jobs and choosing to live on benefit instead'.[28] They went on to note that in a minority of cases, the total income support out of work in the early months of unemployment could be not much smaller than work income. This could result from the combined effects of Unemployment Benefit, ERS, redundancy payments and tax refunds. The last arose if the individual had already paid more tax than he would be liable for if he was not working for part of the year but drawing a non-taxable benefit instead. The DHSS review team said it 'found no evidence, however, that cases with higher levels of benefit in the early months were declining to return to work'. On the contrary, 'people with larger amounts of ERS, redundancy payments and larger tax refunds had previously had high earnings, and they tended to find jobs quicker'.[29] There might be problems in relation to previous low earners, especially where their benefits included dependency additions, but even here little evidence of a preference to remain on benefit, rather than to work, was found.

Throughout this discussion, the level of unemployment (as Table 3.1 shows) was moving upwards at a faster rate than a theory of insurance-induced unemployment could explain, reaching an annual average of 1.475 million in 1978. Moreover, almost 4.4 million claims for benefit for spells of unemployment were made during 1978.[30] While the incidence of long term unemployment was increasing, it was still the case that the majority of claims were short term, and this was so even if a somewhat better level of benefit in the early months enabled some people to spend longer securing what they thought would be the most suitable job or one more likely to be fairly stable. No change of policy on short term benefits was therefore proposed by the Labour government of the time.

A change in policy 1979-85
The Conservative government which took office in April 1979, had been impressed by the evidence which appeared to show an element of insurance-induced unemployment. It therefore set out to reduce the income available for short term unemployment. The first step, in 1980 was to uprate Unemployment Benefit by 5 per cent less than the rate of inflation, pending bringing the benefit into tax. This was achieved two years later in July 1982. Henceforward any tax rebate would not be paid until the end of the period of unemployment or the end of the tax year, when the amount of tax owed, including that on the unemployment benefit (which would have been paid out in full) would be calculated against tax already paid. The 5 per cent abatement of Unemployment Benefit was not, however, immediately restored. This was not done until November 1983.

Also in 1980, the government announced its intention of phasing out the Earnings Related Supplement. The reasons it gave was that the scheme had been 'diminishing in worth and effectiveness over recent years' and that any any one time, it was being paid only to 10-15 per cent of the unemployed.[31]   The maximum rate was therefore reduced in 1981 and the benefit abolished altogether by June 1982.

A third step taken was to reduce and then in 1984 abolish the child dependency additions to Unemployment Benefit. The government's stated objective was to ensure that the children of the unemployed received the same treatment as the children of those in work so that their presence in the household and the benefit they attracted would not create a disincentive to work.[32]

The fourth was to reduce the linking period between one spell of unemployment and another from 13 weeks to 8 weeks. Among other effects, this altered the impact of the waiting days, to the disadvantage of those whose spells of employment fell between 9 and 13 weeks.

Government also made a series of changes to the way in which the figures for the registered unemployed were arrived at. Registration was made voluntary and the count was restricted to those receiving benefit – either UB or SB. As will be seen in Chapter 7, men over 60 were permitted to receive the higher long term rate of SB provided they ceased to register as unemployed. Other statistical adjustments were made from time to time. Although this means that a comparison with earlier figures is defective, it cannot disguise the very large increase in the numbers of unemployed as shown in Table 3.1, passing the 3 million mark in 1983 and remaining at that level until 1987.

Table 3.8 Number receiving Unemployment Benefit November 1978-84. Great Britain and Northern Ireland

000s

1979	467	27.3
1980	940	43.8
1982	-	41.2
1982	975	36.1
1983	906	32.3
1984	896	29.1

Source: *Social Security Statistics 1985* and *Northern Ireland Annual Abstract of Statistics* November 1985.

Table 3.8 shows the numbers receiving Unemployment Benefit in the years 1979-84, including this time figures for Northern Ireland. As the table shows, there was a sharp increase in recipients between 1979 and 1980 and thereafter the numbers stabilise. This stabilisation does not indicate that unemployment levelled out. As Table 3.1 showed, this was far from the case. But the benefit itself lasts only 12 months and as Table 3.9 shows, the additional burden was borne by Supplementary Benefits. The SB figures also show the effects of the real reduction in UB levels and the abolition of ERS as well as the longer duration of unemployment, so that more Unemployment Benefit recipients required supplementation.

Table 3.9 Number receiving Supplementary Benefit, with and without Unemployment Benefit, November 1979-84. Great Britain and Northern Ireland.

000s

	Great Britain		Northern Ireland	
	With UB	Without UB	With UB	Without UB
1979	80	486	3.4	29.6
1980	176	678	6.1	41.0
1982	234	1,084	7.8	63.7
1982	285	1,437	8.8	70.8
1983	205	1,621	7.2	82.0
1984	197	1,688	5.3	85.2

Source: As for Table 3.8

By 1981, the figures for the proportion of UB recipients receiving supplementation, which had fallen to 17.2 per cent in 1979 and 1980, rose again to 23.2 per cent.[33]   After that year, the DHSS ceased to publish the figures in their annual statistics.

The short term unemployed in 1985

Although the debate about benefits for unemployed people in the preceding years had principally concerned the long term unemployed and young people, the position of the short term unemployed in 1985 still warranted consideration.

A proportion of short term unemployed people received no benefits or reduced benefits. The position of married women will be discussed in Chapter 5. A further group has been mentioned earlier – those under benefit suspension. The practice in what are termed 'voluntary unemployment' cases is that if the benefit authorities believe it possible that a new claimant has left work of his own accord or has been dismissed, benefit is automatically suspended pending inquiries. If these show that the suspension was incorrectly applied, then back benefit will be paid. This means that a much larger number than are classified as having been suspended will have experienced a delay in benefit payment. Moreover, it was found in 1983 that back payments were not always made – some 25,000 cases were identified, and pressure had to be brought to bear on the government to try to trace this group and repay them.[34]

If during benefit suspension the individual, especially a person with dependants, would suffer serious hardship, Supplementary Benefit could be paid, but the claimant's benefit (but not that of his dependants) would be reduced by 40 per cent during the period of suspension. Since it was already payable at the short term rate, this implied a severe reduction of an already minimal benefit. Some of those affected might find work during the period of suspension, but others would be beginning a longer spell of unemployment, with resources already under strain.

Unemployment is not evenly distributed across the working population. Chapter 8 will discuss the significantly higher unemployment rates of disabled people when compared with the general population. In 1981 for example when the general rate was 10.3 percent, the rate for registered disabled people was 16 per cent. Table 3.10 shows the unemployment rates by ethnic origin in Spring 1984. This higher level of unemployment among ethnic minority workers has been a persistent feature of the figures for many years.

Table 3.10   Unemployment rates by ethnic origin, all persons 16+, Spring 1984. Great Britain

Per cent

Ethnic origin	Male	Female
All ethnic origins	11.5	10.5
White	11.0	10.1
Ethnic minority of which	21.3	19.1
West Indian	29	17
Indian	13	18
of which E. African Indian	9	20
Pakistani, Bangladeshi	34	40
Others	17	20

Source: Barber, Anne, Ethnic origin and economic status', *Employment Gazette*, December 1985, pp.467-77.

Among the unemployed generally it is the lower paid unskilled workers who are most likely to be out of work. A study undertaken by DHSS in 1978 of people of all ethnic groups entering unemployment found that half the sample group had previous earnings which fell into the bottom 20 per cent of the earnings distribution. Moreover, only one third had spent the whole of the previous year in work. Half had been unemployed for a time, 12 per cent sick and the rest in full time education. A quarter had had three or more spells of unemployment in the past five years.[35] Relatively few, therefore, were well placed to withstand a period on very low income.

For the short term unemployed as a whole, where the periods out of work were brief and infrequent, the limited benefit available could probably be tolerated. However, the evidence was that the typical duration of even short term unemployment had increased. In the 1960s, the *average* duration of male unemployment was 8-10 weeks and if those with employment disadvantage were excluded (age, lack of skills, poor health etc.) the average was 4-5 weeks.[36] By 1982, the *median* duration of completed spells of male unemployment was 11 weeks.[37] By 1984 it was nearly 17 weeks in Great Britain and 22 weeks in Northern Ireland.[38]

At the beginning of this chapter it was suggested that provision for unemployment was based on the assumption that what was required was a short bridge between one job and the next and that the income provided in this period need not and ought not to be too high. It 'need not' because the short term unemployed would have other resources or could manage for the brief period involved. It 'ought not' because too high a benefit would reduce incentive to work. Although in 1985 the longer duration of short term unemployment and the lack of resources of many of the unemployed might suggest the need for upgrading the benefit provision, the presence among the unemployed of so many formerly low paid workers ensured that the work incentive arguments predominated. As the next chapter will show, this disadvantaged group has a key influence on policy for the unemployed.

References
1. Richard Berthoud, Joan C. Brown and Steven Cooper, *Poverty and the Development of Anti Poverty Policy in the United Kingdom*, Heinemann, London, 1981, p.96.

2. *Report of the Ministry of National Insurance 1951*, HMSO, London, 1952, p.7.
3. Ibid.
4. *Annual Report of the Ministry of Pensions and National Insurance 1953*, HMSO, London, 1954, p.20.
5. Ibid., p.19
6. Ministry of Pensions and National Insurance, *Benefits for very short spells of Unemployment or Sickness: Report of the National Insurance Advisory Committee*, Cmd 9609, HMSO, London, 1955, pp.30-1.
7. Ibid., p.32.
8. *Annual Reports of the Ministry of National Insurance* (1949-52) and *Annual Reports of the Ministry of Pensions and National Insurance* (1953-65), HMSO, London.
9. *Social Security Statistics* and *British Labour Statistics Historical Abstract*, op.cit.
10. *National Assistance Board Annual Report 1961*, HMSO, London, 1962, p.32.
11. *House of Commons Hansard*, 26 April 1965, 33.
12. Ibid., p.36.
13. S.R. Parker et al., *Effects of the Redundancy Payments Act*, Office of Population, Censuses and Surveys/HMSO, London, 1971, p.6.
14. Figures from the *New Earnings Survey 1968* shown in Santosh, Mukherjee, *Through no fault of their own*, PEP/Macdonald, London, 1973, p.269.
15. W.W. Daniel, *A National Survey of the Unemployed*, PEP, London, 1974, p.17.
16. *MSC Manpower Review 1982*, Manpower Services Commission, London, 1982, p.20.
17. *House of Commons Hansard*, 7 February 1966, 37.
18. Ibid.
19. Ibid., 40.
20. Ibid., 22 October 1979, 115.
21. *Social Security Statistics*, 1984.
22. *House of Commons Hansard*, 7 February 1966.
23. *Social Security Statistics*.
24. *Social Security Statistics 1985*.

25. Dennis Maki and Z.A. Spindler, 'The Effect of Unemployment Compensation on the rate of Unemployment in Great Britain', *Oxford Economic Papers*, November 1975, pp.440-54.
26. S.J. Nickell, 'The Effect of Unemployment and Related Benefits on the Duration of Unemployment', *The Economic Journal*, March 1979, pp.34-49.
27. For example, M.C. Sawyer, 'The Effects of Unemployment Compensation on the rate of Unemployment in Great Britain', *Oxford Economic Papers*, March 1979, pp.135-46.
28. Department of Health and Social Security, *Social Assistance: A review of the supplementary benefits scheme in Great Britain*, DHSS, London, 1978, p.117.
29. Ibid.
30. *Social Security Statistics 1980*.
31. *House of Commons Hansard*, 26 March 1980, 1461.
32. Ibid., 23 June 1983, 167.
33. *Social Security Statistics 1982*.
34. *House of Commons Hansard*, 22 July 1983, 269-72.
35. Sue Moylan and Bob Davies, 'The disadvantages of the unemployed', *Employment Gazette*, August 1980, pp.830-2.
36. P.R. Hughes and Gillian Hutchinson, 'Changing characteristics of male unemployment flows 1972-81', *Employment Gazette*, September 1986, pp.365-8.
37. 'Unemployment Flows. New Statistics', *Employment Gazette*, August 1983, pp.301-7.
38. *Employment Gazette*, October 1984, p.538 and 'Unemployment Flows: Northern Ireland', *Employment Gazette*, December 1984, pp.550-3.

4 The low paid and the long term unemployed

Low paid workers are both a dominating influence on provision for unemployment, and are ill served by it. This shows itself in two ways, first in the general level of benefit paid and second in the specific rules applied to low paid workers.

As Chapter 1 showed, the less eligibility principle which dictated Poor Law policy towards the unemployed flowed across to the new Unemployment Insurance scheme in 1911 which set a low level of benefit to 'imply a sensible and even severe difference between being in work or out of work'.

When Unemployment Insurance was extended to cover most manual workers and lower paid non-manual workers in 1920, the reasons given for low benefit were twofold. Both related to low pay. First, the level of contribution possible had to take into account the amount low earners could afford to pay and second, benefit levels had to take account of wages. This implied not only low contribution and benefit rates for adult males but lower levels again for women and young workers because of their generally lower earnings. The object was:

> that contributions should not constitute an undue burden on relatively small earnings and that the rates of benefit should not be so high in relation to the usual earnings as to constitute an encouragement to prefer benefit to work.[1]

There was of course a third influence on benefit levels – the cost of the contributions to industry and to the general taxpayer. It was this factor which influenced a change in benefit patterns in 1921 which was to prove significant later in relation to the low paid. Pressure for a general increase in unemployment benefit, on the grounds that it was inadequate to support the recipients, was resisted in order to hold down the cost. Instead, dependency additions were introduced for those with children and non-working wives. This limited the extra expenditure to those in greatest need[2] – but left others with lesser needs unhelped.

The report of the Blanesburgh Committee in 1927 considered the principles upon which contributions and benefits should be based. It suggested that if a contributory scheme was to have any real attractions for the compulsorily insured contributor, benefits must be reasonably adequate. At the same time benefit must be able to be covered by the tripartite contributions on which the scheme was based (employer/employee/State) and the wider interest of the employer and the State had to be taken into account. This produced various criteria, four of which were:

- The workers' contribution must be moderate in amount ... (and) should secure him an insurance sufficient in the great majority of cases to save him, during inevitable unemployment, from recourse to public assistance.
- The scheme must not, by the extent of benefit promised, tempt the insured contributor to improvidence when in receipt of good pay.
- It should provide benefits definitely less in amount than the general labourer's rate of wage, so that there may be no temptation to prefer benefits to work.
- Subject to these conditions, the scheme should be made as attractive in its benefits to the insured contributor, as, on a strictly actuarial basis, it is possible to make it.[3]

The third criterion was the key one in determining benefit rates. Both the Blanesburgh Committee and the Royal Commission on Unemployment Insurance considered the possibility of a system of wage related contributions and benefits so that higher earners could be released from the restrictions imposed by the presence in the insurance scheme of low paid members. Both saw its attractions but both rejected it on what they regarded as practical grounds.[4] Both supported the continuation, though not a wider availability, of dependency additions.[5]

It was, however, the dependency additions which came to be seen as a problem in the 1930s. While the general level of benefit could be set in relation to low wages, the incidence of children in the families of wage earners and the unemployed could not be so easily controlled. Wages took no account of the number of dependants, and there were no social security benefits for the employed. If those out of work received extra benefits on account of their children, the outcome would be contrary to the less eligibility principle and, as some saw it, to insurance principles also.

In 1935, the new Unemployment Insurance Statutory Committee (UISC, chaired by Sir William Beveridge) which was running the reformed insurance scheme, found itself in a financial position – because of declining unemployment – to respond favourably to pressure for increases in the dependency additions. In recommending these to the Minister of Labour it pointed out that the increases could have the 'disconcerting effect' of making a good deal commoner than before, cases where weekly benefit would exceed the wages earned when in employment. It argued that:

> Unemployment benefit is the direct alternative to wages: insurance against unemployment is insurance against loss of wages. It is contrary to the fundamental principle of insurance and the practice of every other form of insurance that the indemnity should be allowed to exceed the loss.[6]

The UISC suggested that one way of dealing with the problem would be to put a ceiling on the benefit receivable. This would have been applied to all claimants, but those disadvantaged by the rule would have been families with 'too many' dependants. This was rejected by the Minister and the dependency additions were increased without constraints being applied. But because the insurance benefit was limited to a duration of 26 weeks, any incentive problem would not, in any case, be long lasting.

The Unemployment Assistance Board (UAB) – which would be supporting many long term unemployed – was faced with the same problem of the relationship of benefits to wages when it had to establish national benefit scales in 1935. It reported that it had considered a number of criteria such as the cost of living, minimum nutritional requirements, other operating scales and so on. It sought a benefit which was more than just 'sufficient to support life' but it considered that:

> It had to keep in mind, however, the necessity of not proposing scales of allowances which would place unemployed persons in a better position than large numbers of persons who were in work.

> Existing wage levels were a fact that had to be recognised as posing
> an upper limit to allowances for households of normal size.[7]

Thus the general rate would be set in relation to prevailing wages
at the bottom end of the scale. This, however, still left the problem
posed by dependency additions which would be essential in a needs
related scheme. The Board noted that the low paid were already
showing 'disquieting signs' of being influenced by the level of benefits
to decline to move to another area to seek work or to undergo training,[8]
but it sought a more pointed tool than the blunt instrument proposed
by UISC of a ceiling on all benefits. It noted that:

> The Board had also to have regard to the obvious objections to
> giving assistance in any particular case which would approximate
> or exceed the net earnings which the applicant could expect to
> receive if he were in work, and it provided that, save in exceptional
> circumstances, no applicant should be assessed at a sum equal to
> or greater than the amount that would ordinarily be available by
> way of earnings for the support of the household, if he and other
> members of the household whose needs have been included in the
> calculation of the scale allowances were following the occupations
> normally followed by them.[9]

At first the Board decided to reduce the children's allowances
where there were more than 5 persons in the household.[10] This,
however, could affect previously well paid workers and in any case
'seemed' like a direct attack on children. After 1936 the Board relied
on the use of what came to be known as the Wages Stop. This put a
ceiling on the whole benefit in individual cases and thus could be
focused more precisely on the low paid.

The Board did not make extensive use of this power. By the end
of 1937 only 6,500 allowances were affected, comprising 5,700 men
and 800 women.[11] There was obviously some unease about using it
at all. In the 1937 report the UAB said:

> The question whether the circumstances of a case are such as to
> justify the partial or complete suspension of the wages stop
> provision is one of great difficulty. Wages are not determined
> primarily, if at all, by reference to the family responsibilities of the
> earner. Needs, however, are directly so determined.[12]

Particular problems arose with women applicants with dependants
'on account of the relatively low earning capacity of many of the
Board's applicants'.[13] In the end the Board devised various rules
which enabled it to pay at a higher rate than the Wages Stop itself

would have required – for example, it decided that the very fact of having four or five children constituted a special circumstance which enabled the Wages Stop to be waived. However, the fact that it was not much used did not mean that the UAB's Wages Stop was unimportant in policy terms. As will be seen later, it established a precedent which was to be much more rigorously used in years to come.

The low paid and the post war reforms

Beveridge brought with him from the UISC his concern about the relationship between benefits and wages. He wanted to improve the position of the unemployed both by extending the duration of the non-means tested benefit (in which he was unsuccessful) and by finding a solution to the problem of ensuring there was a gap between benefits and wages in a way that did not involve paying unsatisfactory benefits.

His goal for benefits was that they should be 'adequate to all normal needs, in duration and in amount'.[14] Moreover, income had to be adjusted to family needs, that is to say dependency additions for children, in particular, would be necessary. But if allowances for children were given only to those on benefit and not to those in work, 'two evils' would arise; first, children in low wage working families would suffer poverty and second, benefits could be higher than wages.[15]

His solution was to support the institution of Family Allowances payable to all families with children. He argued as follow:

> First, it is unreasonable to seek to guarantee an income sufficient for subsistence, while earnings are interrupted by unemployment or disability, without ensuring sufficient income during earning ...

> Second, it is dangerous to allow benefit during unemployment or disability to equal or exceed earnings during work. But, without allowances for children, during earnings and non-earning alike, this danger cannot be avoided ... the gap between income during earning and during interruption of earnings should be as large as possible for every man. It cannot be kept large except by either making their benefit in unemployment and disability inadequate, or by giving allowances for children in time of earning and non-earning alike.[16]

Beveridge's proposal was for subsistence adult benefits and universal children's allowances sufficient to meet the minimum cost of a child, but excluding the first child in the case of working families on the grounds that wages were usually sufficient to support a wife and one child. This would virtually take children out of the wage/benefit calculation. The government went only part way towards realising this plan.

As seen in Chapter 2, the 1944 White Paper rejected the idea of subsistence level benefits for both adults and children. There were a number of reasons given for this but the clinching argument on the insurance benefits was related to contribution levels. These must take account of 'the maximum contribution which the great body of contributors can properly be asked to bear'.[17]

This was later 'translated' by a Labour government spokesman closing the debate on the 1946 National Insurance Bill (and somewhat exasperated by opposition interruptions) who said:

> The Bill gives absolute minimum benefits –what are we asked to do in this Bill? We are asked to provide social security on the ability of the lowest paid worker to pay a contribution ... Within a capitalist system, within a wages system which hon. Members opposite support, that is an absolute impossibility. The result is that we can give a minimum, a very meagre minimum, and that has to be supplemented.[18]

As seen, the object of the supplementation provisions – through the National Assistance Board – was to provide a safety net, at subsistence level, for those without insurance benefits or whose benefits were less than their assessed needs. However, for the low paid worker, this guarantee was to be modified. Regulations introduced in 1948[19] took over from the UAB the old Wages Stop, now losing its final 's' but otherwise little different from its predecessor. Clause 5 provided that unless there were special circumstances, the amount of assistance given should not 'exceed the amount of his net weekly earnings if he were employed full time in his normal occupation'.

The years of high employment

The Beveridge plan to equalise the position of employed and unemployed families with more than one child was further undermined in 1948. Because the Family Allowance was set below subsistence level, the National Assistance Board (NAB) found it necessary to set its child dependency rate above that of the Family Allowance. The first child received the whole of this addition (which was also age related) and subsequent children were paid a sum over and above the Family Allowance.

This not only created an imbalance between those in and out of work, it also affected those on Unemployment Benefit who received no child dependency additions (CDAs) except than for the first child. Those with more than one child could then become eligible for supplementation. The government in 1951 extended the CDAs to all the dependent children of National Insurance recipients. This dealt with part of the problem but, because in subsequent years the Family Allowance was not kept in line with inflation while on the whole National Assistance and National Insurance were, the imbalance between those in and out of work increased. Moreover, National Assistance (and later Supplementary Benefit) recipients received an allowance for their full housing costs, while those in work received nothing, unless they lived as Council tenants in an area with a rent rebate scheme.

National Insurance benefits
The National Insurance benefits, paid by right of contribution, were not subject to a Wage Stop. Because in these years the vast majority of unemployment spells were brief, the lack of such a mechanism was not seen as a serious problem. However, when the Earnings Related Supplement was introduced in 1966 it was felt necessary to put a ceiling on the total benefit of 85 per cent of the wages on which the benefit was reckoned. This was specifically intended to avoid too high a rate of payment being made to low paid workers. The object, according to the Minister (Margaret Herbison) introducing the Bill was 'to secure that claimants generally are not better off when sick or unemployed than they would be at work'. This was particularly needed in the UK because 'the personal rate of benefit can be substantially increased by allowances for dependents'.[20] It was acknowledged that the rule would mainly apply to the low wage earner. 'The higher wage earner unless he had a very great number of dependants, will never be touched by the ceiling'.[21]

The Wage Stop to 1975

Table 4.1 The Wage Stop 1953-70. Great Britain

Year	Number of persons subject to the wage-stop rule in November each year	Number of their dependants
1953	2,400	-
1954	2,700	-
1955	2,300	-
1956	2,600	-
1957	2,900	-
1958	7,000	-
1959	20,700	-
1960	15,300	-
1961	15,000	-
1962	28,400	-
1963	27,600	-
1964	16,600	-
1965	20,500	-
1966	-	-
1967	37,600	179,100
1968	32,400	152,800
1969	24,000	158,300
1970	35,600	158,600

1. The table is based upon information obtained from a sample inquiry held on a particular day in November of each year.
2. No information is available about the number of persons subject to the wage stop rule before 1953, or about the number of their dependants before 1967.
3. Because of pressure of work following the introduction of the supplementary benefits scheme, an inquiry was not held in November 1966.

Source: *House of Commons Hansard*, 4 August 1971, 327.

The ERS ceiling aside, the most overt influence of low wages on benefits was felt in the National Assistance – later Supplementary Benefit – provision. Table 3.4 showed the numbers receiving National Assistance from 1949-65, and Table 3.7 gave the figures from

1965-79. These figures can be compared with Table 4.1 which shows the numbers affected by the Wage Stop from 1953 to 1970 in November of each year. Not all of these were unemployed. The Wage Stop was also applied to the sick on a discretionary basis for the first six months of incapacity. However, the unemployed were the most likely to be affected. In 1963 for example, of 27,600 wage stopped families, 23,000 were unemployed, and in 1965 of 20,500 wage stopped, some 16,000 were unemployed.[22] It should be noted also that these are point in time figures, so that more families would be affected over the whole year.

As Table 4.1 shows, the Wage Stop was not much used in the early 1950s, but by 1963 the figures had become sufficiently high to make the NAB uneasy about its policy, and it began to discuss the question in its Annual Reports. This unease increased in the following two years as a public debate began on poverty, particularly among children.[23] The NAB reported in 1965 that, in its 16,000 unemployed wage stopped families, there were 56,000 children.[24] In some years the figure reached 60,000 at any one time and these children were in families 'with a weekly income below the level of their needs as measured by the normal scale rates'.[25]

The NAB pointed out, however, that the problem was principally one of low wages and of the Board's inability, under the legislation, to supplement the wages of those in work.[26] In so doing it was reminding government that there are two ways to deal with a possible overlap between benefits out of work and wages in work. One is to reduce benefits and the other is to raise wages or improve the social security provision for wage earners.

The new Supplementary Benefits Commission (after 1966), under attack for creating or maintaining child poverty through the Wage Stop, published a report on its operation in 1967. First, it denied that it was in the business of creating work incentives. It said:

> The purpose of the wage stop is not to provide an incentive to a man to get work. The wage stop does not require a man to get less when receiving Supplementary Benefit than he would get when working. What it does is to ensure that an unemployed man's income is no greater than it would be if he were in full time employment.[27] (SBC's italics)

It went on to point out that, since no benefit could be paid to a man in full time employment, even if his wages were below Supplementary Benefit level, it would be wrong in equity to bring the income of a man of a low earning capacity up to that level because he happened to be unemployed or temporarily sick, when there was nothing that could be done for his counterpart in full time work. It was not the Wage Stop which caused family poverty. It was instead 'a harsh reflection of the fact that there are many men in work living on incomes below the Supplementary Benefit standard'.[28]

The option of a National Minimum Wage to deal in the low wages was considered by governments in the late 1960s and rejected. The chosen course of action was to attempt to reduce child poverty in low paid families with children through improved social security, and in the process, reduce the need for the Wage Stop. The first step was taken in 1967-8 by the then Labour government. The Family Allowance was increased for the first time since 1956, but the increase made was too small to have any marked effect. The Conservative government in power from 1970-4 saw a large increase in the Family Allowance as too costly and insufficiently focused on low wage families. It therefore introduced (in 1971) the Family Income Supplement, a benefit designed to supplement the wages of low earning families with children. This was followed in 1972 by legislation to provide rent rebates or allowances for low paid workers and others not on Supplementary Benefit.

Once these two possible benefits were included in the Wage Stop calculations the numbers being wage stopped fell sharply. By 1974 only 1 per cent of the unemployed in Great Britain were wage stopped although 10 per cent of Northern Ireland unemployed were affected.[29] However, by this time the Wage Stop was almost wholly focused on families with three or more children and, as such, was politically embarrassing. In 1975 when only 6,000 families were being wage stopped, it was time for the abolition of the rule.[30]

The Supplementary Benefits Commission (SBC) reporting on the abolition of the wage stop (in July 1975) foreshadowed a continuing influence of low pay in social security benefit rates. It said:

> The Commission recognises that the abolition of the wage stop has given rise to some public disquiet about reports of men whose benefit levels appear to be disproportionately high when compared with the general level of wages.[31]

It urged again the need for action on benefits for working families and on wages. To some extent its wishes were met through new legislation which amalgamated the Family Allowance and a Child Tax Allowance available to taxpayers, and created a new Child Benefit which would be payable in respect of all children, including the first child of the family. The new benefit was particularly helpful to the lowest earners, but its level was not high enough to make a serious impact on the issue of the overlap between benefits and wages. For this, however, a new but as yet not fully recognised weapon had become available from 1973, in particular in relation to the long term unemployed.

The long term unemployed

As seen in Chapter 3, the objective of the post-war Labour government was to eliminate long term unemployment, then defined as 6 months or more out of work. However, in the uncertainties of the immediate post war years, it did not feel sufficiently confident that it could achieve this goal to risk including the long term unemployed in the National Insurance scheme. If the worst happened and there was a return to the level of unemployment characteristic of the depression years, the new National Insurance scheme could be endangered. It was safer to limit the unemployment role of National Insurance to short term unemployment. The support of the long term unemployed should fall on the nation as a whole through a tax supported benefit.

Such a decision did not necessarily require that the unemployed be divided into two classes, one inferior to the other, as had been alleged to be the case in the depression years (see Chapter 1). A tax supported benefit did not have to be means tested. Indeed the Family Allowance which had just been instituted (in 1945) was an example of a non-means tested benefit outside of National Insurance. However, while the Labour government was not prepared to suggest that an indefinite non-means tested benefit might lead to abuse – the position the Coalition government had taken – it was equally not prepared to take the plunge and provide such a benefit by right. Instead, it hoped to avoid the problem by a temporary provision of extended benefit for a 5 year period – to 1953. This was payable to those whose National Insurance entitlements had expired, subject to a tribunal considering the individual's circumstances and the employment conditions in the area. Those found to be ineligible could claim National Assistance.

The minority of the unemployed who required National Assistance for any length of time were almost certainly being viewed by 1953 (when new decisions had to be made for the longer term unemployed), as either not containable in a scheme for unemployment insurance, because they were in and out of work so frequently, or unsuitable for such a scheme. Indeed the description of the long term unemployed (over 6 months out of work) by the NAB in its reports indicated that they bore a strong resemblance to that group in the 1930s which was left to Public Assistance because they were regarded as marginal to the labour market, including a small minority described as 'work shy'.

The 1951 NAB report, for example, noted that the lengthy period some unemployed people had spent on assistance 'must be attributed in large measure to the extent to which they are handicapped physically or mentally'.[32] It went on to say that out of 60,000 recipients of National Assistance – most of whom required more than temporary help – 'the Board's officers were not prepared to say firmly that more than about 7,000 were persons who could be working if they really wanted to work'.[33] The 1952 report reiterated this and went on to discuss in detail how the work shy could be dealt with, without sacrificing the interests of wives and children.[34] With this information before it in 1953, it was perhaps not surprising that the Conservative government of the day decided that there was no need for major change in the benefit arrangements. Extended benefit was ended, additional days for those with a good employment record were increased, and provision through National Assistance for the long term unemployed would be maintained. If there had been any doubts about this decision, a survey of the long term unemployed in Scotland in 1958 which found only 15 per cent completely fit, physically or mentally, to follow their normal occupations,[35] would have laid them to rest.

In 1966 the then Labour government extended the National Insurance benefit duration to 12 months. As seen in Chapter 3, it was presented as a fairer measure than the continuation of the additional days provisions which restricted longer benefits to those who had been in stable employment. It would also be simpler to administer. However, once the redefined group of long term unemployed ran out of NI rights at the end of 12 months, the new Supplementary Benefits scheme would take over responsibility. The principle of provision for the long term unemployed within the general means tested social assistance scheme was thus maintained and indeed did not appear to have been questioned.

In effect, the UK had drifted into a dual system of benefits for the unemployed after 1948 without any serious re-examination of the underlying principles. Throughout the period the numbers involved at any one time had been quite modest and although by 1966 those out of work for more than a year constituted 13-17 per cent of the unemployed, the numbers rarely exceeded 50,000.[36] A problem of this size did not command much attention.

Growing disadvantage for the long term unemployed

Up to 1966 being long term unemployed on National Assistance or Supplementary Benefit was not much worse for most claimants than being sick or elderly. The minority who were wage stopped were disadvantaged, particularly as the provision was applied to people who had been unemployed for many years,[37] but for the rest the basic rates of benefit were the same for all classes of recipients. In 1966 the first step away from this more or less equal treatment was taken. A small additional allowance – a long term addition – was given to all the elderly and to other recipients who had been on benefit for more than two years. The exception to this was the unemployed.

In 1973, what had been a tentative differentiation between the elderly, other recipients and the unemployed, and between long and short term cases, became more fully enshrined in policy. Within the Supplementary Benefits scheme, two rates were established. A long term rate for the elderly from the beginning and for most other recipients after two years on benefit and the short term rate for all but the elderly for the first two years and for the unemployed, no matter how long they were on benefit. It was this new differentiation which came to replace the Wage Stop as the means of avoiding an overlap between benefits and wages.

At first sight, the unemployed were no worse off. They were just not receiving an additional allowance. Indeed, when the Wage Stop was abolished in 1975, the poorest among them were better off. But the reasoning behind the new long term rates indicated that actual disadvantage was involved. The government spokesman in the House explained in 1973 that:

> People receiving the short term benefits often return to work within a few weeks and can postpone longer term requirements – for example clothes and household equipment – until they are back in employment. Moreover they often have, in addition to the earnings related supplement for the first six months, deferred wages, and other savings to help tide them over their period off work. Those receiving pensions and other long term benefits are more dependent, however, on the benefit they received.[38]

Thus a new, higher standard of need was being established for those on benefit for long periods, but the long term unemployed, whose needs were presumably no different, were to be kept at the lower level suitable for people with other resources and/or with early prospects of wage income. The differentiation was compounded after 1975 when a formal policy was introduced to uprate short term benefits to meet inflation, but long term benefits by the higher of two criteria, inflation or wage inceases. In part as a result of this policy and in part because even equal percentage increases to unequal amounts will produce different outcomes, the gap between short and long term supplementary benefit widened year by year. In 1973 it was £1 pw for a single person and £1.20 pw for a married couple. In 1979 it was £5.40 and £7.95 pw respectively. After 1980, the same uprating criteria – inflation – was applied to both rates but the operation of percentage increases ensured that the gap, once established, continued to widen – to £8 and £12.15 respectively in 1985.[39]

This policy, moreover, was no longer being applied to a relatively small group. As general unemployment rose, so did the size of the long term unemployed population. Table 4.2 shows the figures for men from 1968 to 1985.

Table 4.2 Number of men unemployed for more than 12 months, July 1968-85. Great Britain

000s

1968	76.7	1977	254.5
1969	81.8	1978	264.3
1970	88.6	1979	268.2
1971	108.0	1980	268.7
1972	150.1	1981	464.2
1973	137.3	1982	810.4
1974	112.7	1983	832.0
1975	129.2	1984	907.6
1976	201.8	1985	969.2

Source: *Department of Employment Gazette*

The position of women will be discussed in Chapter 5 but here it may be noted that the number registering as unemployed was much lower, in part because so many married women had no benefit entitlement at all, while others would not qualify for Supplementary

Benefit once their NI entitlement ran out. This would only be available as a direct right to woman not living with a husband or other man.

Tables 3.4 and 3.7 showed how the numbers of those dependent on National Assistance/Supplementary Benefit (and not as a supplement to National Insurance), increased in the same period. The figures are for both men and women and include the short term unemployed without NI entitlement, as well as the long term unemployed, but the last group predominated. More and more individuals and families found themselves dependent on the means tested benefit. Moreover, this was a much different group from the 'marginal' workers supported by National Assistance in the immediate post war years. These were men and women with strong labour market attachments, yet, according to the SBC, they were treated 'as if they were an inferior caste'.[40]

The debate about the position of the long term unemployed which took place in the late 1970s, was strongly influenced by the issue of low pay. In its 1976 Annual Report, the SBC said:

> We believe that most claimants, and particuarly those who have been unemployed for long periods, have to live on incomes which are too low ... It does not disturb us if a few cases – very few at the moment – our benefits exceed what may be the very low wages paid to some workers in this country. But democratic governments have to be accountable to the electorate as a whole and it is clear that the British people will not tolerate rates of supplementary benefit for the unemployed which exceed wages on a large scale ... for the unemployed at least, public opinion requires that there should be a gap between the general level of our benefits and the general level of wages paid for less skilled work.[41]

The problem, the SBC said, was principally related to the dependency additions paid to large families and it went on to conclude: 'thus the incomes of low paid workers with several children must rise before it is reasonable to expect any major increase in supplementary benefit'.[42]

As unemployment continued to increase and evidence of the financial problems and hardship being experienced by the long term unemployed became available,[43] the SBC in both Great Britain and Northern Ireland concluded that the proper course of action was to give them access to the long term rate on the same terms as other non-pensioner SB recipients.[44] So also did a report of a review by the DHSS of the Supplementary Benefit scheme carried out in 1977-8.[45]

The Conservative government's policies 1979-85

As Chapter 3 showed, the newly elected government in 1979 had accepted much of the argument about benefit induced unemployment and it took steps to reduce the income of the short term unemployed. It also rejected the recommendation of the DHSS Review Team that the long term rate of Supplementary Benefit should be extended to the unemployed on the same rules as for other non-pensioners, and that this reform should take priority over another proposal, i.e. that the duration of the short term SB rate be reduced to 12 months. Instead the government gave the priority to the general reduction, moving all but the unemployed to the long term rate after a year on benefit. This was on the grounds that families with children needed more help,[46] though not apparently unemployed families with children who, the evidence had shown, were also at a disadvantage.

The huge increase in unemployment generally (see Table 3.1) and long term unemployment in Great Britain (Table 4.2) from 1981 onwards raised serious questions about this policy. There had for many years been prolonged unemployment in Northern Ireland. In 1971 for example 5.5 per cent of the unemployed had been out of work for more than 3 years and by 1980, the figure was 11.2 per cent.[47] But the actual numbers of the individuals involved were relatively small, and could the more easily be discounted for policy purposes.

Until 1980, the Department of Employment's published figures for Great Britain showed only a general category of those unemployed for 52 weeks or more, though Supplementary Benefit data pointed to the existence of a core of very long term unemployed. From October 1980 the *Employment Gazette* began to show figures for those unemployed for 2 years or more. In 1983 the analysis was further extended to show those unemployed for 4 years and 5 years or more. By July 1985, for the United Kingdom as a whole, there were nearly 160,000 men and women registered as unemployed for 5 years or more and this was so even after the majority of 60-64 year old men had been excluded from the count, (a change to be explained below).

The government's natural instinct in 1979 was to keep unemployment benefits low to induce a return to work. But it also resisted the extension to the long term unemployed of the long term rate of SB on grounds of cost and the need to control and, where possible, reduce public expenditure. By 1981, in face of the increased long term unemployment figures, it found it necessary to shift ground a little.

The first report of the Social Security Advisory Committee (SSAC), which replaced the SBC for both Great Britain and Northern Ireland in 1981, noted, with satisfaction, the government's public acceptance of the need to extend the SB long term rate to the unemployed when resources permitted. The Committee described the withholding of the long term rate from the unemployed as 'wholly unjust'. The long term rate had been established by successive governments as the 'minimum level of income for people who had been wholly dependent on social security for more than a year'. It could not be right that a significant proportion of long term recipients had to rely on a rate of personal benefit which was little more than two-thirds of the minimum level.[48]

The SSAC adopted the issue as one of its priorities, making proposals to phase in the extension of the long term rate on a group by group basis, starting with families with dependent children.[49] The position of the children of the unemployed was becoming of increasing concern. By late 1981, nearly 900,000 children under 16 years were in families of the unemployed on Supplementary Benefit, living at the short term rate of benefit.[50] Not all of these were children of the long term unemployed, but a substantial porportion were. Studies, including those by the DHSS itself, had shown that long term unemployed claimants, particularly those with children experienced 'greater financial difficulties' than other claimants.[51]

It was true that certain payments could be available in addition to the basic benefit. Housing costs were met, including mortgage interest (but not capital repayments) for home owners. A large proportion of all claimants received a weekly addition for heating, and some other special needs – for example, dietary requirements – also attracted a small allowance. It was also possible to claim Single Payments for essential items which could not be met out of the weekly allowance, such as house repairs, or a replacement of a worn out cooker. In 1985, for example, just over 2 million Single Payments were made to unemployed claimants at an average payment of £76.58 in the year.[52]

These additions to benefits were sometimes the means to meet essential minimum needs – the allowances for housing, for example, and sometimes a method of keeping pace with rising fuel (and other) costs, without a general benefit increase – the heating allowance, for example. The Single Payments were heavily concentrated on claimants who were experiencing special hardship, and notably on families with children, a large proportion of whom were unemployed and on the short term rate of benefit. They helped the family to survive, but did not make up for the low basic income.[53]

But the government did not respond to this evidence of need among families with children. Instead it turned its attention to another group. In November 1981, men aged 60-64 were permitted to move to the long term rate of SB after 12 months provided they ceased to register for work. In 1983 this was amended to permit these older unemployed to receive the long term rate from the time they came on to benefit, in parallel with the elderly, again provided they did not register for work. The advantage of this step was that it removed virtually the whole group from the unemployment register and it was directed at an age range for whom the issue of work incentives had become largely irrelevant, given the state of the labour market. For the remainder of the long term unemployed, the principal policy initiatives were directed to a series of special employment measures.

The use of such measures had begun in the 1970s as short term, often experimental, programmes to deal with the general rise in unemployment. The largest of these was the Youth Opportunities Programme, which will be discussed in a later chapter, and there were also a number of subsidy programmes to encourage employers to recruit workers. In April 1975 a specific programme was designed for the long term unemployed, defined as out of work for more than six months in the case of 19-24 year olds, and more than 12 months for those 25 years and over. The Special Temporary Employment Programme (STEP) gave employment for 52 weeks on projects of value to the community, and had 12,000 places by 1979.[54] Wages were to be paid at 'the appropriate level for the job', i.e. the local rate payable, with an original maximum (in 1978) of £64.68pw,[55] at a time when average male manual earnings were £80.70pw.[56] In early 1979, average wages having reached £93pw, the maximum rate for STEP was increased to £83pw.

The original plan was that STEP would be expanded by 1981 to reach 35,000 places. However, the incoming Conservative government in 1979 restricted expenditure on the scheme and it remained at 12,000 places. The Manpower Services Commission, which was responsible for the scheme, noted in 1980 that it considered that 'rising unemployment will highlight the inadequacy of the scale of the present programme'.[57]

In 1981, STEP was replaced by the Community Enterprise Programme (CEP) with 25,000 places – at a time when long term unemployment had passed 400,000. In 1982, when the numbers of long term unemployed were moving towards the million mark, CEP was reconstituted as the Community Programme, reaching 45,000 places in April 1983 and 113,000 in April 1984.[58] The limit of 52 weeks on the programme was maintained.

The wage limit set was still supposed to be related to the local rate for the job, and an average £60 pw was to be paid for each place, some of which would be full time and others part time. The actual wage paid would depend on the mix of places on the project. But the chance of a full time worker reaching the old (1979) STEP limit was doubtful, to say the least. The rate was raised in 1984, but only to £63 per place.

An alternative to this kind of special programme was a place on the Training Opportunities Scheme (TOPs), which offered a variety of skill training. In 1979/80 some 75,000 people completed the training of whom nearly two-thirds had been previously unemployed, including one fifth who had been long term unemployed.[59] The Training Allowance paid was £27.55 pw plus an addition for a dependent wife, where appropriate. By 1983/4, the completions had fallen to just over 66,000[60] and the allowance increased only to £35.05 pw plus the dependant's allowance.

Both the Community Programme and TOPS were of value to the individuals involved. They provided a higher income than Supplementary Benefit for a time, training (to a greater or lesser degree), constructive activity and, overall, they improved potential for employment. However, if jobs were not to be had – and for a large proportion they were not – then the next step was a return to dependence on social security. The increased income which had been available for a time was low and left no room for savings or a new accumulation of resources – as for example a period in well paid employment would have provided. In effect, this group found itself moving from low benefit to low wages/allowances and back to low benefit.

The long term unemployed and benefit provision to 1985
In 1948 the Labour government had hoped to deal with the vast majority of the unemployed through National Insurance combined

with extended benefit paid without means test. In 1966, a fresh attempt was made to place the principal emphasis on National Insurance both through the extension of benefit duration to 12 months and through an Earnings Related Supplement for 6 months which could postpone any need for SB supplementation. Table 4.3 shows how the balance of provision shifted during the 1970s and 1980s.

Table 4.3 Proportion of unemployed men supported by three forms of provision[1] 1972, 1979 and 1984. Great Britain and 1983 Northern Ireland

percentages

	1972(GB)	1979(GB)	1984(GB)	1983(NI)
NI Benefits only	41	37	21	15
NI and SB	14	10	9	8
SB only	45	53	70	77t

1. Excluding those not on any benefit

Source: *Social Security Statistics*

It will be recalled (from Chapter 1) that in 1935 the plan for the Unemployment Insurance of the day was that it would support around half the unemployed and that, by 1938, some 60 per cent of the unemployed were in fact on the insurance benefit. After a period when the NI benefit was dominant benefit (see Tables 3.2 and 3.4), by 1972 the balance of provision was very similar to that in 1935. The figures for 1983/4 show to what extent the basic intention of the 1948 provision has been overtaken by the huge growth in long term unemployment and by the fact that so many NI recipients required means tested supplementation.

In its 1981 report the SSAC said: 'We do not believe that means tested benefit should be seen as the normal way of meeting the needs of unemployed people'.[61] It saw the immediate priority as the extension of the long term SB rate to the unemployed but believed that once this was done, options for improving the level and duration of the contributory benefit ought to be considered. By 1985, it had not even managed to reach first base.

References
1. *The Royal Commission on Unemployment Insurance*, op.cit., p.216.

2. Joan C. Brown, *Children in Social Security*, PSI, London, 1984, pp.13-15.
3. Blanesburgh Report, op.cit., p.31.
4. Ibid., p.38 and Royal Commission Report, op.cit., pp.216-17.
5. Ibid., p.68 and p.253 respectively.
6. Cited in Sir William Beveridge, *The Unemployment Insurance Statutory Committee*, LSE, London, 1973, p.40.
7. *Unemployment Assistance Board Report 1935*, Cmd 5177, HMSO, London, 1936, pp.34-4.
8. Ibid., p.12.
9. Ibid., pp.33-34.
10. Ibid., p.292.
11. 1937 Report, op.cit., p.22.
12. Ibid., pp.20-1.
13. Ibid.
14. Beveridge Report, op.cit., p.15.
15. Ibid., pp.7-8.
16. Ibid., p.154.
17. *Social Insurance Part I*, op.cit., p.7.
18. Mr Lindgren, Parliamentary Under Secretary to the Ministry of National Insurance, *House of Commons Hansard*, 7 February 1946, 1982.
19. *The National Assistance (Determination of Need) Regulations 1948*.
20. *House of Commons Hansard*, 7 February 1966, 38-9.
21. Ibid., 47.
22. *Annual Report of the National Assistance Board 1963 and 1965*, HMSO, London, p.38 and p.30.
23. Following the findings of Brian Abel-Smith and Peter Townsend, later published in *The Poor and the Poorest*, Bell and Son, London, 1965.
24. *Annual Report of the National Assistance Board 1965*, p.30.
25. Ibid., p.viii.
26. Ibid.
27. Ministry of Social Security, *Administration of the Wage Stop*, HMSO, London, 1967, p.1.
28. Ibid., p.2.
29. Supplementary Benefits Commission (Northern Ireland), *Annual Report 1974*, HMSO, Belfast, 1975, p.18.

30. Supplementary Benefits Commission (Great Britain), *Annual Report 1975*, HMSO, London, 1976, pp.19-20.
31. Ibid., p.20.
32. NAB, *Annual Report 1951*, p.8.
33. Ibid.
34. NAB, *Annual Report 1952*, p.13.
35. NAB, *Annual Report 1958*, pp.62-3.
36. *Employment and Productivity Gazette*, December 1969.
37. *The Administration of the Wage Stop*, op.cit., and Laurie Elks, *The Wage Stop*, CPAG, London, 1974, pp.24-5.
38. *House of Commons Hansard*, Standing Committee F.17, May 1973, 85.
39. *Social Security Statistics 1985*.
40. SBC *Annual Report 1977*, p.43.
41. SBC *Annual Report 1976*, p.4.
42. Ibid., p.5.
43. Ibid., pp.36-40 shows the results of the Commission's own research.
44. SBC (Northern Ireland) *Annual Report 1977*, p.12 and SBC (Great Britain) Annual Report 1978, P.8.
45. DHSS, *Social Assistance, A Review of the Supplementary Benefits Scheme in Great Britain*, op.cit., p.47.
46. *House of Commons Hansard*, 20 December 1979, 909.
47. Department of Finance, *Social and Economic Trends in Northern Ireland, 1978 and 1980*, HMSO, Belfast.
48. *First Report of the Social Security Advisory Committee 1981*, HMSO, London, 1982, p.26.
49. Ibid.
50. *Social Security Statistics 1982* and John Ditch, *Hard Terms, Unemployment and Supplementary Benefit in Northern Ireland*, National Consumer Council, London, 1984, p.15.
51. *Social Assistance*, op.cit.
52. Social Security Statistics 1987.
53. Richard Berthoud, *Evidence to the Supplementary Benefit Review*, PSI, London, 1984.
54. *Department of Employment Gazette*, April 1979, p.365.
55. Manpower Services Commission, *Annual Report 1977-78*, p.28.
56. *Social Security Statistics*.
57. Manpower Services Commission, *Manpower Review 1980*, p.30.

58. Manpower Services Commission, *Annual Report 83/84*, p.13.
59. Manpower Services Commission, *Review of Services for the Unemployed*, 1980, p.19.
60. Manpower Services Commission, *Annual Report 83/84*, p.21.
61. SSAC Report 1981, op.cit., p.28.

5 Women and unemployment

The unequal treatment of women has been a characteristic of provision for unemployment throughout its existence, and if not in the insurance arrangements, then certainly in the means tested provision. In one period all women were paid less benefit than men. Later, the rules differentiated between single women and married women in the level of benefits paid and, at times, in the eligibility requirements also. The differential treatment of married women was finally eliminated from Unemployment Benefit in the late 1970s but persisted in Supplementary Benefit provision. The early justification for the different treatment of women was related to their low wages but the dominant questions in later years whether married women could be regarded as having a real labour force attachment or should they rather be seen as economically dependent on their husbands. Within the means tested schemes it was the operation of the household means test that had the greatest effect.

Women in the pre-war scheme

Unequal benefit rates
When Unemployment Benefit was first introduced in 1911, no difference was made between men and women in the eligibility rules or in the benefit paid. The number of women involved was relatively small, and both contribution and benefit rates were low even in relation to the women's wages. The extension of the scheme in 1916 to cover munition workers brought in larger numbers of women, but since the government of the day was set on attracting women temporarily into the industry to release men for active service, it was politic to continue equal treatment. This ended with the 1920 Unemployment Insurance

Act, and it took over half a century to restore full equality of benefit rates.

Under the 1920 Act, a substantial number of women were eligible for the insurance scheme. There were now no special reasons in favour of equal treatment. On the contrary, provision for women in the scheme had to be seen alongside that in the National Health Insurance (NHI) scheme which served much the same population and which had differentiated between men and women from the beginning. Thus, a precedent had been established and one to which the NHI wished to adhere, since it regarded women, and particularly married women, with some suspicion.[1]

In planning the new Unemployment Insurance scheme in 1920, policy makers took this NHI factor into account,[2] but had other reasons for introducing differentiation. Benefits generally had to be increased over the old, low, pre-war level. This implied higher costs which would be modified if a lower rate for women was set, especially as they now constituted a notable proportion of insured contributors.[3] The Royal Commission on Unemployment Insurance discussing the 1920 rates for women and juveniles, presented the major policy reason. It said:

> As regards this differential treatment according to age and sex, the legislature appears to have been guided by the principles that, so far as is practicable with flat rates, contributions and benefits should be adjusted in accordance with the broad differences of wage earning capacity so that contributions should not constitute an undue burden on relatively small earnings and that the rates of benefit should not be so high in relation to the usual earnings as to constitute an encouragement to prefer benefit to work.[4]

Women, thus, could be accommodated in a scheme which was basically designed for adult men, but only if they were charged less and paid less in line with their low paid status in the labour force.

Very little objection was raised to this. In evidence before the Blanesburgh Committee in 1927 the TUC said:

> There is a strong opinion in some sections of the Labour Movement that the rates of benefit from men and women should be equal. Provided contributions are equal, we see no objection to equality of benefit; but on the whole we are of the opinion that the low wages paid to many women workers made it desirable that they should pay a lower contribution, in which case a lower rate of benefit is inevitable.[5]

After this ringing endorsement of women's rights from their representatives, it was not surprising that the Blanesburgh Committee saw no need for change.

More effort was put into the evidence of National Union of Societies for Equal Citizenship to the later Royal Commission. The National Union wanted to see wage related benefits for both men and women and argued that 'it is not reasonable to distinguish between men and women on the general ground of difference of normal earning capacity, and not to distinguish between the better paid and lower paid workers of each sex'.[6] The Commission felt it could not propose such a radical change to benefits in time of economic crisis and it noted that it had heard from only one other organisation proposing benefit equalisation. It therefore stood by the practice of unequal contribution and benefits which in due course found its way into the 1934 scheme.

The right to benefit

The benefit rates applied to single and married women alike, who were thus equal in their inequality. Eligibility rules introduced in 1931, known as the Anomalies Regulations, singled out married women for disadvantageous treatment.

The rules were based on the assumption that many married women claiming benefit were not really unemployed and seeking work. The 1920 Unemployment Insurance Act had added the requirement for claimants to show that they were 'genuinely seeking work' and those who could not do so had their benefit disallowed. Women, and in particular married women, found they were more likely to be disallowed on these grounds than men.[7] This rule was ended in 1930 and the Anomalies Regulations were designed specifically to deal with the 'problem' of married women.

They provided that, for those married women with a low contribution record (though sufficient for other categories to receive benefit), additional qualifying conditions should apply:
1. that she is normally employed in insurable employment and will normally seek to obtain her livelihood by means of insurable employment; and
2. that, having regard to all the circumstances of her case and particularly to her industrial experience and the industrial circumstances of the district in which she resides, she can reasonably expect to obtain insurable employment in that district.[8]

The Royal Commission commenting on this, emphasised that the necessity for special conditions for married women:

> arises from the fact that it is the exception rather than the rule for women, after marriage, to earn their living by insurable employment, and that, in the case of married women as a class, industrial employment cannot be regarded as a normal condition.[9]

The Commission's Minority Report, on the other hand, considered the rules unreasonable and a cause of much hardship. It noted that:

> The difficulty of treating married women as a class apart, to whom special regulations apply, has often been pointed out. As a result of the Regulation, the few who were claiming benefit without any particular intention of wage earning have been got rid of, but at the price of disallowing thousands of women, fully paid up contributors, genuinely seeking work, and in many cases in financial need of it. They suffer from the industrial depression in common with the rest of the unemployed, and, like them, would be back at wage-earning again if the opportunity occurred.[10]

The clause related to the industrial circumstances of the district (2 above) was modified somewhat following the Royal Commission report, but the main regulations stood.

The establishment of the Unemployment Assistance Board (UAB) in 1934 institutionalised means tested benefits for the longer term unemployed. Like the Poor Law/Public Assistance before it, the UAB operated the Household Means Test. Unless an unemployed married woman was the head of household (in effect in a one parent family) she was treated as financially dependent on her husband. If he was working, she would have no benefit entitlement and if he was unemployed, he received a dependant's addition for her. If she was employed, his benefit might be reduced. Sons, unmarried daughters or widowed daughters at home were also treated as members of the household. Part of their earnings would be taken into account when benefits for other members of the household were being determined and their benefits in unemployment would be affected by the earnings of other household members.[11]

The Household Means Test was greatly resented, but mainly for its effects on the self respect of the unemployed male head of household who saw his benefit cut if his wife or son or daughter worked. When the means test was modified in 1941 it was principally to reduce the dependence of the father on his children, (and vice versa), not to reduce the financial dependence of the wife on her husband which was regarded as normal.

The Beveridge Report and unemployed women

In his proposals for women in the new insurance scheme, Beveridge, and the subsequent government White Paper on his proposals, distinguished between single and married women.[12] The former were to receive the same rate of benefit as men but would pay a lower rate of contribution. This was not based on the probable lower rates of pay, as before, but on the fact that the male contribution had to cover, not only their own possible claims on the scheme, but allowances for their dependants and pensions for their widows.[13] Single men paid contributions at the same rate as married men, presumably on the assumption that they would marry sooner or later.

Included in the definition of single women were those living with a man but not married to him. They would be expected to contribute to National Insurance at the single women's rate, and thus qualify for unemployment and other benefits in their own right, but they would not be entitled to widow's benefit or old age pension in right of the contributions of their de facto husbands.[14]

In providing greater equality of treatment for the single woman, Beveridge offered a useful step forward for this group and restored to them their pre-1920 position. In his treatment of the co-habiting woman, he accepted the prevailing social insurance rules. His attempts to sort out the position of married women did break some new ground.

He began from the premis that for the majority of married women, marriage was their sole occupation. The position of women who were financially dependant on their husbands had not been adequately recognised in the pre-war schemes (in particular in National Health Insurance which did not cover wives) and this had to be put right. Accordingly, Beveridge said 'the Plan for Social Security treats married women as a special insurance class of occupied persons and treats man and wife as a team ... It treats a man's contribution as made on behalf of himself and his wife, as a team ... and it gives benefit as for the team.[15] In this way the new scheme would provide basic security for a non-working wife from the time of her marriage.

What then of married women who worked? Operating on pre-war data, Beveridge noted that these constituted 1 in 8 married women in 1931 and 1 in 7 just before the war. He made no comment on the quite large scale entry of women into the labour force in the war years. His assumption appeared to be that pre-war patterns would reassert themselves once the unnatural situation created by war had ended. For the minority who did work, rules nevertheless had to be devised if only to deal with the issues raised by the Anomalies Regulations.

The 1931 Anomalies Regulations had been designed to deal with, what Beveridge saw as 'undoubtedly a scandal in unemployment insurance' i.e. 'the drawing of Unemployment Benefit by women who were in no real sense in search of employment'.[16] The remedy for this, Beveridge said, was not special regulations for married women, since there were others who left work with no intention of seeking further employment, but the enforcement of a genuine availability for work test.

Of more importance in the eyes of Beveridge, was the fact that the circumstances of an unemployed married woman removed the economic pressure to return to work. Through marriage, she acquired a legal right to her husband's support. Her home was provided either by her husband's earnings or through his benefit if he was unemployed or sick. Her earnings, therefore, meant less to her than to the single woman. They were 'a means, not of subsistence but of a standard of living above subsistence'.[17] When unemployed, her benefit should be lower than that for a man, or for women who had to provide for themselves, otherwise she might prolong her unemployment unnecessarily.

Beveridge's proposals were for a package of benefits for married women – maternity benefits and widows and old age pensions in right of their husbands' contributions, on the one hand, balanced by lower rates of unemployment and sickness benefit on the other. In addition, taking into account that married women who did work, did not always do so regularly and had to leave work at the time of childbirth, they would be given the option on marriage not to contribute at all in respect of unemployment and sickness and therefore not to be entitled to those benefits. The government accepted these proposals.[18] The reduced rate of contribution subsequently became known as the Married Woman's Option. Women still had to contribute to cover industrial injuries and their employer's contribution had to be paid in full.

Beveridge has been much criticised for his attitude to married women which set a pattern for discrimination against them in social security for the next 40 years. However, it has to be said that there was virtually no objection in Parliament to his proposals, or those of the White Paper and of the National Insurance Bill. Indeed some women Members of Parliament welcomed the new provisions as doing justice to married women at last. Mrs Cazalet Keir (Member for Islington East) welcomed the new status given to housewives and the treatment of men and women as a team.[19] Mrs Ridealgh (Ilford North) wanted to make sure benefits for the household were high enough, in order that the housewife would be sure of a square deal and relieved of the struggle to make ends meet.[20] Mrs Ayrton Gould (Hendon North) agreed that 'married women who are in gainful occupation have an easier life than unmarried women'. They could take a day off if they were not feeling up to the work, where the unmarried woman could not. Moreover even where they were not supporting children they would receive pensions if they were widowed after 55 years whereas unmarried women had to work on till they were 60 years.[21]

In the debate on the National Assistance Act, there was no reference to unemployed married women at all. What was being provided was a means tested minimum income for those with insufficient resources. It would cover the unemployed among others, but by the nature of such a scheme some form of household means test was inevitable. While the new rules would permit a single unemployed woman to receive benefit in her own right, a married woman would be regarded as financially the responsibility of her husband. As before, if he worked he must support her and if he was himself on benefit he claimed for her as a dependant. If she was employed, her income would be taken into account in the means test. Thus here, as in National Insurance, the position of the single woman improved, but the financial dependency of the married woman was reaffirmed.

The effect of the benefit provision

This arrangement for lower benefit rates for married women combined with the right to opt out of Unemployment Benefit operated unchanged for 30 years. So did the substantial lack of personal rights in the National Assistance/Supplementary Benefit schemes.

Table 5.1 shows the growth of employment among married women. Between 1949 and 1976 the numbers doubled. A large proportion of these were part timers and many others were on low wages. In 1971, for example 71 per cent of full time women earned less than £19 pw, a figure equivalent to the lowest decile of male manual earnings.[22] On pay of this level (and its equivalent in earlier years) and with benefits set at roughly three quarters of the male level, there was little incentive to pay full contributions if the option not to do so was available. As Table 5.1 shows, the increased entry to the labour force was not matched by the equivalent increase in the proportion paying full contributions. Taking the Option was the most common practice.

Table 5.1 Married women in employment paying contributions or exercising the Married Woman's Option. Selected years 1949-86. Great Britain

Millions

	Employed(1)	Pay contributions	Married Woman's Option
1949	3.0	2.0	1.0
1952	2.9	1.25	1.56
1955	3.52	1.28	2.15
1960	3.96	1.15	2.75
1965	4.63	1.14	3.44
1970	4.92	1.18	3.70
1976	6.36	2.09	4.16
1980	6.20	2.90	3.23
1984	5.61	3.82	1.78
1985	5.42	3.85	1.59
1986	5.57	4.18	1.39

(1)   Including some self-employed contributors.

Source: *Annual Reports* of the Ministry of National Insurance and *Social Security Statistics.*

Because no Unemployment Benefit would be available to the group taking the Option, and because there were no NA/SB rights for the great majority of unemployed married women, a significant proportion of married women did not bother to register as unemployed. The 1966 census indicated that there were 120,000 women, most of them married, who regarded themselves as unemployed and seeking work but who were not on the register. The 1971 census showed 230,000 such women.[23] The effect was to understate the extent of unemployment among women and, at the same time, to reduce the policy importance of the lack of benefits for this group of unemployed people. Indeed it was difficult to arouse interest in benefit issues of concern to working married women when upwards of three quarters of them chose to opt out of the principal benefit.

The 1970s saw the beginnings of a turn-around in the attitude to women in employment. The Equal Pay Act was passed in 1970, to be implemented in full by 1975. While it has not achieved equal pay, it did bring about some improvement – raising the average proportion of female to male hourly pay from 63 per cent in 1970 to 73 per cent in 1979.[24] Perhaps more important was the fact that more attention was focussed on women's role in the labour force. Figures for 1971 showed that women, both married and single, formed 38 per cent of the labour force and almost two thirds of these were married women. Some 42 per cent of all married women were in paid employment.[25]

The year 1975 saw two other advances, a Sex Discrimination Act and a statutory right to 6 weeks pay at 90 per cent of wages for women taking maternity leave, together with a right to reinstatement into the original job, provided there had been 2 years continuous service with one employer, or longer for women working less than 16 hours per week. Both of these legislative changes acknowledged the labour force attachment of many married women.

The phasing out of the Married Woman's Option

Legislation in 1975 provided for the phasing out of the Married Woman's Option from April 1978. Thereafter any new women employees would have to pay full contributions. Those already exercising the option could continue to do so, but if they left employment for more than 2 years, they must pay full contributions on return. In fact the numbers started their downward trend from 1977[26] whether in anticiplation of the new rules or because married women had become more social security conscious is not clear. As Table 5.1 shows, this decline has continued.

The government's decision to end the Option was, in part, a response to the evidence of the greater role of women in the labour force. It was, in part, the political necessity to equalise social security benefit rates for sickness and unemployment, in harmony with the principles which underlay the Equal Pay Act. This step was also taken in April 1978. The third reason was a practical one. There was to be a shift from flat rate to earnings-related NI contributions, together with a new State Earnings Related Pension Scheme for those not in an employer's pension scheme. The new State pension scheme involved higher contributions for those within it than for those in the private schemes. Amid all these complications, it was undesirable to maintain the further differential for married women. It was therefore convenient to phase it out.

The effect was not immediate but, except for those holding on to the Option, married women at last receive equal treatment with single women and men in the rates of Unemployment Benefit. Given the sharp increase in unemployment which was to follow, it came not a moment too soon.

Access to Unemployment Benefit and Redundancy Pay

With the decline in the use of the Married Woman's Option there was a greater likelihood that married as well as single women would have insurance rights. But Unemployment Benefit has been designed around the working patterns of men and, to a lesser extent, single women. These typically entered the labour force when they left education and worked continuously except during periods of unemployment. As childless married women increasingly stayed in the labour force after marriage, they could fit into the same pattern. All three groups could accumulate a record of NI contributions and be eligible for the insurance benefits. They also had the possibility of accumulating the working years with a single employer which would qualify them for redundancy pay, if they were made redundant.

But for married women with children, the work pattern was (and is) quite different. A 1980 survey *Women and Employment: A lifetime perspective*, showed that almost all women worked until they had their first baby. A minority of women returned to their paid work within 6 months of the birth of the child, some later but before the birth of the second child, while others stopped work until all their children had been born. Some attempted to return to full time work, but then shifted to part time work, or gave up work for the time being, while others went straight into part time work. Only a minority stayed in the labour market throughout the child rearing period.[27] Such a work pattern – persisting until the children were well grown – did not always lend itself to the accumulation of the required contribution record for Unemployment Benefit, though a proportion of such women might have qualified for the reduced rates (for a less than full contribution record) then available.

These patterns of work would also reduce the possibility of receiving redundancy pay, especially as women working for 8-16 hours only per week needed to work for 5 years with the same employer before they could begin to accumulate eligible years under the scheme. Callender, who examined research on this, found that in 1981 only 25 per cent of redundancy payments went to women. The low number of qualifying years, together with the typically low wages earned even by full time women, also served to reduce the amounts of redundancy pay. In 1983, the median payment for men was £1,277, but only £504 for women.[28] As seen in Chapter 3, women also received lower average payments than men under ERS·

Moreover, even in regular employment, there might be barriers to the acquisition of insurance rights. Of the 9 million women in employment in 1984, 4.2 million worked part time.[29] In that year it was estimated that three-fifths of all part time women were earning wages which fell below the threshold at which NI contributions began.[30] This might have been the natural result of the low wages paid for much of the part time work available. But it might also have been the result of a deliberate restriction of hours either by the employer, or the woman herself (or both) to avoid the cost of employer/employee contribution payments.   When such women became unemployed, they had no insurance rights.

Those who were regular part timers prior to unemployment and had paid the necessary NI contributions, could claim Unemployment Benefit, but only for the days they would otherwise have been working. They might also (in time) have to show justification for restricting their availability for work to part time employment only, especially where little part time work was available in the area. If they were considered to be unreasonably restricting their chances of finding employment, they might lose the right to benefit.

Someone who took part time work as a stop gap, having previously worked full time, could claim UB for the days not worked, provided they remained willing to take a full time job if it became available. However, if this situation went on too long, the part time work might be treated as the normal pattern. The individual was then working to the 'full extent normal' for her and would cease to qualify for UB for the non-working days. This could also arise if the right to UB ran out and the requalifying 13 weeks (under the standard rules) were worked part time. On reclaiming, the 'full extent normal' rule would apply.

It should be remembered that some part time workers were men, including those who were allocated part time work on the Community Programme, and were then regarded as working to the 'full extent normal' for them. However, because the majority of part timers were women, then, to the extent that the part time rules proved unsatisfactory, this impinged far more on women than on men. Whether rules are unsatisfactory or not depends to a considerable extent how they are administered. Both the 'availability for work' and the 'full extent normal' rules constitute reasonable requirements in social security provision for unemployment, but they can be applied generously or stringently according to the political climate. A government seeking to reduce the size of the unemployment register (measured by the numbers on benefit after 1982) could make some 'gains' by a stringent application of the part time rules. During 1983 and 1984 it was claimed that the rules were being applied harshly for this purpose[31] though this was denied by government.

Unemployed women and Supplementary Benefit

Single women and men whose entitlement to Unemployment Benefit had expired or who had a deficient contribution record, usually due to frequent unemployment, could claim Supplementary Benefit if they qualified under the means test. A married woman who was separated from her husband could claim benefit in her own right, though the DHSS might pursue her husband for maintenance if he was available. Separation included imprisonment of the husband or his long term hospitalisation. In these cases, the key determinant was the fact that the woman had no man on which she could be seen to be economically dependent.

But a married woman living with her husband and a woman living with a man as his wife would have no separate right to Supplementary Benefit. She would receive benefit only as a dependant of a man who himself was on benefit. The only exception to this was through social security rules which, from late 1983, permitted either partner of a union (whether by marriage or cohabitation) to be the principal claimant, where the woman concerned had been in the labour market in the immediately preceding six months. However, the rules for means tested benefits which aggregate the income of husband and wife would still apply when assessing the rate to be paid.

The effects of this lack of benefit rights can be observed in Table 5.2. Unemployment figures by 1984 counted only those in receipt of benefit, whether Unemployment Benefit or Supplementary Benefit. Whereas for the first 52 weeks of unemployment when Unemployment Benefit was available, the ratio of male to female unemployed was 2:1 or less, after 52 weeks, the ratio rises sharply as married women fall out of the count.

Table 5.2 Duration of unemployment, men and women, January 1984. United Kingdom

Duration		Males	Females
One or less		57,734	37,673
Over 1 and up to 2		60,805	36,702
2	4	75,454	39,954
4	6	85,976	40,299
6	8	82,229	39,801
8	13	183,041	92,496
13	26	378,755	210,814
26	39	222,167	113,749
39	52	170,082	83,908
52	65	131,289	51,435
65	78	119,733	44,948
78	104	171,864	52,360
104	156	228,167	56,045
156	208	156,952	30,097
208	260	56,735	11,000
260		64,376	13,037
All		2,245,360	954,318

Source: *Employment Gazette*, March 1984.

Wives of unemployed men

The rules for unemployment benefits had one further adverse effect on married (and cohabiting) women. Where the husband was unemployed and entitled to Unemployment Benefit, he claimed his benefit by right of his contributions. It would be affected only if he earned more than £2 per day. He could claim a dependency addition for his wife – worth £17.55 in 1984/5 – provided she earned less than the rate of the addition after work expenses had been taken into account. If she earned more, his benefit was unaffected, but the whole of the dependency addition would be withdrawn.

If the unemployed husband claimed Supplementary Benefit, either in full or as a supplement to UB, then different earnings rules applied to both husband and wife. Each could earn only £4 per week if they wished to draw the full benefit. Moreover, the benefit was not made up of separate rates for husband and wife, but was a married couple rate, with dependency additions for children. If the wife earned more than her £4 earnings disregard, it would be deducted £1 for £1 from the whole benefit. It would not be until she earned more than the rate for the whole family that any earnings beyond the £4 disregard would add to the family income.

Figures from the General Household Survey for Great Britain in 1979 showed that, where the husband was working, 62 per cent of their wives were employed, but only 32 per cent where he was unemployed. By 1985, the figures were 62 per cent of wives of employed men working but only 22 per cent of wives of unemployed men.[32] Similar patterns were evident in Northern Ireland.[33]

Researchers have concluded at first tentatively[34] and then more confidently[35] that the social security earnings rules for unemployment benefit had created a disincentive for the wives of unemployed men to work. In Unemployment Benefit, the rules were a disincentive to part time work, but not to full time work. But in Supplementary Benefit, the disincentive applied to all work. As more and more unemployed families came to rely on Supplementary Benefit – see Table 4.3 for the percentage claiming each benefit – so the number of women affected by the SB earnings rule increased. Research showed that a woman who was working when her husband became unemployed was likely to withdraw from the labour force as his period of unemployment lengthened. Other women went out to work after their husbands became unemployed, but gave up when they realised how little this was benefiting the family. Others again looked at the rules and decided it was not worth considering work.[36]

Women and unemployment in 1985

In 1985, single women shared the problems already outlined for men in Chapters 3 and 4. To these were added the inequalities (for example in levels of redundancy pay) which arose from women's disadvantaged position in the labour force. The extent to which married women were seriously disadvantaged by the benefit provisions still depended on their family circumstances. Where their pay was an essential part of the family economy then should both the job and the benefit rights be lost, this could have a marked effect on the standard of living of the whole family. Even where the family could manage, their living standards would be reduced. Women who had been accustomed to having their own income, even if they put the bulk of it into the family economy, were, by the benefit rules, thrust back into total economic dependence. They might adjust to unemployment because they already had an important second job – the running of the household – but where they had worked, albeit part time, for many years, they regarded themselves also as part of the labour force.[37] Unfortunately the benefit system ceased to recognise this if unemployment persisted too long.

At one time, the relative lack of benefit provision for married women could be seen as 'their own fault', because they had taken the Married Woman's Option. Having largely eliminated that problem, so that Unemployment Benefit is more often available to married women, the goal posts had been moved as a result of the onset of high and long term unemployment. The issue of access to the means tested Supplementary Benefit became much more important, and so did the side effects of the benefit rules on married women's ability to add to the family income through work. A reform of the Married Woman's Option was a relatively easy step. To give an entitlement to married women to Supplementary Benefit in their own right would involve a revision of the whole basis on which the safety net provision was founded. This is an obstacle which was substantially less easy to remove.

References

1. *Social Insurance and Allied Services* (The Beveridge Report), Cmnd 6404, HMSO, London, 1942, shows the benefit rates in Appendix B and Joan C. Brown, *The Disability Income System*, PSI, London, 1984, pp.9-13.
2. J.D. Tomlinson, 'Women as "Anomalies": The Anomalies Regulation of 1931, Their Background and Implications', *Public Administration*, Vol. 62, Winter 1984, pp.423-37.
3. Ministry of Labour, *Report of an Investigation into the Employment Insurance History of a Sample of Persons Insured against Unemployment in Great Britain*, HMSO, London, 1927, p.6 said in 1925 women constituted 27.3 per cent of the insured.
4. Royal Commission on Unemployment Insurance, op.cit., p.216.
5. Blanesburgh Report, Second Volume, op.cit., p.172.
6. Royal Commission, op.cit., p.217.
7. Ministry of Labour, *Investigation* ..., op.cit., p.54.
8. Royal Commission, op.cit., pp.241-2.

9. Ibid., p.242.
10. Ibid., p.473.
11. Unemployment Assistance Board, *Annual Report 1935*, Cmd 5177, HMSO, London, 1936, pp.36 and 291.
12. Beveridge Report, op.cit., and *Social Insurance Part 1*, op.cit.
13. *Social Insurance Part 1*, op.cit., Appendix 1.
14. Beveridge Report, op.cit., p.52.
15. Ibid., p.49.
16. Ibid., p.51.
17. Ibid., p.49.
18. *Social Insurance Part 1*, op.cit., p.26.
19. *House of Commons Hansard*, 17 February 1946, 1792.
20. Ibid., 6 February 1946, 1788.
21. Ibid., 11 February 1946, 43.
22. Joan C. Brown, *Low Pay and Poverty*, PSI, London, 1981, p.6.
23. 'The Unregistered Unemployed in Great Britain', *Department of Employment Gazette*, December 1976, pp.1331-6.
24. *Low Pay and Poverty*, op.cit., p.28 drawn from *New Eearnings Survey*.
25. Department of Employment, *Women and Work: a statistical survey*, HMSO, London, 1974, p.5.
26. *Social Security Statistics*, 1978.
27. Jean Martin and Ceridwen Roberts, *Women and Employment: a lifetime perspective*, Department of Employment/OPCS, HMSO, London, 1984, pp.123-5.
28. Clare Callender, 'Gender Inequality and Social Policy: Women and the Redundancy Payments Scheme', *Journal of Social Policy*, April 1985, 14(2), pp.189-213.
29. Equal Opportunities Commission, *Women and Men in Britain: A Statistical Profile*, EOC, Manchester, 1986, p.18.
30. Caroline Glendinning and Jane Millar, *Women and Poverty in Britain*, Wheatsheaf Books, Brighton, 1987, p.143.
31. *Unemployment Unit Bulletin*, June 1984, for example.
32. *General Household Survey*, 1985, HMSO, London, 1987.
33. Department of Social Services and Registrar General Northern Ireland, *Northern Ireland Census 1981*, HMSO, Belfast, 1983.
34. S. Moylan, J. Millar and R. Davies, *For richer for poorer? DHSS Cohort Study of Unemployed Men*, HMSO, London, 1984, Chapter 10.

35. A. Dilnot and M. Kell, 'Male Unemployment and Women's Work', *Fiscal Studies.*, Vol.8, No.3, August 1987, pp.1-16.
36. Moylan et al., op.cit. and McLaughlin Eithne et al.,*Work and Welfare Benefits*, Avebury, Aldershot, 1989, pp.64-5.
37. See Angela Coyle, *Work and the Family*, EOC, Manchester 1983, for a study of unemployed women in the North.

6 The young unemployed

Young people under the age of 18 years have commonly been the subject of special rules during unemployment. As members of the labour force and as the adults of the future, the authorities wanted to teach them the responsibilities of adulthood, which included making provision while in work against periods of unemployment. On the other hand, their low wages could make contributions unduly burdensome, and if benefits were too freely available or too high, they might undermine the willingness to work. Prolonged unemployment could be particularly demoralising, especially where work habits were not well established.

From the early years of the century, therefore, the principal issues have been the age of entry to unemployment insurance and to benefit rights generally, the rates of contributions and benefits which should appropriately be paid by and to young people, and the conditions which ought to be attached to receipt of benefit. Prominent among the conditions discussed over the years has been the undertaking of training in order to maintain and improve employability.

The age of entry to benefits – 1911 to 1948

In 1911 when Unemployment Insurance was first introduced, compulsory education still ended at 12 years of age. In 1921 it was extended to the age of 14 years and remained at that level until 1947. Many children and young people over these compulsory school ages were in the labour force and therefore also capable of being unemployed. The 1911 and 1920 Acts, however, provided only for those of 16 years and over.

In no-mans land – the under 16s

It was understandable that the limited scheme of 1911 did not want to get involved in the provision of contributory unemployment insurance to 12 year olds. The extension of unemployment insurance in 1920 to cover most manual workers and lower paid non-manuals, occurred before the compulsory school leaving age was raised. It was in any case a sufficiently bold move without undertaking the additional difficulty of attempting to cover the very young, especially as in the period between 12 and 14 years, free elementary education was available to all. It might be thought better to encourage these young people to stay at school.

From 1921 onwards, the position became more anomalous. Compulsory education now ended at 14 years and the vast majority left school at this age and sought work. They were recognised as part of the labour force, but only as long as they were at work. No benefit for unemployment would be available until they had paid at least 7 months contributions after the age of 16 years. The insurance rules for adults added a further twist to this. Dependency additions could be claimed by a man (or woman) who was on Unemployment Insurance, but only for children under 14 years of age or those aged 14 and 15 years still at school. Unemployed youngsters of this age were not eligible. They had ceased to be dependants because they had left school.

The Royal Commission on Unemployment Insurance examined the age of entry at the beginning of the 1930s.[1] It noted that the gap between school leaving age and insurable age had been considered by committees in the past, and that when plans were made in 1929 to raise the school leaving age to 15 years, the National Advisory Councils for Juvenile Unemployment (England and Wales) had recommended that the age of insurance should at the same time be lowered to 15 years. Provision for this simultaneous change was embodied in the 1930 Unemployment Insurance Act. However, the Bill to raise the school leaving age was not passed and, the Royal Commission said:

> The position at the moment is, therefore, that, although Parliament has accepted the principle that the gap between school leaving age and entry into insurance should be closed, there is no immediate prospect of the school leaving age being raised and the gap remains.[2]

It therefore recommended that the age of entry into insurance should be lowered to correspond to the age of entry into employment and that the minimum age for insurance be defined as not less than the school leaving age as established by statute from time to time.[3]

The government's response to this in the 1934 Unemployment Act was to lower the age of liability to pay contributions to 14 years but to maintain the age of entitlement to benefit at 16 years. This had the advantage of enabling young people to accumulate a contribution record against later unemployment, but left the benefit gap unfilled. No change was made to the age at which dependency additions ceased in Unemployment Insurance.

Somewhat different rules operated in Unemployment Assistance. Under the Household Means Test, it was the income of the whole household which determined eligibility for benefit. Young people had no independent benefit rights in a household whose income was above the means test line, but if the father was unemployed, he could claim also for unemployed dependants. The UAB scale rates included dependency additions for 14-15 year olds and for 16-21 year olds.[4] There were similar provisions in Public Assistance.

The under-16s in the postwar reforms

At the time Beveridge was reviewing Social Insurance and Allied Services, education policy was also under review. The plan Beveridge put forward for a new social insurance scheme discussed rates of contribution and benefits only for those 16 years and over. But he noted that the position of those under 16 years would need to be considered once educational policy was decided.

As a general principle he stated: 'It is desirable that boys and girls should at an early age be brought into the Social Security Scheme, and become familiar with it'.[5] If they worked for gain under the age of 16, insurance contributions should be paid by them and their employers, and any payment of cash benefit should be combined with continued supervision and education. Thus, the implication was that when the school leaving age was settled, this should become the age for entry into insurance and entitlement to benefit.

The 1944 Education Act provided for the raising of the school leaving age to 15 years and, as soon as practicable, to 16 years. The first of these extensions of compulsory schooling – to 15 years – was implemented in 1947, but no date was set for the second.

The 1946 National Insurance Act in turn provided that:

every person who on or after the appointed day, being over school leaving age and under pensionable age ... shall become insured under the Act and thereafter continue throughout his life to be so insured (Section 1).

Contribution and benefit rates for young people referred only to those under 18 years. Thus there would be no problem in adjusting to a change in the school leaving age.

From 1948, Unemployment Benefit could be drawn after contributions of 26 weeks. This meant that a boy or girl under 16 years could qualify for benefit provided he or she had been in regular work since leaving school. Changes in the regulations for means tested benefit will be discussed later.

Work incentives and training
16 and 17 year olds – the pre-war provision
The 16 to 17 year old group were included in Unemployment Insurance from its inception. They were classified as boys and girls (or juveniles) and paid contributions at a lower rate than those over 18 years who were treated as adults. Benefits were also lower for the younger group, at around half of the men's and women's rates respectively. The intention in setting the rates was to adjust the contribution levels to low wages and to ensure that benefits were not too high a proportion of possible earnings. Since girls earned less than boys, they both paid and received less.

By the mid-1920s there was concern about the incidence of juvenile unemployment amid high general unemployment. There were fears that the benefits available to young people might be creating an acceptance of a state of idleness, undesirable at any age, but particularly in those just starting out in working life. The Blanesburgh Committee in 1927 therefore recommended a still lower proportion of adult benefit for juveniles – down to one third of the adult rate – and the imposition of a condition of attendance at an approved course of instruction, where one was available. In those cases the unemployment benefit would be renamed a training allowance. The Committee said:

It is at this age that industrial workers are made or marred, and we are convinced of the necessity of providing them when out of work with suitable industrial instruction or training.[6]

The later Royal Commission returned to the subject of the juvenile unemployed.[7] It noted that powers to impose a training condition had existed since the 1920 Act but no national funds had been allocated to establish and run appropriate courses and their development depended on local initiatives. It was not until 1930 that some national responsibility (through the Ministry of Labour) was accepted. In spite of the more recent growth in the number of courses only a small proportion of all unemployed juveniles aged 14-17 years attended such courses. Of those who had a benefit entitlement – where attendance could be made a condition of payment – only about half undertook training.

The Commission noted that many of the courses took place 'in dingy, crampled and ill-equipped buildings'. It argued that Local Education Authorities 'should regard them not as a temporary and makeshift, but a serious, part of their responsibilities'.[8] Given this improvement:

> Attendance at a Junior Instruction Centre or at a Course of Instruction should everywhere be regarded and enforced as a normal condition in respect of unemployment, whether through the Insurance Scheme or in the form of Unemployment Assistance.[9]

Juveniles who were suspended from courses for serious misbehaviour or who failed to attend should be suspended from benefit for a period of six weeks.

The 16-17 year old group on Unemployment Assistance after 1935 were treated in the same way as their younger counterparts. If they had not acquired or had run out of insurance rights, they would receive benefit only if they were part of a qualifying household – a factor which, incidentally, restricted the imposition of a training condition. In any case, as the economy recovered after 1935 and more jobs became available, training assumed less importance in benefit control, though the rule remained in use where facilities were available.

The postwar reforms – 16 and 17 year-olds

Under the Beveridge proposals, 16 and 17 year olds would be entitled to unemployment benefit once they had paid sufficient contributions. As seen in Chapter 2, Beveridge wanted to apply a training condition to all those adults who had been unemployed for six months. For young people a training condition should apply from the beginning of unemployment.[10] The government, however, wanted to separate training from devices designed to control abuse of benefit. Training was acknowledged as valuable in its own right, but it was inadequate for purposes of benefit control.[11] Parliament agreed, and no training condition appeared in the 1946 Act.

The 1948 National Assistance Act further improved the benefit rights of 16 and 17 year olds, but not those under 16 years. The Act defined as dependent children only those who were under 16 years of age. A boy or girl under 16 years who had not paid sufficient contributions to qualify for the new National Insurance benefit would not be entitled to National Assistance except as part of a household which itself qualified under the means test. Those aged 16 and over, on the other hand, could apply for National Assistance and be assessed on their own income. The rule, in effect, reduced the age of dependency by 5 years (from 21 years to 16 years), a marked change in the policy for means tested assistance. This also implied that, once the declared intention of raising the school leaving age to 16 years was implemented, then compulsory school leaving age, the age of entry to the labour force, the age at which insurance rights could begin to be acquired, and the age of National Assistance rights to an independent benefit, would all be harmonised at 16 years of age. The catch was that the raising of the school leaving age to 16 was delayed until the 1972-3 school year, leaving the 15 year olds once more in limbo where they did not qualify for Unemployment Benefit.

The young unemployed in the 50s and 60s

Unemployment benefits for young people in the 1950s and 1960s were almost wholly uncontroversial. The rate of unemployment was low, particularly among those under 18 years of age. In March 1955 for example there were 8,600 young people out of work and 8,700 in June 1960. During the 1960s, the numbers rose but except at school leaving time, they were typically under 20,000.[12] Unemployment, where it arose, was usually short term for this age group.

School leavers coming on to the labour market did not, in this period, raise any serious difficulties. The majority were 15 year olds who had no immediate benefit rights, but they found jobs fairly quickly in what was still a favourable labour market for people of this age. Relatively few 16-17 year olds turned to National Assistance for support. Indeed the National Assistance Board reports did not bother to separate them off from the 18-20 year olds until 1965 and when they did, the entry for the younger group was only 3,000.[13] They did not rate any special comment in the reports.

By November 1971 the figures of those under 18 years receiving what was now Supplementary Benefit had risen to 26,000.[14] However, as the unemployment duration figures for July of the same year showed, the problem was still an essentially short term one. Of over 49,000 under 18 year olds who were unemployed, only 2,400 had been out of work for more than 26 weeks and just under 8,000 for over 13 weeks.[15]

The relative ease with which young people found work was probably one of the reasons why the under 18s were excluded from the Earnings Related Supplement introduced in 1966. Moreover, ERS was in part designed to encourage job mobility. The young were naturally mobile and needed no incentives to change jobs. There was also likely to have been a reluctance to increase benefits paid to this age group. All this is speculative because the Minister concerned did not apparently feel it necessary to explain to the House why the age of eligibility began at 18 years. Similarly, no queries were raised about the inclusion of the younger group in the extension of Unemployment Benefit duration to 12 months, also in 1966. Since they had paid the requisite contributions, there was, presumably, no obvious reason to exclude them and long term unemployment among this group was not yet an issue requiring separate consideration.

The raising of the school leaving age and its consequences

In the 1972-3 school year, the step foreshadowed in the 1940s – the raising of the school leaving age to 16 years – was finally taken. Its immediate impact was to help to reduce the number of unemployed under 18 years from 77,000 in July 1972 to 25,000 in July 1973.[16] There was in any case a general fall in unemployment at that time (see Table 3.1) but the removal of a whole year's school leavers from the labour market had a useful additional effect. It was, however, only temporary.

The numbers of 16 and 17 year olds out of work rose once more in July 1974 – to 33,000 – and more markedly in July 1975, when they reached 104,000.[17] Figures taken in July are inevitably higher than at other times of the year because they include school leavers. In terms of the general pattern of unemployment, therefore, the high July figures did not in themselves create concern. But the raising of the school leaving age had had another effect. School leavers now fell within the eligibility criteria for Supplementary Benefit.

In its Annual Report for 1976 the Supplementary Benefits Commission (SBC) pointed out that, in July 1976, there were over 199,000 school leavers registered as unemployed and large numbers of them were claiming benefit.[18] This huge influx of claimants was disruptive administratively, but it also, in the SBCs view, raised questions of principle.

School leavers inevitably took time to become absorbed into the labour market. Some had jobs to go to but would not start until the end of the summer vacation. Some found jobs during August and September. Others failed to find work and decided to return to school or enter non-advanced education. Some remained on the unemployment register beyond the vacation period. All of these could claim SB and a large proportion did. This situation had arisen, not because of any change in the typical circumstances of school leavers, but as the direct outcome of the raising of the school leaving age.

Commenting on this, the SBC said in the 1976 report:

> We accept that young people of this age group should be encouraged to be as independent of their parents as possible and to manage their own financial affairs, making a contribution towards their keep ... Nevertheless, how far should young single people living with their parents be encouraged immediately on leaving school to look to the State rather than their parents for support?[19]

The SBC went on to raise the possibility that entitlement to benefit be deferred until the end of the school holidays, when their employment position would be clearer.

The Labour government of the time referred the matter to the new inquiry into Supplementary Benefit, established in 1977, and being undertaken by DHSS officials. The officials examined three propositions. First, that the qualifying age for SB should be raised to 18 years – which since 1969 had been the age of majority – on the grounds that the majority of 16 to 17 year olds lived with their parents and were not yet fully independent. This option was not recommended because provision would have to be made for 16 and 17 year olds who for good reasons did not live at home or who had a child to care for. To differentiate between categories of young people might have undesirable social repercussions.

The second proposition was that the eligible age should be lowered, to take account of the fact that some children actually left school before their sixteenth birthday because of the way statutory school leaving dates operated. This was not favoured because, the report said, there never had been a direct link between the date of school leaving and benefit age. If it was introduced it could encourage early leaving and it could 'reinforce a socially undesirable trend for children to enter adult life by moving straight from school onto benefit'.

The third proposition was the one that was recommended. This was to deal with the practical problem created by school leavers for the Supplementary Benefit scheme, as described in the SBC's 1976 report, and also with 'temptations to abuse the scheme', which arose when the child claimed to have left school, in order to get benefit, but had every intention of going back to school at the end of the holiday. The deferment of benefit entitlement to the end of the school holidays would deal with both problems.[20]

The report was published in 1978, but before any of its proposals were implemented, there was a change of government. In 1980, the new Conservative government introduced legislation to defer SB payments to school leavers until the end of the vacation which followed the date of leaving. Once this period was over, 16 and 17 year olds would be eligible for SB in the normal way. Later developments made this appear to be the beginning of a Conservative government drive against SB payments to the young unemployed. But it is very likely that a Labour government would have taken the same step, in order to ease the administrative disruption being experienced by the SBC, at a time when unemployment generally was high.

Training for the young unemployed
Because of the continuous high employment levels among young people from 1948 onwards, the issue of training in relation to unemployed 15-17 year olds had hardly arisen. Training for young people who had left school had been regarded as an employer responsibility and State-provided training (other than through the education system) was geared almost exclusively to those aged 19 years and over.[21]

The increase in the numbers of young unemployed, and in the length of time many of them were out of work particularly from 1975 onwards, brought renewed political interest in the training question.

Table 6.1 gives the unemployment figures in January each year, that is, at a time of year when school leaving did not markedly inflate the numbers.

Table 6.1 Unemployment among 16 and 17 year olds, January 1976-9. Great Britain

	Males	Females
1976	57,505	48,605
1977	62,863	59,503
1978	66,978	67,869
1979	55,345	52,495

Source: *Department of Employment Gazette*, February 1976-9

Initially, the Manpower Services Commission (MSC) (which had the responsibility for the development of training), sought to open up the main adult scheme – the Training Opportunities Scheme (TOPS) – to the young unemployed.[22] However, the persistence of unemployment among this age group turned the MSC's attention to the planning of specific schemes for young people. The first, established in September 1976, and as a temporary measure, was the Work Experience Programme (WEP). This offered those under 19 years of age, six months work experience during which they were paid a training allowance, rather than a social security benefit. The scheme offered opportunities for 'learning by doing' and aimed to make the young people more employable. If, during the course, they found employment, there was no objection to their abandoning WEP in favour of paid work. Indeed, the average length of stay on WEP was 21 weeks and the MSC reported that the majority of those who left the scheme early, did so to get a job.[23]

Even as WEP was being established, the MSC had doubts about whether it would be sufficient to meet the need. The Commission reported that it considered that:

> the problems of unemployment amongst young people are so serious (and likely to remain so) that it should become an objective of the Commission to ensure that all young people of 16-18 years of age who have no job or who are not engaged in further or higher full-time education should have the opportunity of training, of participation in a job creation programme or of work experience.[24]

The outcome was a decision to establish a Youth Opportunities Programme (YOP) in 1978. This would have a much stronger training content than WEP, and its aims would be to improve the employability of unemployed young people, and help them to find suitable permanent employment.[25] Whereas WEP, by March 1978, had involved nearly 60,000 young people,[26] the goal set for YOP, now including work experience, was for 187,000 places in the first year of operation.[27] As with WEP, a training allowance would be paid.

Although YOP was the product of the manpower planning arm of government, it nevertheless had an important role both in relation to social security policy, and to wider social policy. Young people who went direct from school to Supplementary Benefit (or after only a limited period of employment) were not learning the duty of self-support on which the economy is based. On the contrary, they were acquiring habits of dependency on the State and in the process were being unfitted for employment. Spending their time, not in the disciplines of education or of work, but in unstructured idleness, they had, moreover, the potential to become a social threat. The fact that, (as with adults) unemployment fell disproportionately on young people of the ethnic minorities, was seen as an additional cause for alarm because of what Solomos refers to as 'the supposed linkages between black youth, crime and unemployment'.[28]

YOP was seen as a constructive way to counter these undesirable developments, pending an upturn in the economy which would return young people to the labour force, without the need for special interventions. At that stage, it was not regarded as a form of benefit control. There was no penalty for refusing a YOP place. The aim was to make it an attractive alternative to Supplementary Benefit or Unemployment Benefit, offering a higher allowance than either of these, interesting activity and a route to a permanent job. As with WEP, no tears were shed if young people did not need to enter YOP, because they had found work before the Easter after school leaving, when a guarantee of a place would come to be applied, nor were there any bars to leaving YOP if a job came along. The priority was employment, and not training in its own right.

Policies for 16 and 17 year olds after 1979
With the change of government (in 1979) came the change to the Supplementary Benefit rules, discussed earlier, postponing eligibility for benefit until the end of the school holidays. At the same time, as

Table 6.2 shows, after a brief dip, the unemployment figures among those under 18 years moved upward again and so did the numbers receiving Supplementary Benefit. To the figures shown in the table must be added those for Northern Ireland which began to be available after 1980. In 1984, for example, around 7,000 would have to be added to the unemployment figures and 5,600 to the SB figures to account for the under-18s in Northern Ireland.[29]

Table 6.2 Unemployment among 16 and 17 year olds. Selected years January 1978-86. Great Britain

	Unemployed in January	On SB in preceding November/December
1978	134,847	87,000
1980	105,656	na
1981	190,775	126,000
1982	220,545	150,000
1983	215,277	168,000
1984	198,191	161,000
1985	192,633	169,000
1986	181,815	na

Source: *Employment Gazette* and *Social Security Statistics*

Unemployment and the youth wage

In March 1980, a report was published by the Department of Employment which took a fairly pragmatic view of the level of youth unemployment. Summarising this report in the *Employment Gazette*,[30] the author related unemployment among the young to the general level of unemployment. As adult unemployment rose, youth unemployment rose also, but at a faster rate, because one of the first steps employers took in times of recession was to reduce or cease new recruitment of young people. Conversely, as adult unemployment fell, youth unemployment fell faster, because recruitment recommenced. This relationship between adult and youth unemployment was described as the major explanation of the variations in the youth rate, so that the cure for youth unemployment, like that of adults, lay in an improvement in the economy. There was, the author added, no obvious need to introduce 'other hypotheses' such as the effects of pay increases or unemployment benefit as they were not shown as having any effect.

Before long it was clear that the government wanted a more active explanation. It took the view that the youth wage was too high and was deterring employers from offering work. In August 1981, it announced a new Young Workers Scheme, to come into operation in January 1982. This offered a subsidy of £15 pw for 12 months to an employer who recruited an unemployed person under 18 years of age at a gross wage of less than £40 pw. A half rate subsidy would also be given for jobs paying £40 to £45 pw. These rates of pay were said to be appropriate because they reflected the lack of training and relative inexperience of young people.[31]

In 1983, the Department of Employment published a report which gave some support to the government's position.[32] It showed that after 1969, the youth wage, as a proportion of the adult wage, had risen. Following the lowering of the age of majority to 18 years (from 21) in 1969, there had been a gradual wage rise for 18+ males as unions and employers shifted the age for the payment of the adult rate downwards to 18 years for males, bringing it into line with the female adult rate which had already been established at that age. This had had a flow-on effect to junior rates. A more direct influence had been the raising of the school leaving age in 1972-3. This had not only created a temporary shortage of young recruits (as seen earlier) but new school leavers were in future one year older and presumably better educated. The report went on to suggest, though with some caution, that the higher wage rates which has resulted had an adverse effect on the availability of employment for young people.

The government hoped that besides inducing more employment for young people, the Young Workers Scheme would have the effect of lowering youth wages more generally.[33] One disadvantage, from its point of view, was that some youth wages were set at a statutory minimum, i.e. those in Wages Council Industries. From 1982 onwards, the government began to talk of the possibility of abolishing the Wages Councils. No steps were taken until 1986 when the Wages Act removed young workers from the scope of the Wages Councils, though it left those for adults in operation.

The pros and cons of the government's thesis have been fiercely argued, but will not be discussed here.[34] What is important, from the point of view of benefits for the young unemployed, was that the next stage of the discussion was the relationship between the allowances paid to them and the hoped for lower youth wage. The downward pressure on wages would have to be accompanied by a downward pressure on allowances.

The Youth Training Scheme

During 1980 and 1981, steps were taken to expand the intake of the Youth Opportunities Programme. In the year from April 1980 to March 1981, 360,000 unemployed young people entered the scheme.[35] Its goals were unchanged.

Later that year, faced with the increasing unemployment which was creating even greater demands on YOP and at the same time providing fewer opportunities for permanent jobs on leaving YOP, the MSC presented a new plan. This was to offer young people under 18, the 'opportunity either of continuing in full time education or of entering training or a period of planned work experience combining work-related training and education'.[36]

The new Youth Training Scheme, as it was to be called, was not simply a 'constructive alternative to unemployment', but a means of creating a better trained work force for the future. It would be directed to all young people, not simply to the unemployed. It would provide the normal first entry point to the labour market for 16 year olds, other than those who remained in full time education. However, the initial drive would be to absorb the young unemployed. The new scheme came into operation in 1983 (1982 in Northern Ireland) and was to provide one full year of training to 16 and 17 year olds, with a goal of extending to two years as soon as feasible. To the MSC it was an important training initiative. The government had additional goals.

During 1981 the government had begun to suggest that it was undesirable that 16 year olds should have a Supplementary Benefit entitlement in their own right. It indicated that it believed 'it would be right for young people, whether in education, the new training scheme or unemployed, to be regarded in general as dependent on their parents for the first year after reaching minimum school leaving age'.[37] The change would be made at the point when the government was in a position to guarantee that no 16 year old need be unemployed – i.e. when the new training scheme was introduced. At the same time, the government rejected the MSC's proposal for training allowance of £28 pw (higher than the YOP allowance of £25) and proposed instead to pay £14.40 pw to 16 year olds and £24 pw to 17 year olds.[38]

Both propositions aroused opposition, in particular from a Youth Task Group of the MSC which sought an allowance at the same level as for YOP but uprated to take account of inflation. The rate it proposed was £26.90 pw with provision for an annual review. It was against the withdrawal of the right to SB, first because it would introduce an undesirable element of compulsion into participation in the training scheme, if refusal to do so carried such a severe penalty. The scheme should be able to attract voluntary participation, while 'reluctant recruits' could be a disruptive influence. Its second reason was that inevitably there would be periods when young people, through no fault of their own, were not on the training scheme. A safety net was essential to deal with this.[39]

Around the same time a Select Committee of the House of Lords was reaching similar conclusions. The government's proposed allowance was inadequate and ought to be increased. The objective ought to be to make the training option attractive and the option of unemployment irrelevant. If this was done, there would be no necessity to withdraw SB from 16 year olds.[40]

The government gave way, though it reiterated its view that it was not the job of the government to offer, with taxpayer's cash, the option of being unemployed.[41] The Youth Training Scheme allowance for both 16 and 17 year olds would remain at the £25 pw provided under YOP, and SB would not be withdrawn at least until the scheme had been one full year in operation, when the policy would be reviewed. However – in a return to the policy for young people pursued in the 1930s – unreasonable refusal of a place on the scheme would be penalised by benefit reduction for a period of six weeks.[42]

By April 1986 the Youth Training Allowance had reached only £27.30 pw. But as the second year of YTS began to be introduced (in 1986), a separate second year rate of £35 pw was established. This higher rate would also be paid to new 17 year old entrants after the first 13 weeks. From 1984, new 16 year olds entrants to the Young Workers Scheme were not to be accepted, so that it did not compete with YTS.

Supplementary Benefit

For 16 and 17 year olds, the principal benefit during unemployment was Supplementary Benefit. The NI contribution rules did permit 17 year olds to qualify for Unemployment Benefit, provided they had had a full year's work after leaving school. Separate figures for this age group are not given in the Social Security Statistics, but it can be expected that the numbers involved were modest. The rules attached to Supplementary Benefit, and the rates paid, were therefore of considerable importance to the young unemployed.

Young unemployed people on Supplementary Benefit faced three possible hazards. The first related to YTS. Those who refused a place on a scheme or who left a scheme prematurely could find their benefit reduced for six weeks by around 40 per cent. In a 6 months period up to May 1984, just over 7,000 young people were affected by this rule.[43]

The second also had a training connection. The decision in 1948 that training would *not* be made a condition for benefits for the unemployed had produced a clear separation between education and training – for which the education and manpower authorities respectively were responsible – and benefits which the social security authorities paid to those neither in work nor in full time education or training. This sharp division, however, had the potential for creating problems for those who were pursuing part time education.

In the three decades after 1948, little was heard of any problem. There was some evidence of flexible arrangements made by the SBC to allow newly unemployed young people to complete day release courses they had begun or to undertake limited studies, provided they remained available for work.[44] But the combination in the early 1980s of the increase in unemployment among young people, the formalisation of many Supplementary Benefit rules by the 1980 Social Security Act (now to be operated by DHSS direct, and without the mediation of the Supplementary Benefits Commission), brought the issue into greater prominence. Decisions made by Social Security Commissioners, adjudicating on individual cases sometimes introduced extra difficulties.

The rules provided for two possible situations. For the first three months on Supplementary Benefit, 15 hours study per week was permitted, including homework. Generally speaking it was expected that this would cover young people just leaving school, who were seeking work but were finishing off parts of their education or seeking to improve their qualifications. The object of the 15 hour rule was to distinguish between those who were really still in education and should therefore be claiming Child Benefit and education allowances from the Local Education Authority, and those who were in the labour market and available for work. For this reason it was restricted to those 18 and under, i.e. the Child Benefit age limit.

The 15-hour rule ran into difficulties when a decision of a Social Security Commissioner gave the right to SB to a young person doing 13 hours course work and 4-5 hours homework. The DHSS felt that this opened the way for an upward drift in the permitted hours of study which could be combined with SB. In 1984, it introduced a revised rule permitting 12 hours study, excluding homework.

After three months on benefit, the second element in the rules came into operation. This permitted 21 hours per week study, again provided it did not interfere with immediate availability for work. This, too, ran into definitional difficulties. In 1981-2, following legal advice, DHSS began interpreting the 21 hours as including meal breaks and homework. The apparent discouragement this gave to young unemployed people (as well as older unemployed who also qualified) who were trying to improve their employability aroused some controversy. Later, the rule was modified, retaining the total figure of 21 hours, but clearly relating this to class work and tuition.

Although these difficulties arose at the same time as the government was discussing the possibility of withdrawing Supplementary Benefit from the young unemployed altogether, it need not be assumed that they were part of the same policy. The problems stemmed from the poor provision being made for young people of 16 and 17 years who stayed in full time education. Where allowances were available – and they were not so universally – they were frequently below the level that could be obtained by claiming SB as an unemployed person. Government, however, resisted the introduction of mandatory allowances, either for those still at school (Education Maintenance Allowances) or those in non-advanced further education (Minor Awards), because of the cost.[45] The DHSS, for its part, was determined that Supplementary Benefit should not be allowed to develop into an education subsidy.[46] Its task was to provide for those who were unemployed and available for work. The Department was willing to be moderately flexible, but wanted to draw clear lines so as to emphasise the proper purpose of benefits. The young people concerned fell into the gaps created by the failure to develop a coherent policy on education, training and benefits.

The third hazard was, however, much more clearly part of the government's distaste for paying Supplementary Benefit to young unemployed people. Among the payments available from SB was a higher rate of benefit for those unemployed and other recipients who lived away from home in board and lodgings. The level of these payments was determined at local DHSS offices, on local criteria, resulting in quite wide variations from place to place.

Government concern about the operation of the rules governing board and lodgings arose from a 60 per cent (from 23,000 to 37,000) increase during 1983 in the number of young people of 25 years and under claiming SB board and lodging payments. The belief that the policy required an early review was re-inforced by a press campaign alleging that unemployed young people were taking extended holidays in seaside resorts, under the guise of seeking work and that this was being done at the taxpayers expense. This campaign was, in its essence, supported by a number of Conservative MPs representing seaside constituencies and by evidence from DHSS offices in these areas of increased claims from unemployed young people from other areas of the country.[47]

The government's first set of proposals, in November 1984, were designed, not simply to tackle the local problem being experienced in the seaside resorts, but to reduce the level and the quantity of board and lodging payments across the whole country. In particular it was intended to place limits on the eligibility of 16 and 17 year olds to claim board and lodging payments in their own right, and to restrict severely the length of time for which a board and lodging allowance would be available to all unemployed people, without dependants, outside their own local area.[48]

These proposals were referred to the Social Security Advisory Committee (SSAC) which received over 500 submissions (a peak not reached before) mainly in opposition to the goverment's plan. The SSAC report, in turn, indicated very serious misgivings about the proposed policy. Nevertheless the government decided to proceed. The new policy, somewhat revised, was announced in March 1985, to come into force on 29 April 1985. New national payments limits would be set, moving from a current range of £40 to £110 pw, to six standard amounts ranging from £45 to £70 pw, depending on the area. Within these limits, no restrictions would be placed on those 26 years and over, or on exempt categories such as the chronically sick or disabled or those who had a dependent child. The idea of special rules for 16 and 17 year olds was not pursued. Limits would apply to all those 25 and under, permitting stays in board and lodgings of up to 2, 4 and 8 weeks only, depending on the area and including their home area. When this period expired, the normal SB non-householder rate would apply. Those now in board and lodgings would have between 4 and 13 weeks to find cheaper alternative accommodation. No limit was placed on the length of stay in hostels where the £70 pw maximum would apply nationally.[49]

The new rules had a chequered career. In August 1985, they were ruled to be illegal by the High Court. In October 1985, they were re-imposed only to be disallowed within Parliament itself. They re-emerged in November 1985, this time in more permanent form.

Throughout the controversy, those who opposed the new rules argued that the problem was created by high unemployment, the government's cuts to the housing programme which had led to shortage of suitable accommodation and increased homelessness, and by family conflict, often due to the stress of unemployment, which forced large numbers of young people to leave home. The rules, therefore, attacked the symptoms, not the cause.

The government, for its part, rejected the possibility that the sudden and rapid increase in board and lodging claims could be attributed to these wider causes. It asserted – though without hard evidence – that there was widespread abuse by both landlords and young people who were exploiting the willingness of the DHSS to meet board and lodging costs, and that the system gave excessive encouragement to young people to leave home. Moreover, and this was used as the clinching argument, if an unemployed young person found work, it was highly unlikely that they could earn enough to pay high board and lodging charges themselves. Thus, a disincentive to work was in operation, and not only in the seaside places which had aroused the original concern, but nationwide. Limited action would therefore be insufficient.[50] Some concessions were made - rather more generous exemption rules and deferred application of the rules to existing claimants until 28 July 1986 – but apart from this, the government pursued its goals with determination.

The young unemployed in 1985

In mid-1985, the young unemployed aged 16-17 years fell into one of three benefit categories. First were those who had had a period of work long enough to pay contributions for Unemployment Benefit (UB). These would normally be 17 year olds and they would receive UB at the adult rate of £25.45 pw. Second were those on the Youth Training Scheme, receiving a Training Allowance of £26.25 pw. Most of these were 16 year olds but a proportion were 17 year olds. (A higher rate for 17 year olds would be introduced in the following year.) Third were 16 and 17 year olds on Supplementary Benefit. As unemployed people they would receive only the short term rate and as young people they were only entitled to dependency rate for their age group of £19.30 pw.

Government policies towards this age group were both positive and negative. They were positive in that very substantial sums of money were being expended on the Youth Training Scheme which the MSC sought to make of real value to young people, though it was not always successful in meeting this goal. The policies were negative in that government sought to exert social control over the young unemployed through the social security system.

This took two forms. The first was pressure to undertake training through the sanction of reduced benefits. To the extent that government was attempting to establish a new social pattern – that is, that 16 and 17 year olds would not normally be in the labour force but be engaged in education or training to equip themselves for a technologically-oriented future – this could be seen as a necessary part of the process. Unfortunately it was not accompanied by a guarantee that good standards of training would always be available in YTS or by a policy of financial support for those who could benefit more by remaining in the education system.

The second approach to social control was to attempt to raise the age which had marked the end of full dependency. The government repeatedly expressed its desire to withdraw the right to Supplementary Benefit from 16 year olds who, it considered, should be the responsibility of their parents. In the initial plans for the Board and Lodging regulations, it wished to place particular limitations on 16 and 17 year olds, to deter them from leaving home. In the outcome, the rules were applied not only to the youngest unemployed but to all those, without dependants, up to the age of 25 years. They marked the beginning of differential rules, not only for 16 and 17 year olds, but for those above and well above the age of majority.

References

1. Royal Commission on Unemployment Insurance, op.cit., pp.184-8.
2. Ibid., p.185.
3. Ibid., p.187.

4. *Report of the Unemployment Assistance Board 1935*, Cmd 5177, HMSO, London, 1936, p.291 and the *Beveridge Report*, op.cit., p.231.
5. Beveridge Report, op.cit., pp.152-3.
6. The Blanesburgh Report, op.cit., p.39.
7. Royal Commission, op.cit., pp.312-22.
8. Ibid., p.319.
9. Ibid., p.320.
10. Beveridge Report, op.cit., p.58.
11. *Social Insurance Part 1*, op.cit., p.17.
12. *British Labour Statistics Historical Abstract*, op.cit., Table 175.
13. *Report of the National Assistance Board 1965*, HMSO, London, 1966, pp.58-9.
14. *Department of Health and Social Security Annual Report 1971*, HMSO, London, 1972, pp.339-340.
15. 'Duration of Unemployment and Age of Unemployment', *Department of Employment Gazette*, September 1971, p.830.
16. Ibid., August 1972, p.738 and August 1973, p.778.
17. Ibid., August 1974, p.746 and September 1975, p.886.
18. *Supplemetary Benefits Commission Annual Report 1976*, pp.53-20.
19. Ibid., p.54.
20. DHSS, *Social Assistance*, op.cit., pp.26-8.
21. *Unqualified, Untrained and Unemployed: Report of a Working Party set up by the National Youth Employment Council*, Department of Employment/HMSO, London, 1974, Chapter 3.
22. Manpower Services Commission, *Annual Report 1976-1977*, p.26.
23. Ibid., *Annual Report 1977-78*, p.30.
24. MSC, *Towards a Comprehensive Manpower Policy*, 1976, p.22
25. MSC, *Review and Plan 1977*, p.37.
26. MSC, *Annual Report 1977-8*, p.30.
27. MSC, *Annual Report 1978-9*, p.23.
28. John Solomos, 'Problems, but whose problems: The social construction of black youth uneployment and State policies', *Journal of Social Policy*, 14/4, October 1985, pp.527-54.
29. *Social Security Statistics Northern Ireland, 1984*.
30. Peter Makeham, 'The anatomy of youth unemployment', *Employment Gazette*, March 1980, pp.234-6.

31. Department of Employment, *Press Notice*, 'Young workers scheme starts next week', 31 December 1981.
32. William Wells, *The Relative Pay and Employment of Young People*, Department of Employment, London, 1983 also summarised in an article with the same title in *Employment Gazette*, June 1983, pp.230-7.
33. Robert Bushell, 'Evaluation of the Young Workers Scheme', *Employment Gazette*, May 1986, pp.145-52.
34. See for example, 'Youth wages and unempoyment', *Unemployment Unit Briefing*, May 1983.
35. MSC, *Annual Report 1980-1*, p.23.
36. MSC, *A New Training Intiative: A Consultative Document*, London, May 1981, p.4.
37. Past policy statements summarised in a Department of Employment, *Press Notice*, 'Government adopt wider youth training scheme', 21 June 1982.
38. *A New Training Initiative: A Programme for Action*, Cmnd 8455, HMSO, London, 1981.
39. MSC, *Youth Task Group Report*, London, April 1982, paras 4.22-36 and 7.14-15.
40. *Report from the Select Committee of the House of Lords on Unemployment*, 142, HMSO, London, 1982, pp.109-15.
41. Department of Employment, *Press Notice*, 6 May 1982.
42. Ibid., 21 June 1982.
43. *House of Commons Hansard*, 4 June 1984, 27.
44. John Pelican, *Studying on the Dole*, Youthaid, London, 1983, pp.16-17.
45. *House of Commons Hansard*, 30 October 1984, 1150.
46. *Studying on the Dole*, op.cit., p.13.
47. *House of Commons Hansard*, 29 November 1984, 1098-1107.
48. Ibid.
49. Ibid., 2 April 1985, 1165-7.
50. Ibid., 1168-86.

7 The older unemployed

The definition of an older worker (or older unemployed person) in policy discussion tends to move in relation to two factors: the age of retirement and the level of unemployment. The age of retirement is determined principally by the availability of retirement income, and in particular, State benefits. Pension age, that is, the year State pensions become available, is an important watershed in the social security system. Differing rules may apply to those above and below pension age. This age changes infrequently and has been stable since 1940. It has, since that time, come to set the age beyond which it is more normal to be out of the labour force than to be within it. It also influences attitudes to those who are within a few years of retirement age, should they become unemployed. As the age of retirement has fallen since the beginning of the century, so the definition of being near retirement has fallen and since the age of retirement now differs between men and women, this affects women at an earlier age than men.

The level of unemployment, on the other hand, is a much less predictable factor and it produces a variety of policy responses. In long periods of low unemployment, a high value is placed on all age groups in the labour force, including those over pension age. Prolonged high unemployment, on the other hand, may suggest the need to reduce the size of the labour force or the need to set priorities for action to assist certain categories of the unemployed. At such a time, the older worker has a lower priority for special assistance to return to employment than younger married men with children, or younger adults generally. The older age group may be viewed as dispensable, if the labour force is to shrink. Early retirement under various guises may be seen as one 'solution' to unemployment. It may be informally encouraged, but not necessarily to the extent of altering State pension provision.

Governments are reluctant to make a formal change in the pension age. In times of full employment, when there is a labour shortage, proposals to raise the retirement age will be rejected, partly because this would be politically unpopular, and partly because a proportion of the age group concerned will no longer be physically fit for work or will not be needed in the labour market. These would have to be catered for through other forms of social security. In times of high unemployment, proposals to lower the retirement age will equally be rejected. A proportion of older workers will still be needed. Others are in a position to take voluntary early retirement because they have occupational pensions and there is no need to incur the substantial cost of providing State pensions for this group. Moreover, it may be that unemployment will subsequently fall and a pension age once lowered cannot easily be raised, at least in political terms. Better, therefore, to maintain an unemployed group pending developments in the labour market.

Typically no clear policy is developed by governments for the older unemployed. They are identified as a problem group but no action is taken unless it suits the government of the day to do so.

The depression years

Prior to 1908, the only resort for an unemployed person without income was the Poor Law. The introduction of means tested old age pensions in 1908 was designed, in part, to permit workers over 70 years of age to retire with dignity. A few years later, the 1911 Unemployment Insurance Act provided entitlement to benefit regardless of age for all those in insurable employment who had paid the requisite contributions. The boundary between old age pensions and Unemployment Insurance was fluid and while the latter lasted, it could be chosen in preference to retirement.

The onset of high unemployment in the 1920s, focused attention on the older worker. The definition was a stringent one and distinguished between the 'older' worker, defined as over 45 years for men and over 35 years for women and the 'elderly' worker, defined as at or near pensionable age. The first group, it was found in 1926, were less likely than younger workers to become unemployed, but once out of work they had greater difficulty in getting a job and consequently spent longer on benefits.[1] This was treated as a fact of life which an insurance scheme had to deal with and where eligible, older workers could qualify for extended benefit without too much difficulty[2] (see Chapter 1).

Elderly unemployed workers, on the other hand, were seen as an insurance problem. In areas of high unemployment where their chances of securing a job were low, they might be refused Unemployment Insurance on the grounds that, at their age, they were unlikely to be employed again.[3] The TUC, giving evidence to the Blanesburgh Committee, wanted to see elderly workers removed from the labour market to make room for younger workers. It argued, therefore, for a more generous old age pension to enable them 'to leave the world of labour with an assured pension'.[4]

This proposal was only partly met by the introduction of contributory old age pensions in 1925, payable from the age of 65 years. Unlike the earlier means tested pensions (which remained for those of 70 years and over) they were payable whether or not the recipient worked. At the same time the right to Unemployment Insurance after the age of 65 years was withdrawn. Since the pension was lower than Unemployment Insurance this was a loss to the unemployed, though a gain for those who could work.

The Blanesburgh Report made no specific proposals for older workers, but its recommendation that, after initial qualification, continued benefit be made dependent on the payment of at least 30 contributions in the previous two years,[5] was bound to affect adversely the older unemployed more than the younger, because of the greater difficulty they had in finding work.

The proposals of the Royal Commission on Unemployment Insurance and the legislation which established the reformed insurance scheme and the Unemployment Assistance Board (UAB) also presented difficulties for older workers. Under the new provisions the insurance scheme was designed to deal with short term unemployment (around 6 months) and the means tested assistance scheme with longer term and chronic unemployment. The provision that a worker with a good contribution record could get extended Unemployment Insurance was likely to assist older workers with good employment records. On the other hand, the difficulties older workers experienced in getting back into work once unemployed was likely to result in their accumulation in the UAB scheme.

This proved to be the case. By 1937 some 48 per cent of men receiving UAB were over 45 years of age (and 40 per cent of women).

Among those men unemployed for 3 years or more, the proportion was 62 per cent (39 per cent for women).[6] Others were rejected by the UAB as unlikely to work again and these had to turn to Public Assistance for support. These numbers on UAB moreover, did not prompt a programme directed to their re-employment in what was, by then, an improved labour market. Instead, in 1938, the Board examined means by which the long term unemployed under 30 years of age could be assisted. It did acknowledge that 'the view that at 45 or 50 a man is, by reason of age, past work is ... one that cannot be held with complacency'. The problem was one of 'importance and urgency' – but for practical reasons attention was first to be given in cases of younger applicants.[7]

With the onset of World War II in 1939, the bulk of unemployment was soaked up within a few years including that affecting older workers. Indeed, by the end of the war, 750,000 old age pensioners were in work and nearly 300,000 had returned to the labour force after having retired.[8]

Older workers and the post war reforms
This practical proof that it was not necessary to 'write off' the older long term unemployed and the adoption of the goal of maintaining full employment in the post war years, was perhaps reason enough for the attitude taken by Beveridge to this age group. No reference was made to the older worker as a problem of unemployment. Instead Beveridge, in his pension proposals, was aiming to raise the average age of retirement to save pension costs. This was because in future a higher proportion of the population was expected to be over retirement age and means had to be found 'to lighten the burden that will otherwise fall on the British economy'. He made it clear that 'early retirement of men on pension is not wanted or useful as a cure for unemployment'. While it was not considered feasible to raise the pension age – because the individual capacity to work varied so much – incentives could be offered for those over pension age to stay in the labour force as long as work was available to them.[9] The retirement pension would be paid only to those who had retired from work. Those who worked on could pay National Insurance contributions and could earn a higher pension in this way. If they became unemployed, they could claim unemployment benefit, but unlike the proposals for the

rest of the unemployed, only for a limited period. The reason for these provisions was given as follows:

> ... to make the age of retirement flexible is one way of adjusting the supply of labour to fluctuations in demand. In time of good trade the older men will find it easier to keep their work and postpone retirement. In times of bad trade they will tend to retire earlier and reduce the supply of labour; it is an essential part of the proposal that the period for which unemployment (and disability) benefit can be drawn after the minimum age of retirement should be restricted.[10]

The government, in any case, rejected an indefinite unemployment benefit, substituting a 6 months benefit for all, followed by means tested National Assistance, but the view that the older worker was an asset, not a problem, was maintained in the adoption of the other Beveridge proposals. Indeed, in the 1944 White Paper there was a declaration of confidence in the elderly worker, who was to be encouraged to work because of the growth in the proportion of the elderly in the population:

> it may well become a matter of vital importance to keep up the national income by encouraging the continuance of productive work by those who have reached pensionable age. In the war elderly people have turned to and served the country well, in many capacities, paid and voluntary. In peace, there may be a similar call upon their readiness and ability to play a constructive part in the national effort.[11]

As seen in Chapter 3, the UK rate of unemployment remained low in the 1950s and 1960s, except in Northern Ireland where it ranged from 5 to 10 per cent. Some older workers did experience problems of unemployment and they commonly formed a large proportion of those out of work. In surveys undertaken by the Ministry of Labour in 1961 and 1964, in Great Britain over half the unemployed men and a lower proportion of the women were over 45 years. Those who were within five years of retirement age were the most likely to be classified as difficult to place in employment. In Northern Ireland, in 1964, age was identified as a problem in 12.7 per cent of men and a very small percentage of women.[12]

Age, then, was regarded as one of the obstacles facing the older unemployed, but mostly from 55-60 years onwards. Even so, the absolute numbers involved (in a period of low general unemployment) did not suggest a need for a policy change in benefit provision. For those aged under 65 years for men and 60 years for women, there would be an entitlement, under the same conditions as for younger men and women, to Unemployment Benefit. When this expired, National Assistance would be available to the men and single women on a means tested basis, and at the same rates as paid to other recipients, though married women (as seen in Chapter 6) would be less well covered.

The Redundancy Payments Act 1965

From 1965 onwards unemployment rose and with periodic fluctuations reached just short of 1 million in 1975 and remained in excess of 1 million for the remainder of the 1970s. This in itself could be expected to prejudice the position of the older worker, but their situation was worsened by what was probably an unexpected side effect of the Redundancy Payments Act of 1965.

The main provisions of the Act have been described in Chapter 3. On the face of it, they favoured the older worker. It was true that those over retirement age (65/60) were excluded, since they were seen as having the option of a retirement income. It was also the case that the use of the scheme by employers or employees as a form of early retirement was discouraged. The employee's entitlement was reduced by one twelfth for each month his age exceeded 64 years or her age exceeded 59 years, i.e. just short of pensionable age in each case. But in most other respects the intention of the Act was to favour those over 40 years. Whereas half a week's pay was payable for years worked between 18 and 21 years and 1 week's pay for the years 21-40, from 41 years the time worked counted for 1.5 week's pay. Moreover, an older worker who had been employed for many years with one company might be able to accumulate the maximum 20 years service entitlement set by the Act. An OPCS report in 1971 (on a survey undertaken in 1969) said:

> The case for introducing the age factor in the compulsory national scheme, by providing special weighting for the older worker, was felt to be a strong one, since redundancy could often be a particularly serious blow for him in several ways. For the older worker, redundancy can bring with it a particularly severe period of anxiety prior to dismissal, greater difficulty in the search for alternative employment, and greater problems in the re-adjustment to the change of environment.[13]

In addition to this weighting of the payments, employers could reclaim a higher percentage of redundancy pay (seven-ninths instead of two-thirds) from the Redundancy Fund for those over 40 years. The intention was to encourage employers to hire older workers because they would attract a larger refund if it was later necessary to make them redundant. However, it also had another effect. Given two workers with equal length of service, it could cost the employer no more to make the older than the younger worker redundant, even though the rate of redundancy pay for the older worker was higher.[14]

The OPCS survey endeavoured to find out if there had been any change in the criteria used to select workers for redundancy, following the Act. Prior to the Act the most common rule was that known as 'last in, first out', followed by efficiency at work and skill level. Older workers with good employment records would not be first in line under such rules. Age as a criterion ranked fourth and well below the other three in proportional terms. Last in, first out as a criterion was mentioned by 62 per cent of employers, whereas age was given by only 19 per cent. By 1969, the use of age as a criterion had risen to 38 per cent of the employers surveyed.[15]

Further studies in the 1970s confirmed this trend. An examination of redundancy practices in the period 1974-7 by Daniel and Stilgoe found that, in cases of enforced redundancy, last in, first out, remained the top criterion (at 53 per cent of firms) but 28 per cent selected those over retirement age and 21 per cent those near retirement age.[16] The study also noted a trend which had also been identified by OPCS, in the use of voluntary redundancies. Here it was found that schemes were designed to attract certain categories of worker. Some 37 per cent of schemes were intended to appeal to older workers.[17]

A British Institute of Management study of 350 companies, published in 1974, identified a third form of payment in the shape of special redundancy provisions within the occupational pension scheme.[18] These enabled the payment of a more generous pension than would otherwise be available and were, again, directed to older workers.

In 1977, the government made some effort to counter this tendency to over emphasise on age as a criterion by reducing the rebate from the Redundancy Fund for older workers and setting a new, uniform level. By this time, the trend was probably too well established to be affected.

It was noted earlier that older workers were less likely to become unemployed than younger men and women, but once out of work, they took longer to find employment. The Redundancy Payments Act made the first half of this proposition less valid, but the second half remained true. The OCPS study found that of those who had received statutory redundancy pay (during the 18 months preceding the survey), 18 per cent of those aged 50-59 years and 53 per cent of those aged 60-64 years had not found another job. Of those who did find employment, the average time spent acquiring another job was 4 weeks for 20-29 year olds, but 15 weeks for 60-64 year olds.[19]

The increase in the number of older unemployed in the 1970s was not, of course solely due to the effects of the Redundancy Payments Act. The general growth of unemployment to around 1.4 million in 1979 inevitably affected older workers considerably. Of particular concern was the high proportion of older workers unemployed for more than twelve months. Table 7.1 shows the figures for men.

Table 7.1 Proportion of men unemployed for more than 52 weeks, 1973, 1976 and 1978. Great Britain

Percentages

	1973	1976	1978
All	14.8	19.6	25.4
45-49	36.5	27.8	37.0
50-54	39.6	31.6	41.4
55-59	45.9	34.5	43.9
60-64	49.0	39.2	45.9
65 and over	33.2	42.4	50.4

Source: *Department of Employment Gazette*, August 1973, August 1976 and August 1978

The position of women was a little better but the figures would be distorted by their lower registration as unemployed. Data by age on the much longer duration of unemployment in Northern Ireland did not become available until 1980, but it can be expected that the same adverse patterns were evident in the 1970s.

The benefit provision in the 1970s

As Chapter 3 showed, these comprised four elements – Redundancy Pay, Unemployment Benefit, Earnings Related Supplement (ERS) and Supplementary Benefit, either as supplementation or as the main income. The older unemployed were well placed to receive redundancy payments, though if they had been unemployed more than once in a period of two years, the second period would not qualify. A PSI study of the unemployed in 1979 found that around 73 per cent of men over 45 years had received redundancy pay, some of quite small sums (less than £200) but the mean figure was in the region of £1,000 to £1,600.[20] Data by age for the payment of ERS was not published, but the rules did not disadvantage older workers who had a good record of employment.

Apart from these, Unemployment Benefit (UB) after 1966 was potentially available for 52 weeks, with or without SB supplementation, and Supplementary Benefit could be paid to those without UB entitlement or whose rights had expired. The older unemployed men who usually had fewer dependents than young people, were not heavily represented among those receiving supplementation of Unemployment Benefit. The real call on SB came from those without NI entitlement and here the pattern of long term unemployment among the older men showed up.

Table 7.2 Receipt of Unemployment Benefit (UB), Earnings Related Supplement (ERS) and Supplementary Benefit (SB) by unemployed men aged 55-64, 1972, 1976, 1979 . Great Britain

Thousands

	1972	1976	1979
UB only	34	41	31
UB + ERS	34	46	55
UB/ERS + SB	1	2	1
UB + SB	9	11	6
SB only	54	48	67
None	51	54	58
Total	183	196	198

Source: *Social Security Statistics*

Table 7.2 shows the source of social security income for 55-64 year old unemployed men in 1972 (the first year when age related statistics were published), 1976 and 1979. The figures for women were much smaller – in 1979 for example there were 24,000 in all, including 12,000 on SB either as a supplement or on its own. These lower figures are in part due to the fact that once any UB rights have expired, married women are treated as financially dependent on their husbands, and in part because for women they cover only the years 55-59. At 60 years they would usually be classified as retired.

For the long term older unemployed, the key figure is that for SB only – 67,000 men and 11,000 women in 1979. In the 1960s being on SB as an unemployed person was little different from the same situation after pensionable age. However, as Chapter 4 showed, the introduction in 1973 of the long term rate for pensioners served to improve their position as against those on the short term rate. Most other SB recipients proceeded in time (after 2 years) to the higher long term rate, but no matter how long the unemployment, the unemployed were never permitted to do so.

Concern about the older long term unemployed was tempered by evidence that a large number of them were receiving occupational pensions. Thus it could be suggested that many were not suffering particular hardship and/or were not truly unemployed. The occupational pensions sector had enjoyed substantial growth in the 1950s and 1960s, and a proportion of the pension schemes, particularly in the public sector, set a retirement age for men at 60 years. A group who had ceased their normal employment under these provisions began to emerge in the unemployment statistics in the late 1960s, and were reinforced by those whose redundancy provisions included payment of an earlier occupational pension than would otherwise have been available.

By the early 1970s, a signficant proportion of the 60-64 year old men shown in the unemployment statistics were occupational pensioners who were registering as unemployed, because work was desired or needed for financial reasons, or in order to obtain Unemployment Benefit and/or credits for the National Insurance Retirement Pension. The 1973 survey[21] of the unemployed found 50,000 male occupational pensioners including 46 per cent of unemployed men aged 60-64 years and a smaller proportion of those aged 55-59 years. In a 1976 survey, 75,000 occupational pensioners were identified among unemployed men aged 55-64 years. This included 49 per cent of those men aged 60-64 years.[22] (Only 2,000 of the women under 60 years had such pensions.)

The income available to those men in 1976, would have depended on the size of the occupational pension and the length of time unemployed. In 1976, average male wages were £71.80 and Unemployment Benefit for a married couple was £18 pw plus a maximum of £9.37 for six months in Earnings Related Supplement (ERS).[23] In the same year, more than half of the male occupational pensioners aged 55-64 years in the survey received less than £20 pw in pension and nearly 16 per cent received less than £5 pw. Without Unemployment Benefit and ERS, many would have had to apply for Supplementary Benefit. With the NI benefits, while they lasted, their position was more satisfactory although still far below average earnings. Those with pensions over £20 pw, plus the NI benefits were not too badly off. Once the NI benefits ran out, then their income could be supplemented by Supplementary Benefit, provided they fell below the minimum income prescribed, after a disregard of £1 of their occupational pension. At a time when the SB rate for a married couple was £17.65 pw plus housing costs, those who had a low pension would be little better off than an unemployed couple with no occupational pension rights.

Although a closer examination of the data on the occupational pension group did not suggest that there was any grounds for complacency about their financial position, the bald figures nevertheless reinforced the tendency to neglect the older unemployed. The policy of maintaining low benefits to give a financial inducement to return to work was applied to this older group even though their chances of obtaining work were considered to be very low. The 1976 unemployment survey,[24] for example, rated only 19 per cent of men aged 55 years and over as having a good, fair or reasonable chance of employment. Moreover, little attempt was made to assist them to find work through a submission for a job vacancy by the Employment Service. The same survey found that 83 per cent of men aged 55 and over had not been put forward for any job during the time they had been unemployed, including 80 per cent of those out of work for more than 12 months.[25]

In effect, whether nor not the older unemployed were 'really retired', because they had an ample occupational pension, or were in financial need, requiring Supplementary Benefit, they were beginning to be virtually written off for purposes of re-employment. The 1970s saw the introduction of a series of schemes to provide temporary work for the unemployed. They were principally designed for those under 25 years. There were also two training schemes – the Youth Opportunities Programme introduced in 1978 and the Training Opportunities Scheme in 1972. The latter was theoretically available to all those over 19 years, but in 1980 less than 3 per cent of the trainees were over 50 years of age.[26] The only scheme directed specifically to older workers was one designed to encourage them to give up their jobs in favour of someone younger.

The Job Release Scheme

In 1977 a new scheme was introduced which emphasised the view of the older worker as dispensable, to be moved out of the labour force when demand for labour was low. The Job Release Scheme offered workers within a prescribed number of years of retirement, a tax free allowance if they agreed to withdraw from the labour market and the employer agreed to recruit someone from the unemployment register to replace them – though not necessarily in the same job. Originally the scheme was restricted to Assisted Areas – that is those entitled to special aid because of high unemployment – but later it was extended to the whole country. For the first six months of the scheme both unemployed and employed could apply, but then the unemployed were excluded, since they did not have a job to vacate.

The scheme was described in the *Department of Employment Gazette* as a means of reducing the level of unemployment:

> The objectives of the scheme is to allow older workers to leave the labour force and be replaced by those otherwise unemployed in time of recession. It reduces the labour supply temporarily ...[27]

Its other advantages were said to be that it was voluntary, that it could be used selectively, by age or area, and that it could run for a limited period without altering existing arrangements for retirement or seriously disrupting other employment practices.

Its flexibility was demonstrated by frequent alterations of the age of eligibility. At first this was set at 64 years for men and 59 years for women. Later in 1977 it was extended to men over 62 years and registered disabled men over 60 years. By February 1979, 48,000 persons in Great Britain and a smaller number in Northern Ireland had retired under the scheme.[28]

That the scheme was not more popular was attributed to the low level of the allowance offered. In late 1977, at £23 per week, it was slightly lower than the rate for a married man with a dependent wife on Unemployment Benefit (then £23.80) though higher than the single rate (£14.70). From July 1978 the rate was increased to £35 for a married man and £26.50 for single men, still a very modest offering when the average manual wage for men was £78.60 pw.[29] However, it could be attractive to those who had the possibility of a small occupational pension, not enough in itself to retire on, but acceptable if combined with a JRS allowance. A survey in 1979 found that over half of JRS applicants had an occupational pension averaging £19 p.w.[30]

The impact of high unemployment 1980-5

Table 7.3 Duration of unemployment of older men and women. United Kingdom, October 9, 1980.

Duration of unemployment in weeks	Males			Females	
	55-59	60-64	65+	55-59	60-64
MALE					
One or less	2,979	3,528	40	840	34
Over 1 and up to	3,919	4,799	58	1,134	55
2	5,394	6,095	76	1,653	85
4	6,230	7,468	79	1,899	85
6	4,109	4,598	56	1,172	53
8	9,125	11,705	136	2,671	130
13	15,759	22,823	286	5,089	252
26	10,194	15,655	245	3,533	201
39	6,592	11,878	201	2,438	132
52	5,087	10,695	191	1,921	119
65	3,641	6,619	140	1,287	82
78	5,037	9,439	254	1,988	136
104	7,151	15,180	426	2,872	224
156	17,741	26,133	1,135	5,792	368
All	102,958	156,615	3,323	34,289	1,956

Source: *Employment Gazette*, November 1980

Table 7.3 gives the numbers of older unemployed on October 3, 1980. This shows the length of time they had been out of work when the count was taken. Some of these may have been able to return to employment. A DHSS study of the unemployed, which interviewed men in 1978 and again in 1979, found that by the second interview, 22 per cent of those aged 50-59 years and 7 per cent of those over 60 years had full time jobs, while 3 per cent and 5 per cent respectively had part time jobs. But 61 per cent of those aged 50-59 years and 79 per cent of those over 60 years had been continuously unemployed throughout the period.[31] The proportion of 55-59 year old men within the 50-59 year old group, who did not find a job could reasonably be expected to be higher than the overall figures show.

As Table 7.3 shows, by late 1980, 26,000 men aged 60-64 had been unemployed for 3 years or more and 17,700 aged 55-59 years. In Northern Ireland, it was found necessary to extend the figures presented to cover those unemployed for 5 years or more in 1980, though given the relatively small size of the Province's labour force, the actual numbers were small.[32] The level of UK unemployment by mid-1980 had passed the 2 million mark and was still climbing, reaching 3 million in 1982 and remaining above that level until 1987. Thus it could be expected that the chances of the older unemployed finding work would be further diminished·

As seen in Chapter 5, the government's first response to the higher level of unemployment was to reduce benefits to increase work incentives, first by the abolition of ERS and then by uprating the benefits by 5 per cent less than the rate of inflation, pending bringing the benefits into tax. Moreover, it was resisting pressure to give the long term unemployed access to the long term rate of Supplementary Benefit.

In November 1981, it modified its views somewhat, but only in relation to men over 60 years. Where such men were on SB and had been unemployed for more than one year, they could move onto the long term SB rate, provided they ceased to register for employment. In 1983, this was extended to all men in this age group on SB, and this time, like those of pension age, they could receive the long term rate as soon as they claimed benefit, again provided they did not register for work. The policy helped to contain the size of the unemployment register, but it also served to recognise the reality of the position of these older unemployed and to pay benefit accordingly. For a time the Northern Ireland unemployed were expected to continue to serve

52 weeks on the short term rate before becoming entitled to the higher rate.[33] The reason for this was not evident.

No such recognition was given to the equally parlous position of men and women aged 55-59 years, whose chances of re-employment were low. These must serve out their time on the short term rate, until they reached 60 years, when the women would qualify for the Retirement Pension and the men for the long term rate of SB. By mid-1985 over 210,000 men of this age group were unemployed and over 68,000 women. Of these, 132,000 and 43,000 respectively had been unemployed for more than a year, and 22,000 men and 6,000 women for more than 5 years.[34]

The older unemployed in 1985

If the position of an unemployed man or woman over 55 years was compared with that of an employed man or woman of the same age, and in a stable job, a range of disadvantages became evident. Few of these individuals would have young children dependent on them, though they might have older sons or daughters in extended education. In the case of the employed aged 55-64 years, both parties to the marriage might be free to work and the reasonable income which resulted could be used to build up the material resources of the home, pay off any mortgage and other credit commitments, and to accumulate some savings. It is true that if the jobs were low paid, this facility would be limited but nevertheless it could be expected to be a decade of modest affluence. At the same time, those in occupational pension schemes were accumulating pensionable years which would enhance their income in retirement and other employees, after 1978, would be paying contributions to the State Earnings Related Pension Scheme (SERPS) which, on retirement, would also give them an addition to their National Insurance Retirement Pension.

Unemployed men or women aged 55-64 resembled this group only in their lack of young dependants. At 55-59 years, they would have suffered a sharp fall in their income. Not many of this group could expect to receive an immediate occupational pension, unless it was negotiated as part of a redundancy agreement. They would usually have an entitlement to 52 weeks of Unemployment Benefit and possibly had redundancy money when they left work. Once out of work for more than 52 weeks, the income of the men and single women would be derived principally from Supplementary Benefit, and for married women, the wife's dependency addition to that benefit, where relevant. These benefits would be paid at the short term rate.

While this period of unemployment persisted, then far from being able to build up material resources and savings for retirement, their resources would be gradually drained away. Moreover, although the provision of credits for the NI Retirement Pension preserved their entitlement to the basic pension, they could no longer contribute to an occupational scheme or to SERPS, thus affecting their their ultimate retirement income.

Once over 60 years, the position improved somewhat. The women would be regarded as retired and the NI pension would be paid. Any SERPS entitlements would also be paid and in the case of occupational scheme members, there might be a right to a preserved pension left behind when the job was lost.

A larger group of the 60-64 year of men than the younger group would have an occupational pension. In 1980, however, the government introduced new rules for this group. If the pension exceeded £35 pw, Unemployment Benefit would be reduced £ for £ for any amount in excess. In addition the £1 disregard of the occupational pension for SB claimants was withdrawn. Occupational pensioners who had been in schemes with a pensionable age of 60 years and whose full term pension was fairly ample, could still be reasonably comfortable. They would retain a right to credits for the NI pension which would become payable at 65 years.

For those without an occupational pension or a rather low pension, there would be an entitlement to full Unemployment Benefit for 52 weeks. Thereafter they might have to turn to Supplementary Benefit. This would be payable at the long term rate. However, though better than the short term rate, the income would still be low and leave little room for savings. Indeed if they had had savings in excess of £3,000 it would be necessary to live on the surplus for a period, since SB would not be available to them.

Finally, there would be a group who had retired under the Job Release Scheme. The qualifying age for this was raised again to 64 years for men in 1984, though it stayed at 59 years for women and 60 years for disabled men. However, men of 62 and 63 years who had qualified before 1984 might still be receiving the allowance. By 1985, 293,000 people had retired under the scheme and of these 57,000 were still receiving the allowance in August 1985, all but 5,000 of whom were men.[35] The allowances payable were a little higher than the long term rate of Supplementary Benefit and preserved the right to the NI pension. They might also be supplemented by a small occupational pension, but other recipients had to drop out of SERPS or their occupational pension scheme.

The payment of the higher rate of SB to men after 60 years and the limited Job Release Scheme, could not be described as a well developed policy for the long term older unemployed. The government continued to resist the formal lowering of the pensionable age, but it placed no impediment in the way of what had become a drift to earlier retirement. This had occurred through the provision of occupational pensions, either in schemes with a retirement age of 60 for men, or for individuals whose pensions were high enough to permit taking early retirement on a reduced pension, or where redundancy had included an occupational pension deal. In so far as the government participated in the downward drift of retirement age, it was by requiring the 60s and over on long term SB or Job Release to withdraw from the unemployment register as a condition of benefits.

No policy had been developed which fully protected the future retirement income of those who become unemployed late in working life. The current pension system is designed to produce an adequate income in retirement through a second pension built upon the basic NI pension. For the unemployed the NI pension is protected, but the lost years of contribution to the second pension, are lost forever. Finally, no policy at all was developed for the 55-59 year olds. If in 1985 the prognosis for the future was a fall in unemployment to pre-1979 levels, such a passive policy stance might have been understandable. Given the gloomy prospects for continued high unemployment, it appeared rather an evasion of responsibility.

References

1. Ministry of Labour, *Investigation* ..., op.cit., pp.48-9.
2. Ibid., pp.52-3.
3. The Blanesburgh Report, Vol. 2, op.cit., p.169.
4. Ibid.
5. The Blanesburgh Report, op.cit., p.32.
6. *Report of the Unemployment Assistance Board 1937*, Cmd 7552, HMSO, London, 1938, pp.68-76.
7. *Report of the Unemployment Assistance Board 1938*, Cmd 6021, HMSO, London, 1939, p.3.
8. *House of Commons Hansard*, 6 February 1946, 1749.

9. Beveridge Report, op.cit., p.59.
10. Ibid.
11. *Social Insurance Part I*, op.cit., p.22.
12. 'Characteristics of the Unemployed', *Ministry of Labour Gazette*, April 1962, pp.131-7 and 'Characteristics of the Unemployed: Survey Results', *Ministry of Labour Gazette*, April 1966, pp.156-7.
13. *Effects of the Redundancy Payments Act*, op.cit., p.5.
14. 'Age and Redundancy', *Department of Employment Gazette*, September 1978, pp.1032-9.
15. *Effects of the Redundancy Payments Act*, op.cit., p.49.
16. W.W. Daniel, and Elizabeth Stilgoe, *The Impact of the Employment Protection Laws*, PSI, London, 1978, p.19.
17. Ibid., p.18.
18. Catherine M Smith, *Redundancy Policies: A survey of current practice in 350 companies*, British Institute of Management, London 1975, p.23.
19. *Effects of the Redundancy Payments Act*, op.cit., pp.89, 107 and 187.
20. David J. Smith, *Unemployment and Racial Minorities*, PSI, London, 1981, p.90. The lower figure of the two was the mean for ethnic minority workers.
21. 'Characteristics of the Unemployed: Sample survey June 1973', *Department of Employment Gazette*, March 1974, pp.211-21.
22. 'Characteristics of the Unemployed: Sample survey June 1976', *Department of Employment Gazette*, June 1977, pp.559-74.
23. *Social Security Statistics*, 1984.
24. 1976 Survey, op.cit., p.863.
25. Ibid., p.656.
26. House of Commons Social Services Committee, *Age of Retirement: Evidence*, HC 26-11, HMSO, London, 1982, p.448.
27. 'The Job Release Scheme', *Department of Employment Gazette*, April 1978, pp.422-3 and 425.
28. Ibid.
29. Ibid.
30. 'An increase in earlier retirement for men', *Employment Gazette*, April 1980, pp.366-9.

31. Moylan, S. et al, *For Richer or Poorer?*, op.cit., p.29.
32. *Northern Ireland, Annual Abstract of Statistics*, No.1 - 1982, HMSO, Belfast, 1982.
33. *House of Commons Hansard*, 1 May 1986, 467.
34. *Employment Gazette*, September 1985.
35. Ibid., November, 1985.

8   The disabled unemployed

The concept of special labour market disadvantage has been used quite widely in recent years to refer to those groups who experience more and/or longer unemployment than the average. Older workers are one such group, though it was not until the last decade that the disadvantage of age attracted any special measures and then only of a strictly limited nature. One group for whose labour market disadvantage a policy was developed was the unemployed who were disabled. But it relied heavily on parallel policies which ensured low levels of general unemployment and therefore high labour demand. When general unemployment rose, the weaknesses in the policy for the disabled unemployed were exposed.

The pre-war years
The pre-war social security arrangements made a clear distinction between those regarded as wholly incapacitated for work – in which case the Poor Law/Public Assistance or National Health Insurance would provide – and those whose disabilities were partial and who therefore had residual working capacity. Within this second category, there were three groups for whom some special provision was made.

Two of these were uncomfortably placed on the boundaries of the disability and unemployment provisions. In the case of war pensioners, their pensions were directly related to the severity of their disability and not to income. The assumption was that a partially disabled pensioner would be able to work and the pension would either supplement a wage that was below normal level because of the disability or would simply act as compensation for the hurt suffered. This seemed a legitimate arrangement as long as work was available but proved a difficulty at the time of the depression because some war pensioners could neither get work nor support themselves on their pensions. The Blanesburgh Report (in 1927) noted that this group had particular difficulty in qualifying for Unemployment Insurance, because this required at least a minimum number of contributions while in work. The Unemployment Insurance authorities were sympathetic, but reluctant to modify their rules for a minority group, while the Ministry of Pensions (which was responsible for war pensions) did not want to make changes to the structure of pensions.[1] This gap in war pension provision was not filled until 1943, in the middle of another war, when an Unemployability Supplement was introduced, payable when the equivalent civilian benefit was not available.[2]

A similar situation arose under Workmen's Compensation. This provided that a man or woman totally disabled from work due to industrial injury or illness, would receive half their average weekly wage prior to the injury up to a maximum fixed from time to time. Provision for partial incapacity took the form of an allowance fixed in relation to the wages earned prior to the industrial injury and the average amount the worker was able to earn after the accident. This could be commuted for a lump sum payment. Either way, the payment was likely to be inadequate if the worker was unemployed and had no insurance entitlement. No solution – other than means tested supplementation – was found for this until 1948 when a new improved Industrial Injuries Scheme was introduced.

The third group which attracted some attention was the blind. The main provision – from 1920 – was to permit blind persons to qualify for means tested old age pensions at the age of 50 rather than 70 years. In 1938, the qualifying age was reduced to 40 years. The assumption was that blindness after that age severely limited the possibility of training or re-training for employment and the most convenient way of meeting this problem administratively was to regard the older blind as prematurely retired. Young blind persons might qualify for local government assistance for training or through supplementation of low wages earned in blind workshops or in home employment.

Apart from these groups, disabled people with residual working capacity were expected to cope in the labour market or claim Unemployment Insurance. If they were not eligible for the latter, then they would be given Unemployment Assistance if they were regarded as potentially employable or Public Assistance if they were not.

The disabled unemployed and the post-war reforms

The disabled unemployed did not get a great deal out of the new post-war social security arrangements. Several improvements were embodied in the new Industrial Injuries Scheme. This now adopted the war pension approach to its new Disablement Benefit, that is, the level of weekly benefit would depend on the percentage of disability which resulted from injury at work. This would be paid whether or not the injured worker returned to employment and regardless of other income, since it was compensation for the injury rather than income replacement. In addition a Special Hardship Allowance was introduced to supplement wages which were lower than had been previously earned because of the industrial injury and an Unemployability Supplement would be available for an injured worker who was unemployed but did not have insurance rights. Also, in the post war years, war pensioners were given the equivalent of the Special Hardship Allowance, in the form of a Lower Standard of Occupation Allowance.

But on Beveridge's recommendation, the right of the blind to obtain an old age pension prior to normal retirement age was withdrawn. Beveridge did comment on the need to consider a partial incapacity pension for the blind. He noted that:

> Blindness may not prevent earning wholly and should not be treated on the assumption that it means total loss of earning power. Some kind of provision for partial incapacity is required.[3]

He made no specific recommendation, however, and the idea was not taken up in subsequent legislation.

The blind, from 1948 on, were to be treated in the same way as other disabled unemployed, who in turn were to be treated like all other unemployed. If they were not sufficiently disabled to qualify for a benefit for incapacity for work, and if they had paid contributions, they would receive Unemployment Benefit. If this ran out before a job was secured, they could receive means tested National Assistance. Those disabled before they could pay any or sufficient contributions relied on National Assistance throughout.

There was, however specific legislation which was intended to give disabled people access to employment oppportunities. A committee on the rehabilitation and resettlement of disabled persons (the Tomlinson Committee) reported in 1943 on ways in which, through energetic policies, the majority of disabled people could be ensured employment. It wrote:

> In a highly industrialised country such as Britain, the number of separate occupations is so large and their demand on physical activity so varied, that it is possible to find an occupation within the physical capacity of all save a minority of the disabled. This does not mean that the problem is easy of solution; it means only that disablement need not be a bar to economic employment.[4]

On this basis, it was not necessary to make special social security provision on the assumption that disabled people would have difficulty in finding employment. Instead the Disabled Persons (Employment) Act (with a Northern Ireland equivalent) was enacted in 1944. It provided for the voluntary registration of disabled people. The most severely disabled would be placed in sheltered employment. Those capable of open employment would be assisted by specially appointed Disablement Rehabilitation Officers (DROs) and if necessary by a period in an Industrial Rehabilitation Unit – later renamed Employment Rehabilitation Centres. In addition, and this was seen as a key provision, every employer of 20 or more employees was required to employ at least three per cent of workers who were registered as disabled. This became known as the Quota Scheme. Those who chose not to register would be expected to compete in the labour market in the normal way.

The period of high employment

The twenty years of high employment that followed the war ought to have been an ideal period for the kind of programme envisaged by the Tomlinson Report, and to an extent it was. But it remained the case throughout that, being in poor physical or mental health, of limited intelligence or having a physical disability, increased the chances of figuring among the unemployment statistics, and, in particular, among the longer term unemployed who were dependent on National Assistance. A study undertaken by the Ministry of Labour in 1962 of a sample of all unemployed found that a quarter of them would be difficult to place in employment because of their physical condition or mental instability. The only other group which came near to this in proportional size was the 15 per cent who were difficult to place because they were over 55 years of age.[5]

For many of the disabled group, unemployment was prolonged. Almost every year from 1951 to 1965 the Annual Reports of the National Assistance Board (NAB) commented on their presence on benefit. They formed, the Board reported, the vast majority of those on benefit for six months or more. Some were registered as disabled, and many who were not, 'were suffering from some disability which greatly reduced their prospects of regular work'.[6] Others had been off work with fairly lengthy illnesses and were now recovered, but had not found work.

Towards the end of the 1950s, the NAB began to adopt a more active policy towards this group. It was not convinced that all of them needed to be unemployed in a period when jobs were available. A large proportion had low skills or had been classified by the Ministry of Labour as only fit for light work, but the NAB felt that 'the longer they remain unemployed the greater is the tendency for them to accept such a life as a normal condition'.[7] The Board therefore instituted a programme of medical reviews after the individual had been on benefit for six months. Some ceased to claim benefit before the date of the medical, including those who would have found work in this period anyway, and some were found fit to work and found employment soon after. Others, not registered as disabled, agreed to be registered in the hopes of facilitating employment, some were referred for employment rehabilitation and a proportion were found incapable of any work and reclassified as long term sick.[8]

In the 1960s, classification as unemployed or sick involved no change in income one way or another. However, being regarded as long term sick meant a removal of pressure to seek employment and of the requirement to register and show availablility for work.

The effect of increased unemployment

Official figures for unemployment rates among disabled people have usually been restricted to the registered disabled. These are people who fulfilled the definition of disabled under the 1944 Act – that is someone who:

> on account of injury, disease or congenital deformity, is substantially handicapped in obtaining or keeping employment, or in undertaking work on his own account of a kind which apart from that injury, disease or deformity would be suited to his age, experience and qualifications.

It was also necessary to show that the disablement would last for 12 months or more and that, though handicapped for employment, there was nevertheless a reasonable prospect of obtaining and keeping some form of employment, including sheltered employment.

Table 8.1 Rate of unemployment among the registered disabled, compared with the general unemployment rate. Selected years 1970-81. Great Britain

Percentages

	Registred disabled	General rate
1970	11.3	2.5
1975	12.0	4.1
1977(1)	14.0	6.3
1979(2)	13.3	6.0
1980(3)	13.0	6.2
1981(4)	16.0	10.3

1.   October
2.   January
3.   September, rough figure
4.   April

Source: MSC Reports, *The Quota Scheme for the Employment of Disabled People*, 1979; *Development and Training Services for Disabled People*, 1978; *Review of Assistance for Disabled People*, 1982; *House of Commons Hansard*, 21 July 1977, 719

By restricting the unemployment figures to the registered disabled, there was a reasonable basis for the count, but it excluded persons who were registrable (in the view of Disablement Resettlement Officers (DROs)) but who preferred not to register. It also excluded people with lesser handicaps who might nevertheless be disadvantaged in the competition for employment when unemployment was high, and like all the unemployment figures, tended to under count married women. Thus the official figures could be regarded only as the minimum level of unemployment affected by disability.

Early figures have not been published, but the Manpower Services Commission (MSC) estimated in 1979 that from 1965, the unemployment rate for registered disabled people varied between 2 1/2 and 5 times the general unemployment rate. Table 8.1 shows the rate in selected years from 1970. Annual figures are not always available. Instead there are month by month figures.

The fact that these minimum figures were so high suggested that the total problem of disabled unemployment was even more severe. It also has to be noted that the closing of the gap between the disabled and the general rate in the early 1980s was more the effect of large scale general unemployment than any relative improvement in the job opportunities of disabled people.

In addition to these high point in time figures, the disabled unemployed experienced another problem, a longer duration of unemployment than was generally the case. In 1979, for example, the MSC reported that while 24 per cent of all unemployed had been out of work for a year or longer, 60 per cent of registered disabled unemployed were among the long term unemployed.[9] This higher figure was still persisting in 1981, when the median duration of unemployment for non-disabled unemployed was 25 weeks, but for the disabled, excluding those classified as awaiting sheltered employment, it was 50 weeks.[10]

To some extent, the lengthy duration of unemployment was a problem of age, that is, it affected those 55 years and over most severely. Even in this case, the position of the disabled older worker was worse than that of other older workers. Among the unemployed generally, 14.1 per cent were 55 and over in October 1981, whereas 27.3 per cent of the disabled unemployed were in this age group. Median unemployment duration for the over 55s who were not disabled was 40 weeks while the median duration for the disabled of this age group was 68 weeks.[11]

Table 8.2 Registered Disabled Unemployed (RDU) and Unregistered Disabled Unemployed (UDU) May, 1978-81. Great Britain

Numbers

Year	Open Employment		Sheltered Employment	
	RDU	UDU	RDU	UDU
1978	59,749	67,870	9,828	3,988
1979	53,298	68,404	8,503	3,751
1980	52,661	77,917	7,891	3,688
1981	68,391	113,492	7,429	4,337

Source: *Department of Employment Gazette*, July 1978, 79, 80

From 1978 to 1981 figures for the unregistered disabled unemployed began to be published alongside those who were registered. These are shown in Table 8.2. This still did not provide a total of all disabled people who were unemployed because some did not contact the DRO, and thus get assessed as registrable, and others were less severely disabled than would warrant this assessment. Nevertheless, the figures did offer a fuller picture of those out of work.

The special employment measures for the disabled unemployed
As Chapter 7 showed, few programmes were developed to improve the employment opportunities of older workers. This has not been the case for disabled people. In 1976, the MSC took over the full responsibility for the special provisions for disabled people and in the next couple of years added to these. By 1978 there was a battery of measures in place – the Quota Scheme, access to employment rehabilitation, special consideration in the allocation of training places on TOPS courses, the attention of Disablement Resettlement Officers, financial support for sheltered employment, as well as a number of other special schemes. These last included grants for special aids for employment (tools and equipment); payments to employers to enable them to adapt their premises in order to recruit or retain a disabled person; fares to work for those who could not use public transport; a limited scheme to assist in setting up a business and a Job Introduction Scheme which paid a subsidy for six weeks to an employer taking on a disabled person.

In 1978, the MSC reviewed these programmes and declared that its 'future strategy must be to help as far as possible to reduce the high rate of unemployment among disabled people and to reverse the present trend for increasing numbers of disabled people to become long term unemployed'.[12] But it also issued a warning about the future. Judgements would have to be made about 'how much of the available resources should be channelled towards disabled job seekers and how much they must concentrate on meeting general employment and training needs...'[13]

By 1979, the MSC was already having doubts about one element of the package of special measures. The Quota Scheme was restricted to registered disabled people and the numbers registering had declined over the years. Apart from eligibility for the quota, there was no need to register because the DROs were prepared to give equal attention to unemployed people they regarded as registrable. This group were also given access to the range of special schemes. Some disabled people disliked the label 'disabled' for personal reasons, while others saw it as an impediment to employment. As long as they were not registered, they were free to present themselves to employers as they thought fit. Moreover, the quota itself was of declining value. In 1961, employers complied with the scheme to the full 3 per cent required. By 1978, employer compliance had fallen to 1.7 per cent.[14] The MSC, indeed, pointed out that, with the decline in registrations, full compliance could not exceed the 2.1 per cent mark, even if the almost 495,000 then on the register were given work. By 1981, there had been a further decline in the register – to 460,000 – with a possible rate of 1.9 per cent for the quota. The actual rate by then was 1.5 per cent.[15]

In 1981, faced with high general unemployment, the MSC undertook another review of its programmes for the disabled unemployed. As Table 8.2 indicated, their numbers were increasing. But the report of the MSC review showed that the numbers benefiting from the special programmes were not large. In 1980/1 some 775 aids were issued under the Special Aids to Employment Scheme, 80 grants were made for the adaptation of premises, 240 people received fares to work, 11 grants were made to assist self-employment and 1,100 people were placed in employment though the Job Introduction Scheme, 60-70 per cent of whom retained their jobs at the end of the trial period.[16]

In the same period, some 4,100 disabled people completed training under either TOPS or the Youth Opportunities Programme, about 35 per cent of whom were in employment three months later. A larger number, 14,400, had been though employment rehabilitation and three months later 15 per cent were in employment and 15 per cent in further training.[17] Of those eligible for assistance by DROs, an analysis in 1981 showed that 40 per cent had not seen a DRO or one of their assistants for a period of six months and 65 per cent had not been submitted for a job at any time during the past two years.[18]

The review found that three times as much resources were being expended on the job placement of disabled people as on the unemployed in general.[19] Given the continued growth in unemployment and pressure to cut expenditure, the MSC 's main concern now was how to get the best out of more limited resources and how to encourage employers to open up job opportunities to disabled people. A new Fit for Work campaign was launched and a Code of Practice for employers published. A vain attempt was made to get rid of the Quota Scheme altogether, on the grounds that it could not be effectively operated either voluntarily or compulsorily. This idea was withdrawn because it aroused so much opposition, but no serious attempt was made to enforce the quota. A decision was taken, mainly on practical grounds, to expand sheltered employment only to a modest extent. High general unemployment and public expenditure cuts also meant a reduced market for the goods produced in sheltered work.

Within the MSC based services, the policy was to concentrate specialist provisions (for example, DRO time) on the more severely disabled. The MSC took the view that the whole service for the disabled unemployed would be reduced in effectiveness if it was spread too thinly. For the less disabled, there were to be efforts to ensure they received adequate attention from the mainstream services.[20]

The disabled unemployed and benefits

This brief description of the services for disabled unemployed people forms the context in which their benefit provision can be discussed. For the majority of the disabled unemployed, the benefit provision, and the rules under which it operates, was no different from that applying to all other unemployed people. Unemployment Benefit was available for those who met the requirements, supplemented by or followed by Supplementary Benefit where need was shown. This would be at the short term rate as long as the individual was classified as unemployed.

The effect of this was to apply to disabled unemployed – with their additional labour market disadvantages – the same policy of low benefits as a means of inducing an early return to work, which was thought appropriate for unemployed people without these disadvantages. There were however, two elements in the policy which could ease the situation. First were the extra SB allowances which could be claimed for heating and, where a need could be shown, for special diets and high laundry costs, as well as a small extra weekly allowance which was payable to blind people. Second were the lump sum Single Payments which could be claimed for special expenditure which could not be covered out of the weekly allowances. In both of these cases, it was not necessary to be classified formally as a disabled person, so that those on SB as unemployed people were also eligible.

In addition, the claiming process for the more severely disabled person could be modified for both Unemployment Benefit and Supplementary Benefit. Normally the unemployed individual must sign on for either UB or Supplementary Benefit each fortnight to show availability for work. A disabled person who had difficulty in travelling could be permitted to claim by post. Someone who had been signing on fortnightly, had been out of work and receiving benefit for a year, and was handicapped in search for work by mental or physical disability, could be permitted to sign on quarterly. If the handicap was severe, the requirement to sign on could be waived altogether on the recommendation of a DRO. If this occurred, the individual might become eligible for the long term SB rate after 12 months on benefit, and the period of quarterly signing could be counted as part of the waiting time.

There was, as before, a certain amount of movement between benefits for unemployment and provision for those incapacitated for work. An individual might be reclassified as sick/disabled rather than unemployed. In this case, an entitlement to Invalidity Benefit might be established or a claim, sooner or later, to the long term SB Rate. However, this process could also operate in reverse.

Individuals on Sickness or Invalidity Benefit might be reclassified as fit for work – and therefore unemployed if no job was available – after examination by a Regional Medical Officer (RMO). This change of status could be made even where the RMO's finding was that the claimant was 'fit within limits', i.e. capable of certain types of employment only, and even where no such work of this kind was available in the area. The change of status could then involve a drop in social security income from the long term benefits – Invalidity Benefit and the long term rate of Supplementary Benefit – to the short-term SB rate available to an unemployed person.

To some extent, as unemployment rose, it might be expected that there would be a greater propensity to reclassify an unemployed disabled person as unfit for work. But according to the Disability Alliance in 1980 it was receiving an increasing number of reports of disabled people being reclassified as unemployed.[21] The Disability Alliance estimated that in 1981 between 30,000 and 80,000 claimants lost the right to Invalidity Benefit and that the procedures which determined the benefit rights were deficient in themselves and were, in any case, based on rules unsuited to a period of high unemployment[22] – for example the 'fit within limits' rule referred to above. Government, for its part, insisted that no change in policy had taken place.

One of the issues this raised was the need to get away from the sharp distinction between capacity to work and incapacity to work. But provision for partial incapacity could be found only in the War Pensions and Industrial Injuries Schemes. It will be recalled that Beveridge in 1942 had pointed out the desirability of considering a benefit for partial incapacity in the main scheme. This had never been taken up, but the idea was revived in the early 1980s. Reports from the Economist Intelligence Unit (EIU)[23] on behalf of the Multiple Sclerosis Society and from the Social Security Advisory Committee[24] put forward various options for the implementation of such a benefit. Some of these were geared to those with severe disabilities, but others would have included those with less serious conditions, but which nevertheless were a barrier to employment. The government acknowledged the need for a benefit of this kind, but took no immediate action.

Being disabled and unemployed in 1985

Disabled people in the labour market in 1985 had a higher rate of unemployment, a longer duration of unemployment and a greater likelihood of forming part of the long term unemployed than the average worker. As a result, the deficiencies in provision for the unemployed and, in particular, for the long term unemployed, fell particularly heavily upon them. This had always been the case, but the persistence of high unemployment had worsened their position in the labour market and raised many questions, not least about the suitability of a work incentive-based policy, relying on low benefit payments to spur a return to work, when applied to those with additional labour market disadvantages.

In 1978, the DHSS review of Supplementary Benefits, in recommending that the unemployed be given entitlement to the long term rate on the same basis as other non-pensioners, drew particular attention to the fact that many of those concerned had low skills or some disability and were 'often the claimants experiencing the greatest hardship'.[25] Similar concerns were expressed by the Social Security Advisory Committee in its first report in which it endorsed comments by its predecessors, the SBCs of both Great Britain and Northern

Ireland, who had drawn particular attention to those unemployed who were in poor health or partially disabled.[26] However, except for those men who were 60 years and over, to whom the long term rate was extended, and the earlier age of eligibility for disabled people in the Job Release Scheme, the government in 1985 was offering no improvement in policies for the disabled unemployed.

References

1. Blanesburgh Report, op.cit., pp.75-6.
2. G. Woolton, *The Official History of the British Legion*, Macdonald and Evans Ltd, London, 1956, p.263.
3. Beveridge Report, op.cit., p.69.
4. *Report of the Inter-departmental Committee on the Rehabilitation and Resettlement of Disabled Persons*, (The Tomlinson Report), Cmd 6415, HMSO, London, 1943, p.6.
5. Characteristics of the unemployed, *Ministry of Labour Gazette*, April 1962, p.133.
6. NAB *Annual Report 1951*, p.8.
7. NAB *Annual Report 1961*, p.32.
8. NAB *Annual Report 1961*, pp. 33-4, 1962, p.40. 1964, p.41.
9. Manpower Services Commission, *The Quota Scheme for the Employment of Disabled People: A discussion document*, MSC, London, 1979, p.3.
10. Manpower Services Commission, *Review of Assistance for Disabled People*, MSC, London, 1982, pp. 14-15. These figures appear to include unregistered but registrable disabled unemployed.
11. Ibid., pp.10 and 15.
12. 'The foreseeable future. The new development programme for employing disabled people', *Department of Employment Gazette*, March 1978, pp.292-3.
13. Ibid.
14. MSC, *The Quota Scheme*, 1979, op.cit., p.10.
15. MSC, *Review of the Quota Scheme for the Employment of Disabled People*, MSC, London, 1981, pp.6-7.
16. MSC, *Review of Assistance to Disabled People*, op.cit., pp.106-7.
17. Ibid., pp.29 and 33.
18. Ibid., p.21.
19. Ibid., p.35.

20. MSC, *Review of Assistance to Disabled People*, op cit., pp.98-9.
21. Disability Alliance, *A very high priority? The impact on people with disabilities of government policies since the last election*, London, 1980, p.11.
22. Disability Alliance, *Invalid Procedures? A study of the control system for Invalidity Benefit*, London, 1983.
23. Economist Intelligence Unit Ltd., *Benefits for Partial Incapacity*, EIU, London, 1982.
24. *Second Report of the Social Security Advisory Committee 1982/83*, HMSO, London, 1983 pp.33-6.
25. DHSS, *Social Assistance*, op.cit., p.48.
26. *The First Report of the Social Security Advisory Committee 1981*, HMSO, London, 1982, p.26.

9 Social security reform, 1984-86 and after

In April 1984 the government announced the establishment of a Social Security Review. It suggested that it would be 'the most substantial examination of the social security system since the Beveridge Report forty years ago'.[1] This proved to be the case but the exercise was not comparable with the Beveridge inquiry. The Review neither looked at the social security system as a whole nor the whole of the social security system. There were four separate review committees, one each for provision for retirement, Housing Benefit, Supplementary Benefit, and benefits for children and young people. There was to be no immediate review of the full range of benefits for disabled people. This would await the outcome of a national survey of disabled people about to be undertaken.

As the Review developed it became evident that there would be other important gaps. No examination of the functioning of the National Insurance scheme was intended. The Review would concentrate on the means tested benefits and, in the case of the elderly, on the second pension provision. No review of the provision for the unemployed as a separate subject area would be undertaken. As a large population group dependent on means tested benefits, their position within those benefits had to be considered, as well as the relationship between these various benefits and between the unemployed and the low paid working population. But the balance between contributory and means tested benefits in provision for the unemployed was not part of the brief given to the review teams.

This would not (and did not) prevent witnesses to the Review giving evidence which discussed these wider issues, but there was little likelihood that the teams would depart significantly from their briefs.

While the Beveridge inquiry had a significant degree of independance from government, three out of four committees in the Social Security Review were chaired by Ministers and the fourth (Housing Benefit) had a very specific task - to examine the Housing Benefit scheme. The co-ordinating committee which was established at a later stage to look at the outcome of the four separate elements of the Review was made up of civil servants. Thus, the review was substantially controlled by government at all its stages and the decisions on how the subject of the provision for the unemployed would be handled were government decisions.

The structure of provision

In 1984/85, benefit expenditure on the unemployed was around £6.4 billion or 17 per cent of all social security expenditure. This was made up of around £1.6 billion in Unemployment Benefit, £4.5 billion in Supplementary Benefit and related Housing Benefit, and the balance in sundry benefits such as Child Benefit and war or industrial disablement pensions.[2] Whereas at the end of 1970, 240,000 or 41 per cent of the unemployed on benefit had been wholly or partly dependent on Supplementary Benefit, by the end of 1984, 1.95 million unemployed or 65 per cent of the unemployed on benefit were receiving SB. Of these, 202,000 were receiving supplementation of Unemployment Benefit and 1.75 million were on SB alone.[3] This pattern of expenditure raised obvious questions about the benefit structure. Among the evidence given to the Review, three approaches can be considered.

The first sought to remove the unemployed from Supplementary Benefit almost entirely. The evidence of the Society of Civil and Public Servants (SCPS), which represented executive and managerial administrators in the DHSS social security divisions is an example of this. It said:

> Unemployment benefit in a time of mass and long term unemployment must as a first prerequisite continue to be payable for the duration of an individual's unemployment. The absurdity of limiting benefit to only one year is cruel and irresponsible. There should be no limit to the duration of benefit.[4]

It also sought a level of Unemployment Benefit set at 20 per cent above the SB level, and wished to see the Earnings Related Supplement (ERS) restored, to cushion short term unemployment and the early months of long term unemployment. In addition there were proposals to credit-in school leavers to National Insurance so that they had UB entitlement while neither in work nor on a training scheme.

This plan would upgrade the income of the unemployed and reduce the use of means testing quite substantially, but it had obvious cost implications. The SCPS acknowledged that its plan involved extra expenditure but it believed this should not be a deterrent. It said:

> Social Insurance, because it rests on a pooling of risks and a sharing of benefits between the whole national community, is the sound way to pool the risks of unemployment. We firmly believe that those who are in work would be willing to pay the increased cost of national insurance contributions to raise benefits for the unemployed in the way we have described above.[5]

A quite different point of view was put forward by the Institute of Fiscal Studies (IFS) in a plan for social security reform which would have involved abolishing the National Insurance scheme altogether.[6] IFS argued that to meet what it considered should be the primary goal of a social security system – poverty prevention – it was necessary to concentrate resources on those in need and withdraw payments which it described as 'wasted'. IFS assumed, for the sake of its argument, that the prevailing SB level was adequate to prevent poverty and it based its estimates of 'wasted' benefits on this. It calculated that, in 1981, nearly 76 per cent of Child Benefit expenditure, 26 per cent of pension costs and 45 per cent of sickness and unemployment benefits went to the non-poor. If these benefits were not paid, the resources released could, in part at least, be used to raise the level of benefits paid to those in need.[7]

The new scheme proposed by IFS would be based on a universal means test applied through tax assessment mechanisms. A minimum income line would be drawn taking into account the number of adults and children in the household and housing costs. Those with zero income would receive a Benefit Credit, reduced as income rose until the minimum income line was reached when it would cut out. Thereafter tax would be payable, increased as income rose.

The Institute saw no reason why Unemployment Benefit should be an entitlement based on contributions, payable regardless of current income and resources and, in the case of the short term unemployed, regardless of future income. In the proposed scheme, an unemployed person would not be eligible for a Benefit Credit while he had resources above his minimum income line. Moreover, since assessment for Benefit Credit entitlement or tax liability would be on an annual basis, someone who returned to work after a brief spell of unemployment and secured a reasonable wage, might, in a full tax year, find himself repaying the Benefit Credit through tax. In effect the benefit would operate as a loan.

This proposal would concern itself, therefore, only with immediate need. Unemployment Benefit would no longer act to cushion a sharp fall in income. No account would be taken of the problem of meeting commitments undertaken while in work, which could not immediately be abandoned. No action would be taken until the income fell below the minimum level. On the other hand, if the proposed redistribution of resources in favour of the poor produced a Benefit Credit higher than current benefits, it would provide a better standard of living for the longer term unemployed.

A proposal which fell between these two extremes came from the National Consumer Council (NCC). It wished to retain the National Insurance scheme and Unemployment Benefit, but to improve their functioning. First, the Council sought the relaxation of the contribution conditions which at present excluded from UB those who could not show a sufficient contribution record in the previous tax year. It looked at various alternatives and favoured adopting a test used under the Equal Treatment Regulations to determine the right of a woman to claim benefit as the breadwinner in a married or cohabiting couple. This was known as the 'contact with employment' test, under which it was necessary to show employment of eight hours or more per week for the six months prior to the claim. Applied to all adults, it would remove the barriers to UB for a large proportion of those now excluded. For young people, the NCC proposed that NI credits should be given for education or training so that on seeking work, and failing to find it, they had an immediate entitlement to Unemployment Benefit.[8]

This would reduce the extent of means testing, but the NCC were not prepared to recommend an indefinite right to a non-means tested benefit as an immediate goal. This was partly a question of cost and partly because for some groups – for example young people who had never been in work – this might have undesirable side effects. Its proposal was for a one year entitlement only, for those who had just left school, college or a training course. However, for adults, while benefit would begin with a one year minimum duration, it might be increased in respect of years of prior work. The NCC envisaged that a worker made redundant at 50 years could, if necessary, draw Unemployment Benefit until retirement.[9] In all cases the availability for work rule would apply.

In the event, none of these (or other) propositions were accepted by government. The Social Security Review produced no comprehensive report, but in late 1985 a Green Paper was issued in which the government laid out its plans. Subsequently a White Paper confirmed most of these proposals.

The government had decided it did not want to abandon the contributory principle which it regarded as an important link between contributions paid in, and benefits received. In the case of unemployment, it saw the contributory principle not so much as social insurance (i.e. the pooling of risks) but as a social compact, between those in work and those not.[10] The government saw 'a clear continuing role for unemployment benefit as a contributory, national insurance benefit'.[11] It went on to say:

> Alternatives to the present arrangements would involve either extending unemployment benefit or replacing it with a wholly income-related approach. The Government do not believe either course to be appropriate or sustainable. The former would require substantial extra resources which are neither justified nor affordable without adding to the already heavy burdens on contributors or taxpayers. For example, paying unemployment benefit for an unlimited period could cost over half a billion pounds extra... Relying on a wholly income related approach would reduce expenditure and ensure that resources were targeted on those who need financial help during unemployment. But this would be a step away from the contributory principle and would have the effect of depriving anybody with more than modest savings from benefits. We propose, therefore, to leave the present arrangements for unemployment benefit as they are.[12]

Any additional help for the unemployed would come from reforms to the means tested (income related) schemes. The government had no proposals to open up unemployment benefit entitlement to some or all of those currently excluded, and no comments to make on the desirable balance between social insurance and means tested provision for the unemployed.

Although the Green Paper said that the government's intention was to leave the present arrangements for unemployment benefit 'as they are', this decision did not last for long. Subsequent to the Social

Security Review, it took four steps which would have the effect of reducing entitlement to the benefit.

The first of these was the abolition of the reduced rates of unemployment benefit available to those with a less than full contribution record. Provision to end this right was added to the 1986 Social Security Act – the legislation which implemented the Review proposals. Two reasons were given; the administrative costs of the payment were high (over 20 per cent), while the low rates required supplementation from Supplementary Benefit for around half the recipients, who thus gained nothing from the payments.[13] The main losers from the change were married women who could have qualified for the partial Unemployment Benefit on the basis of their contributions, but were not eligible for the means tested benefit.

The second change formed part of the 1987 Social Security Bill (the 1988 Act). The contribution rules for Unemployment Benefit were made more stringent. As they stood before the Act, contributions on earnings of at least 25 times the lower earnings limit (ie the threshold for NI contributions) must have been paid in any one tax year since 1975, and in some circumstances, contributions in two tax years could be joined. In addition, contributions on earnings of at least 50 times the lower earnings limit must have been paid or credited in the tax year prior to the year of claim. The credit rules, though limited in some respects, gave access to Unemployment Benefit to those who had spent some time on disability related benefits (including carers receiving the Invalid Care Allowance) as well as to those who had been in approved education or training. They also assisted those who had had a period of unemployment in the recent past but had met certain minimum contribution conditions. Under the new rules, the required contributions must be paid in the two tax years immediately prior to the claim and no other contributions could be taken into account. In these two years, contributions must have been paid on earnings of 25 times the lower earnings limit in one year and contributions on earnings of at least 50 times the limit must have been paid or credited in both years. In addition, credits would no longer be awarded to people entering the National Insurance scheme for the first time, a provision which had helped them to satisfy contribution conditions at an early stage. These rules would come into force in October 1988. Their immediate effect would be to exclude 350,000 people from Unemployment Benefit, all but 50,000 of whom were likely to qualify for the means tested benefit.[14] The rules would also reduce the access of young people to the insurance benefit.

The link between recent employment and entitlement to Unemployment Benefit was further tightened in the 1989 Social Security Act. Where a person had exhausted his/her entitlement to the insurance benefit, it would be necessary to have worked 16 or more hours in at least 13 of the 26 weeks immediately before the new claim.

The government presented these various changes as 'measures that emphasise the contributory principles in qualifying for national insurance benefits and re-inforce the original purpose of unemployment benefit'.[15] This purpose was defined as 'to insure those who are accustomed to earnings from employment for short periods of unemployment while they seek work'.[16]

But the method chosen to emphasise the contributory principle was to link benefit rights with paid contributions in the immediate past. The government appeared to be recalling a former 'purer' period in National Insurance, but it chose to ignore the fact that the scheme had always sought to be flexible and to give recognition to the earlier years of contributions where this was needed to give access to insurance benefits. Indeed, as the account in Chapter 3 of the practice immediately following the original National Insurance Act indicates, not only was the early record part of the reckoning, but it was used to extend the duration of benefits through the additional days provisions. The credit rules were a later development. They sought to increase the access to insurance benefits. For the unemployed at least, the government chose the opposite course.

The fourth step taken to limit Unemployment Benefit rights also appeared in the 1988 Social Security Act. This extended downwards, from 60 to 55 years of age, the rule requiring pound for pound deductions from Unemployment Benefit of any occupational pension in excess of £35 per week. This would apply from January 1989.

The government's argument was that, by drawing their occupational pension rights, the 55-59 year old unemployed were signifying that they were really retired. Since Unemployment Benefit was not intended for those who were retired and no longer seeking work, it was 'consistent with the original intention of unemployment insurance'[17] to abate (ie reduce) the benefit. It was pointed out in the debate on the Bill that the pension income at which reductions began – £35 – had not been increased since 1980 and should now stand at £48 to take account of inflation. But the government argued that no uprating was needed since the full benefit would not cut out until income reached £66.50 for a single person and £88.90 for a married couple on 1987 benefit rates.[18]

No proof was offered that the 55-59 year old unemployed saw themselves as retired. Indeed the opposition quoted a government survey showing that only 3.5 per cent of them did so.[19] Moreover, it has to be assumed that these men and women were meeting the availability for work rules required of the unemployed. It was just as likely that they had claimed their occupational pension, even though this may have meant accepting an actuarially reduced rate, in order to cope better with low income in unemployment. Unless the pension was an ample one, the benefit reduction, therefore, was another blow to an already disadvantaged group. It was expected to extinguish the benefit rights of 400,000 claimants and reduce the benefits of a further 300,000,[20] and it would reduce public expenditure by £65 million.[21]

The adequacy of benefits

By 1984, a good deal of evidence had accumulated to show that the long term unemployed on the short term rate of Supplementary Benefit were suffering financial hardship. As early as 1976 the Supplementary Benefits Commission in its Annual Report presented evidence on the severe difficulties experienced by unemployed families with children in particular, in managing on the short term rate of SB for extended periods.[22] The report of the DHSS review of the Supplementary Benefits Scheme in 1978 also referred to the unemployed as 'often the claimants experiencing the greatest hardship'.[23] The DHSS team were concerned not only at the denial of the long term rate to the unemployed, but also with the inadequacy of the children's scale rates which compounded the problem for families with children.[24] Some changes were subsequently made to the rates for children, but they remained inadequate, and especially for older children.[25]

Studies in the early 1980s confirmed these earlier findings. Reporting in 1983 on an examination of the living standards of the unemployed, Bradshaw et al concluded that:

> the cumulative weight of evidence suggests that the living standards of the long term unemployed are lower than those in short term employment and that the living standards of both are below those of the poorest families in work.[26]

In 1984, Ditch reported for the National Consumer Council on the unemployed on Supplementary Benefit in Northern Ireland where long term unemployment was at its worst. He noted evidence of concern about the diet of unemployed families, and of debts for rent, heating, electricity and hire purchase.[27] Evason, too, found hardship among the long term unemployed in Northern Ireland in 1983/4.[28]

In light of these and many other reports and studies, it was not surprising that the income of the unemployed was a central issue for many witnesses to the Social Security Review. However, they were not all in favour of increasing benefit rates. The issue of work incentives and the relationship between benefits and wages so prominent in the 1970s continued to be raised.

The Institute of Directors revived the old principle of 'less eligibility' which the Poor Law had used as the basis for benefit rates for the unemployed in particular. Its evidence said:

> since on the principle of less eligibility the income of a low paid worker should be more (or at least not less) than the income of a non-working recipient of welfare payments, the market thus imposes a ceiling on the amount that should be paid in benefits.[29]

The 'fundamental anomaly', the Institute went on, was that welfare support was too large a proportion of low pay. Supplementary Benefit was too high and should be reduced for both adults and children. This, it claimed, would strengthen work incentives.

A more common approach was to recommend the extension of the long term rate of Supplementary Benefit to the unemployed on the same terms as other SB recipients. This was, for example, the highest priority of the National Consumer Council, pending more extensive reforms.[30] It also appeared in the evidence of such groups as the Scottish Convention of Women,[31] the Association of County Councils,[32] the Child Poverty Action Group[33] and many others. This was often accompanied by recommendations for improvements in the rates paid to children or for a significant increase in Child Benefit.

The Social Security Advisory Committee, in its evidence to the Review, introduced a new element. It noted recent research evidence that new SB claimants, going on to the short term rate, experienced considerable financial problems while adjusting to a lower income, and did not necessarily have financial reserves to cushion the changeover.[34] The SSAC also thought the differential between the long and the short term rates, now 25-27 per cent, had become far too great. It wanted, therefore, to see a staged transition to a single rate, set at the higher long term rate.

In the event, the government rejected all of these recommendations, though elements of each of them appeared to have some influence. The government began from the position that any social security reform had to be undertaken without additional expenditure - a no-cost basis. So money for any benefit increases had to be found by shifting resources from one group or one form of benefit to another. This clearly limited the options for change.

The government acknowledged that some of the unemployed were suffering financial hardship. In the Green Paper it declined to formulate a definition of poverty, as some witnesses to the Review had urged, but it set out a basis for the determination of priorities for the reallocation of resources, through a definition of low income. It said:

> Families whose needs are likely to be greatest may be defined as those falling into the bottom 20 per cent of the national distribution of income, with family incomes being adjusted for differences in family size and composition to allow for the greater requirements of large families.[35]

The composition of the bottom 20 per cent had changed in the past decade. Fewer pensioners were to be found in this group than in 1971 and more families with children. In 1982 those in the bottom 20 per cent of income as defined were proportionally: 19.2 per cent pensioners, 57.1 per cent one and two parent families with children, 8 per cent couples without children and 15.7 per cent working age single persons. The Green Paper went on to say that 'higher unemployment was the single most important cause of the shift in composition of the low income group' and that, 'unemployment has now displaced old age as the main reason for low income'.[36] The quite substantial group (15.7 per cent) of working age single persons were, however, dismissed on the grounds that 'many of them are non-householders living in households with higher incomes'. The real cause for concern was families with dependent children who, the Green Paper said, 'now account for over half of individuals living on low income'.[37]

A decision to improve benefits for unemployed families with children might, however, have undesirable consequences for work incentives. The Green Paper said:

> While it is one of the functions of the social security system to help those who are unemployed, it is self defeating if it creates barriers to the creation of jobs, to job mobility or to people rejoining the

labour force.   Clearly such obstacles exist if people believe themselves better off out of work than in work...[38]

The rates of support, therefore, could not 'be isolated from consideration both of the returns and the rewards that are available to people in society generally'.[39]

The government, therefore, set out to create a structure of benefit provision for unemployed families with children which would operate in harmony with provision for low income working families, but would ensure that working families would always be better off than those not working. As part of this process, it would restructure the Supplementary Benefits scheme – to be renamed Income Support – not only for the unemployed, but for other population categories also.

In the new scheme the distinction between long term and short term cases and between householders and non-householders would be ended. There would be a standard personal allowance for all claimants varied only by age and marital status. Child Dependency Additions would be unchanged, but a new feature would be introduced. There would be 'premiums', i.e. additional allowances, paid to certain categories – families with children, the elderly, one parent families and disabled people.

The family premium would be available to unemployed families with children – thus improving their income. The structure of their benefits – a basic allowance, plus a family premium, plus Child Dependency Additions – would then be 'matched' with a similar structure for the low paid in a new Family Credit Scheme to replace Family Income Supplement. This would also have three tiers – wages, a family benefit and child additions. But this 'matching' need not be exact. Higher payments could be made within Family Credit to ensure that those in work had a disposable income which was higher than for those not in work.

The plan for better matching also involved modifications to other benefits. Housing Benefit for those in work would be improved. Under the prevailing arrangements, a different means test was applied to those in and out of work. Moreover, while those on Supplementary Benefits received full housing costs, those in work received allowances in the region of 60 per cent of the rent and rates payable. In future, the operating means test would be the same, both groups would receive 100 per cent of rent but only 80 per cent of rates. The lower percentage for the rate rebate did not relate to the work incentive issue. It was introduced because the government believed that freedom from the responsibility to pay rates induced irresponsible voting in local elections.

Further steps were necessary within the new Income Support Scheme to achieve a full alignment and these involved a reduction in the benefits available to the unemployed and other recipients. Water rates and other residual housing costs would no longer be paid in the new Income Support scheme, as they had been under SB, though allowance could be made for them on the setting of benefit rates. SB families who were owner occupiers, had received an allowance to pay the interest on the mortgage (but not for capital repayments), from the time they came on to benefit. Low paid families received no such help. The Green Paper said of this situation:

> The specific extra help through Supplementary Benefit can create an incentive problem and raise the question of fairness between those in and out of work. For a claimant with a sizeable mortgage there may be little financial reward from a return to work.[40]

Help with mortgage interest could not be withdrawn altogether or the home could be lost. The government, in due course, compromised by ruling that only half of the mortgage interest would be paid for the first four months of unemployment. During this time, the unemployed home owner would be expected to arrange with his Building Society or other mortgager for the deferment of payments if this was necessary. If a re-scheduling of the loan led to higher interest payments at a later stage, these would be met for individuals still remaining on benefit.

It was also necessary to deal with those additional payments in the Supplementary Benefits scheme for which there was no equivalent in the scheme for the low paid. Additional weekly allowances for such items as heating, diet and for other special needs of disabled people would be ended and the Income Support rates adjusted to take account of these costs. A further problem was the Single Payments, which could be claimed for home repairs, replacement of large items such as cookers, certain items of furniture and other essential outlay which could not be met out of low weekly allowances. The Green Paper said of these:

> The rapid growth in payments in the last few years had raised considerable questions of fairness with those not on benefit. The availability of payments stands in sharp contrast to the position faced by many others, on what may not be a very different level of disposable income, who have to budget for such items.[41]

Single payments would therefore be ended and replaced (from April 1987) with loans from a new Social Fund. These would have to be repaid from benefit.

Finally, those 25 years old and under were singled out for special treatment. The Green Paper argued that while there was no one age dividing line relevant to all claimants, it was clear that, at the age of 18, the majority of claimants were not fully independent, and that the great majority of claimants above the age of 25 were. In the SB scheme as it then operated, nearly 90 per cent of all claimants over 25 years were getting the householder rate, while 'a clear majority' of the under 25s were living in someone else's household.[42] However, if the non-householder rate was to be abolished, this younger group would receive a higher rate of benefit than before – inappropriately in the Green Paper's view. The solution adopted was to pay a lower rate of personal allowance to all those 25 years and younger, other than lone parents. Originally the intention was to apply this rule to married (and cohabiting) couples as well as single people and to the young married with children also. This aroused a good deal of opposition and the later legislation restricted the lower allowance to the single people of 25 and under and couples under 18 years. This would apply whether or not they were in fact householders.

The provision for unemployed women was not addressed by the review at all. Apart from changes to the benefit arrangements which would affect them as dependent wives, their position was basically unaltered. If they were single, their treatment would be on all fours with that of single men. If they were married, the rules prevailing under SB would apply, with minor modifications to the disregard rules (to be discussed later).

The social security reforms offered some improvement in the position of unemployed families with children after 1988, when the family premium was introduced. Moreover, this would be payable from the time the family came on to benefit in the Income Support scheme rather than after a year's wait, thus assisting both short and long term recipients.

However, taken in conjunction with all the other changes proposed, the improvement has been quite modest. In late 1987, the DHSS published estimates of the effect of the social security reforms, based on notional rates of benefit, but sufficiently close to the implementation date (April 1988) to be reasonably reliable. The figures showed that, on average, unemployed couples with children would gain around £1.50 pw and those unemployed without children would, on average, lose £0.70 pw.[43] But these figures did not take account of the loss of Single Payments. In 1986, over 2 million unemployed recipients received Single Payments, at an average of £82.20 per head. Tighter rules were introduced for 1987, cutting the numbers to around 1 million, but still at an average payment of over £82.[44] Thus the abolition of Single Payments would have a considerable impact on the unemployed, and especially on the longer term unemployed with children who were among the heaviest users of Single Payments.[45] Unemployed people who were owner occupiers suffered a specific disadvantage through the reduction in mortgage interest support for the first four months – a provision which could become extremely burdensome if the claimant had frequent spells of unemployment.

As the figures given above suggest, unemployed people without children tended to be losers. They are effectively to be maintained on the equivalent of the old short term rate, while losing access to the various additional payments. Particular note may be taken of three categories. An older worker who has children when he comes on benefit and whose children move out of the age of dependency while he is still unemployed, will lose not only the dependency additions, but eventually the family premium also, and his income will fall accordingly. An individual classified as disabled and with entitlement to the disability premium may be reclassified as unemployed and lose that premium. Moreover, as a disabled unemployed person in the SB scheme, he might still have had rights to additional payments in relation to the disability, but these will no longer be available to cushion the loss of the premium. Someone who comes on to Income Support as an older childless unemployed person – for example a 50-59 year old – will be offered only the equivalent of the short term SB rate until the age of 60 years when the pensioner premium will become payable.

Notable among the losers is the 18-25 year old age group. As seen these are to be paid a lower rate of personal allowance in Income Support as long as they are single, or if married (or cohabiting) while they are under 18 years. This proposal had raised quite widespread opposition. One of the concerns was that the lower rate of benefit would enforce dependence on young adults just at the time when they are moving towards greater independence. The SSAC noted 'the steady trend' towards the formation of independent households at younger ages and did not think the proposal took account of 'social realities'.[46] The National Union of Teachers argued that the proposed change would 'not only have an impoverishing effect on young people who are currently living independently, but will also prevent others from choosing to live independently'.[47] These and other respondents to the Green Paper also pointed out that the proposal would place an unfair burden on the parents of these young unemployed adults.

The difficulties the younger (18-25) unemployed would experience if they attempted to live independently were reinforced by later changes in the Board and Lodging rules. Most people on low incomes, including the low paid, got help with housing costs through Housing Benefit. Government believed it was unsatisfactory that for one group – those claiming SB – special rules were in operation within the Supplementary Benefit scheme. The rules, moreover, were complicated, not only in relation to whether or not the charges made included food and other non-accommodation costs, but also by the time limits imposed on those under 26 years since 1985.

In the context of the new Income Support scheme and the revised Housing Benefit provisions, it was decided, therefore, that from April 1989, new rules for boarders would be introduced. In future, except for those living in hostels (who were included from October 1989 with some additional protective provisions),[48] boarders would make a claim from Housing Benefit for that part of the boarding costs which related to the accommodation. Other costs – mainly for food – would have to be met from the Income Support benefit.

These new rules were not seen as wholly unwelcome. They would simplify claims for those 26 years and over and they would remove the time limits on the younger age group. But, taking the 18-25 group as an example, but the rules would imply that single unemployed people attempting to live independently would have to manage on £27.40 per week (in 1986) after accomodation costs had been met, instead of the £34.90 available to those over 25 years. Moreover since the rate of Housing Benefit was linked to the rate of benefit under Income Support to which the individual would be entitled, the 18-25 year old would have a lower entitlement to Housing Benefit than would someone over this age.

Commenting on these provisions in their 1988 report, the SSAC said they regretted that the structure of Income Support and Housing Benefit would not only retard the natural development of this 18-25 age group towards greater independence, but would 'cause inevitable hardship to some who may leave home not just on account of domestic tension, but also, in areas of high unemployment, to find work'.[49]

The measures affecting the 18-25s introduced in this period were presented by the government as necessary and desirable simplifications of the social security rules. But it is reasonable to assume that there was no reluctance on the part of government to reduce the benefit income of the single unemployed of this age group. There was some evidence (confirmed in a report published in 1989, but based on a 1984 survey)[50] that a minority of the 18-25 year old group had ceased to search for employment or to do so actively. Exerting pressure to work through the benefit system would have been in accord with the government's general policy stance.

16 and 17 year olds
The brief of the review team on benefits for children and young people included an examination of the range of benefits for 16-17 year olds. Although plenty of evidence was submitted on this point – looking at the confused network of Education Maintenance Allowances, Minor Awards for non-advanced further education, YTS Allowances, Unemployment Benefit and Supplementary Benefit – there was no discussion of this age group in the Green or White Papers.

But the government had not overlooked the young unemployed on benefit. It was awaiting the right moment to act. As seen in Chapter 6, the government had repeatedly expressed its desire to withdraw from 16 and 17 year olds the right to claim Supplementary Benefit, which it saw as the right to opt for unemployment at public expense. In September 1988, the development of the Youth Training Scheme had reached the point that a guarantee of a training place could be given to all 16 and 17 year olds not in education or employment. The time had come to withdraw benefits for unemployment for most of this age group.

The 1988 Social Security Act raised the normal minimum age for entitlement to claim Income Support in one's own right, from 16 to 18 years. Section 4 of this Act provided for some exceptions to this. The Secretary of State was also given power to make discretionary Income Support payments in cases of 'severe hardship'.

In future, in the normal regime, when a young person left school, the parents could continue to claim Child Benefit – to be known as Extended Child Benefit – for 4 further months (September to December) for Summer school leavers and 3 months for Christmas and Easter leavers. This right would be dependent on the young person's registration at a Careers Office or Job Centre as looking for a YTS place or a job. The benefit would stop if a job or YTS place was found, but could be paid again, during the extended period only, if the young person left the job or YTS, and it would not be cut for refusal of such opportunities. But no other benefit would be payable after the extended period was over.

Once in a YTS place, a weekly training allowance of £29.50 for the 16 year olds and £35 for 17 year olds (1988 and 1989 rates) would be paid. Some one who left a job or a YTS place could claim a Bridging Allowance of £15 pw., but only if they were registered as seeking work or another YTS place, and only for a maximum of 8 weeks in any period of 52 weeks. This allowance could be stopped for refusal of a YTS place.

Clearly the rules were principally designed for young people, living at home, whose families could, if necessary, afford to support them in an extended period of dependence, on low benefits or no benefits. The rules were expected to cover the vast majority of 16 and 17 year olds, but various exceptions were recognised to be necessary.

Provision had to be made for the point of changeover to the new rules. There were roughly 70,000 16 and 17 year olds on Income Support as unemployed people at that time.[51] These were transferred to the Bridging Allowance for 8 weeks or until they took up a YTS place, whichever was sooner. Thereafter, the new normal rules would apply.

Another group retained the right to claim Income Support, because they were not expected to be available for work. These included single mothers, pregnant girls (from the 11th week before the expected birth), young people who were registered as blind, disabled young people likely to be incapacitated for work for at least 12 months, and a number of other people whose circumstances (usually relating to caring responsibilities) would prevent them from working.

Where the 16 or 17 year old had parents who were on Income Support or Family Credit, the parents could claim a topping up benefit for the young person as a dependant, but only during the Child Benefit extension period. A further group could also claim Income Support for a time. These were young people without parents; those who were in local authority care or youth custody immediately before their 16th birthday; young people who were mentally or physically handicapped or mentally ill, whose parents could not cope with them, but who were capable of work; those at risk of physical or sexual abuse at home as well as some other equally difficult situations. But again, the benefit rights lasted only during the Child Benefit extension period.

Beyond this period, Income Support would only be given where 'severe hardshiip' could be shown. Initially this was not defined. It would be judged by the Secretary of State, but would not automatically include cases of family estrangement. Later the Minister (Nicholas Scott) described the criteria in this way:

> Examples of the factors that are taken into account include the young person's health and vulnerability – for example, the risk of being led into crime, the risk of eviction and subsequent homelessness as a result of inability to meet accommodation costs, the availability of any income which would normally fail to be disregarded, the availability of any savings, the prospect of speedy entry into YTS, the prospects of casual work, the young person's financial commitments and prospects for postponing payment, and whether the young person has any friends or relatives who could help.[52]

The object of the new regime was to remove any 'perverse incentive for people of this age (16/17) to leave home needlessly'.[53] Young people who had the option to live at home must either do so, or manage as best they might on the new normal benefit provision. For 16 and 17 year olds who had a responsibility for paying rent and or rates this included a right to claim Housing Benefit. YTS trainees in board and lodgings might still be able to claim Income Support to top up the training allowance.

Both the government's interpretation of leaving home needlessly and the stringency of the severe hardship criteria proved controversial. Voluntary organisations in direct contact with young people, including the increasing number of young homeless, were particularly critical and made many representations to government.

In March and April 1989, some concessions werre announced[54] mostly operating from July 1989. Cases of genuine family estrangement would be eligible for Income Support during the Child Benefit extension period. Those receiving Income Support during this period would, because of their vulnerability, be considered for severe hardship payments if at the end of the period they had not found a job or a YTS place. Young people seeking emergency accommodation in night shelters would get severe hardship payments. And any young people on Income Support, who for good reason had to live independently, would be eligible for the 18-25 rate of allowance. The amount available for 16/17 year olds in Housing Benefit would also be increased. This package was expeced to cost a further £3.7 million. But the Minister (Nicholas Scott) said:

> Our wider policy of encouraging such youngsters (16/17) to stay in the parental home and, if they are not in education or employment, to take up the offer of a YTS place, remains appropriate for the vast majority of young people of this age.[55]

One other point should be noted. The effect of the new NI contribution rules, requiring 2 years contributions to qualify for Unemployment Benefit, will be to exclude 17 year olds from this benefit. Whereas after a year's work, they could qualify at 17 for the insurance benefit, now there is no possibility of qualifying before the age of 18 years. For those who have spent 2 years on YTS, which gives no insurance credits for unemployment, it will not be possible to qualify until the end of their 20th year. During this time, only Income Support will be available.

Disregards
Returning to the outcome of the Social Security Review, if benefits for the unemployed were not to be increased to any extent and might be decreased, were there other ways in which those on benefit could add to their income?

It has been the practice for many years to allow benefit recipients to earn a little extra money without loss in benefit. A certain level of earnings is therefore disregarded when benefit entitlements are calculated. Earnings higher than the disregard level are deducted pound for pound from benefits.

The rules in force at the time of the Social Security Review were described in Chapter 5, but are repeated here, for convenience. While on Unemployment Benefit alone, the claimant might earn £2 per day, six days per week without benefit loss. The wife of an unemployed man might earn up to the level of her dependency addition, i.e. £17.55 per week in 1984/85 (£21.40 in 1989). Because this disregard takes work expenses into account, the amount it is possible to earn might be higher, though still limited. If she earns more than her dependency addition, the whole of the addition is withdrawn. These rules still apply. Once on Supplementary Benefit, either as a supplement or as the main income, the SB rules applied. At the time of the Review these permitted only £4 per week in earnings by the claimant and the same for the wife of a claimant, though again work expenses were taken into account.

The policy on disregards was explained by the DHSS in 1981. Disregards were designed 'to provide a modest encouragement to those who are able to help themselves by part time working to do so'.[56] For the unemployed, it was considered that disregards 'should not be at a level where the total income from earnings and Supplementary Benefit would discourage claimants from moving back into full time work because the net gain would be small'.[57]

The earnings disregard for Unemployment Benefit was last uprated in 1982 after standing still for almost a decade, though that for the wife moved with each uprating of the dependency addition. For Supplementary Benefit, the last increase for both partners was in 1980, after a 5 year lapse. Thus the value of these disregards, and the number of hours which could be worked before loss of benefit, had fallen. This affected not only the unemployed on SB, but their wives also, whose contribution to the family budget was thus severely limited.

During the early 1980s, there were many recommendations for a review of disregard policy. The SSAC, for example, urged in several reports (1981, 82/3, 84 and 85) that, at the least, the prevailing disregards should be uprated in line with inflation so that they retained the same proportional relationship to the benefit as when they were first instituted. The Committee also argued that changes in the economy made it more desirable to facilitate efforts by the long term unemployed to keep in touch with the labour market. A more flexible disregard policy could contribute to this.

These and similar proposals were rejected by the government on the grounds of cost. The first call on additional resources should be to improve the benefit rates for all claimants, rather than to assist those who could earn a little extra.[58] The Social Security Review, which heard further evidence on the need for a more generous disregard policy, did have some proposals to make on disregards in the new Income Support scheme, to be implemented in 1988.

For the first two years of unemployment, the earnings disregard would be set at £5 per week each. This was not transferable between husband and wife. The apparent increase was, however offset by a reduction in deductible work expenses. These would now cover only tax, NI contributions and half of occupational pensions contributions, but would exclude fares to work, child care costs and other work expenses. After two years of unemployment, a £15 per week disregard would apply jointly to husband and wife where neither was working. One could claim the whole if the other did not work. Single people, on the other hand, would remain on the £5 disregard indefinitely.

To this was added an even less favourable rule change which was designed to exclude couples from entitlement to benefit under the Income Support scheme if either was in regular work. Regular work would now be defined as 24 hours per week or more. Couples with children could instead claim under the new Family Credit scheme. Couples without children would have to subsist on the part time earnings of husband or wife, even if these were very low. This, the government argued, had become necessary following the introduction of the equal treatment rules, under which either the man or the woman can claim benefit.[59] It would prevent an unemployed woman claiming benefit while her partner worked part time and, in effect, had his earnings subsidised by her benefit·

All of these proposals aroused considerable criticism as being both too limited and too inflexible an approach to disregards at a time when unemployment was so high and the chances of full time work so limited for so many people. The SSAC, for example, said that it did not think the government had 'responded adequately to the need for benefit change to cope with a high unemployment society in which part time work assumes increasing economic and social importance'.[60] The Northern Ireland Assembly drew attention to the higher disregards being offered to other claimant categories (£15 per week for disabled people and one parent families) from the beginning of benefit receipt and could see 'no justifiable rationale for disbarring the unemployed from the same earnings disregard'.[61] It went on: 'If the government are serious about encouraging the unemployed to maintain contact with 'the world of work' then they must recognise the illogicality of this proposal'.[62]

The National Consumer Council was, if anything, more critical. It said:

> These earnings disregards are not enough to enable the unemployed to maintain their skills and their sense of purpose. Unemployed people are given a choice – either they can lapse into apathy and idleness, or be driven into the black economy by claiming while doing casual work. It is a trap affecting not only the claimant but their partners as well. Having set up the trap, the

government is putting increased efforts on to 'fraud drives' in which claimants are pressured to withdraw the claims to benefits.[63]

The NCC's alternative strategy was higher disregards and the encouragement of part time work. The government's decision was to adhere to its proposals within Income Support and to make no change to the disregards for Unemployment Benefit.

Concluding Comments

In the White Paper the government wrote:

> It cannot be said too often that social security cannot remove the causes of poverty. it can and should give protection from the effects of unemployment. But unemployment itself will only be tackled by creating the conditions for sustained economic growth. Social security must not hinder that growth – either in the way the system affects individuals or in the burden it places on the economy generally.[64]

In the social security reforms, the government showed a much stronger interest in giving effect to the latter part of this statement than in protecting poeple from the effects of unemployment. The benefit provision cannot, however, be considered as an isolated policy. It must be seen in the context of a range of other policies towards the unemployed. It is to these that the next chapter will turn.

References

1. *House of Commons Hansard*, 2 April 1984, 652-3.
2. *Reform of Social Security: Background Papers*, Vol.3, Cmnd 9519, HMSO, London, 1985, pp.106-7.
3. *Social Security Statistics*, 1986.
4. Society of Civil and Public Servants, *Social Security for all the People*, London, 1985, p.35. (This was the response to the government's Green Paper but affirmed and expanded on its earlier evidence entitled, *From the Cradle to the Grave*, 1984.)
5. Ibid., p.36.
6. A.W. Dilnot, J.A. Kay, and C.N. Morris, *The Reform of Social Security*, IFS/Clarendon Press, Oxford, 1984.
7. Ibid., pp.54-5.
8. National Consumer Council, *Of Benefit to All*, NCC, London 1984, pp.131-3.
9. Ibid., p.134.

10. *Reform of Social Security*, Vol.1, Cmnd 9517, HMSO, London 1985, p.40..
11. Ibid., p.37.
12. Ibid.
13. *Fifth report of the Social Security Advisory Committee 1986/7*, HMSO, London 1987, pp.35-6.
14. *House of Commons Hansard*, 2 November 1987, 670.
15. Ibid, 659.
16. Ibid.
17. Ibid, 660.
18. Ibid.
19. Ibid, 671.
20. Ibid.
21. Ibid, 21 December 1988, 306.
22. Supplementary Benefits Commission, *Annual Report 1976*, pp.36-40.
23. DHSS, *Social Assistance*, op.cit., p.48.
24. Ibid., p.39.
25. David Piachand, *Children and Poverty*, Poverty Research Series No.9, CPAG, London, 1981.
26. Jonathan Bradshaw, Kenneth Cooke, and Christine Godfrey, 'The impact of unemployment on the living standards of families', *Journal of Social Policy*, Vol.12, No.4, pp.435-52.
27. John Ditch, *Hard Terms: Unemployment and Supplementary Benefit in Northern Ireland*, National Consumer Council, London, 1984.
28. Eileen Evason, *On the Edge: a study of poverty and long term unemployment in Northern Ireland*, CPAG, London, 1985.
29. Institute of Directors, *The Welfare State (1) Submission to the Review of Benefits for Children and Young People*, London, 1984.
30. *Of Benefit to All*, op. cit., p.126.
31. Social Security Review, *Evidence of the Scottish Convention of Women*, March 1985.
32. *County Councils Gazette*, September 1984, p.166.
33. Child Poverty Action Group, *1984: Changed Priorities Ahead: Evidence to the Review of Benefits for Children and Young People*, CPAG, London, 1984.

34. *Third Report of the Social Security Advisory Committee 1984*, HMSO, London, 1985, p.18 quoting Richard Berthoud, *The Reform of Supplementary Benefits*, PSI, London, 1983.
35. *Reform of Social Security*, Vol.1, op.cit., p.13.
36. Ibid.
37. Ibid., p.14
38. Ibid., p.3
39. *Reform of Social Security: Programme for Change*, Vol.2, Cmnd 9518, HMSO, London, 1985, p.21.
40. Ibid., pp.20-1.
41. Ibid., p.49.
42. Ibid., p.23.
43. *The Impact of the Reformed Structure of Income-Related Benefits*, DHSS, London, October 1987.
44. *Social Security Statistics*, 1988.
45. Richard Berthoud, *The Examination of Social Security*, PSI, London, 1985, p.98.
46. *Fourth Report of the Social Security Advisory Committee 1985*, HMSO, London, 1986, p.21.
47. National Union of Teachers, *Reform of Social Security*, (response to the Green Paper), London, 1985.
48. *House of Commons Hansard*, 16 March 1989, 546-8.
49. *Sixth Report of the Social Security Advisory Committee 1988*, HMSO, London, 1988 p.10.
50. Michael White and Susan McRae, *Young Adults and Long Term Unemployment*, PSI, London, 1989, p.209.
51. *House of Commons Hansard*, 21 January 1989, 749-50.
52. Ibid, 5 December 1988, 148.
53. Ibid, 13 March 1989, 62.
54. Ibid, and 24 April 1989, 771.
55. Ibid, 13 March 1989, 27-8.
56. Quoted in the *First Report of the Social Security Advisory Committee 1981*, op.cit. p.62.
57. Ibid.
58. *House of Commons Hansard*, 26 July 1983, 424; 10 July 1984, 870 and 14 June 1985, 599.
59. *Reform of Social Security: Programme for Action*, op.cit. p.26.
60. *Fourth Report of the Social Security Advisory Committee 1985*, HMSO, London, 1986, p.28.

61. Northern Ireland Assembly, *Report: Green Paper on the Reform of Social Security*, Volume 1, HMSO, Belfast, 1985, p.18.
62. Ibid.
63. National Consumer Council, *The long-term unemployed still at the bottom of the heap*, NCC, London, 1985.
64. *Reform of Social Security: Programme for Action*, op.cit., p.2.

10 Special employment measures and benefit administration

Discussions of post-1984 developments has concentrated so far on benefit reform, but as seen in earlier chapters, other measures for unemployed people such as training programmes, often contain aspects which affect the income of the unemployed. In addition, there are a variety of benefit control measures, which form a legitimate element of social security policy, but which can be stepped up or eased off as the circumstances are deemed to demand.

Rational discussion of these policies has been handicapped by the running dispute about how many unemployed there really are. It will be recalled that in the 1970s, this debate focused on allegations that unemployment was artificially inflated by benefits which were too high and that the numbers shown as unemployed included those who were really retired and those making fraudulent benefit claims. These elements of the debate have not gone away but attention has also been directed to the way in which the unemployment statistics have been managed by the government since 1980 and on whether the regular count of the unemployed over or under estimates the true state of unemployment.

For purposes of a discussion of benefits for the unemployed, it is not necessary to enter into a detailed account of the many minor and more major changes to the way the unemployed are counted. It is important to note that, since 1982, only those who are receiving benefit are counted as unemployed and each time steps are taken to reduce access to benefits, the unemployment count goes down accordingly. But while the non-benefit population may 'disappear' from sight, it does not necessarily mean that they cease to be unemployed.

Because of the changes in the way the unemployed are counted there is inevitably suspicion that some government policies are more concerned with getting people off benefit in order to reduce the unemployment count, than with helping the unemployed individual or controlling benefit abuse in a legitimate way. Whether this suspicion is well founded or not, it has certainly soured the policy discussion.

As Table 3.1 showed, the unemployment count continued to rise until 1986, when it reached 3.3 million. It then began to fall, and faster than could be wholly accounted for by any manipulation of the figures, reaching just over 2 million in January 1989, and continuing to fall in the months following. Government policies in this period, therefore, need to be viewed in the context of declining unemployment, even if the true figure for those out of work is higher than the published figure.

The two kinds of policies discussed in this chapter – special employment measures and benefit control provisions – are theoretically separate entities. The first are the responsibility of the manpower and training authorities and the second of the DHSS (now Department of Social Security DSS) or of the Employment Department acting as an agent for social security in the payment of benefits for unemployment. The first seek to help unemployed people to get back into employment; the second act to withhold benefit from those not regarded as genuinely unemployed. But, in practice, the two have always been linked in that, under certain circumstances, refusal of a training place could lead to benefit suspension. These links have been greatly strengthened in recent years. It will be convenient to discuss these policies separately here, but at the same time to draw attention to the interaction between the two policy streams.

The Special Employment Measures

When the present government came into office, it appeared to have mixed feelings about the special employment measures instituted by the previous administration. Indeed, its first step was to cut or freeze the levels of some of the programmes. Since that time a wide range of schemes have been tried out, some later abandoned but others expanded. These measures now form a significant part of the government's policy towards the unemployed.

Youth Training Scheme – 16-17 year olds
In 1983-4, when YTS was mainly for 16 year olds, there were 242,300 trainees. The two year scheme began in April 1986 so that by 1987-8

there were 376,000 trainees[1] and by January 1989, 413,000 young people were in training.[2] By 1988, of 1.67 million 16 and 17 year olds in Great Britain, 39 per cent were in full time education, 30 per cent were in employment (or other activities), 24 per cent were in YTS and 9 per cent were unemployed.[3] The YTS was thus playing an important role for the 16-17 year old age group, though not perhaps the dominating role that government Ministers sometimes claimed for it, as the normal route from school to work.[4]

The quality of the training provided improved over time. There were many claims in the early years that YTS trainees were simply providing cheap labour. A survey undertaken in 1986 found there was still some evidence of this. Most firms made a serious attempt to provide good training and much of it was said to be of impressively high standard. But some companies, particularly in the retail sector, offered tasks which required only a few weeks training and used the trainees simply as substitutes for staff they would otherwise have had to recruit.[5]

In the same year (1986) between April and August, some 52 per cent of those leaving the 1 year YTS programme, had gained a nationally recognised qualification.[6] In March 1988, of those leaving the 2 year programme, 54 per cent were reported to have gained a qualification. In late 1987, the MSC declared that its goal was to give every young person taking part the opportunity to obtain a recognised vocational qualification or a credit towards one.[7] It reported that from April 1988, all YTS training providers would have to hold or obtain Approved Training Organisation status, a step described as 'probably the single most important contribution to quality control in YTS'.[8] Efforts were also being made to ensure that disabled young people were given access to training opportunities. In addition, Approved Training Organisation (ATO) status included the requirement to operate equal opportunities policies for ethnic minorities. In January 1989, it was reported that 5 YTS managing agents had failed to achieve ATO status on grounds which included an unsatisfactory equal opportunities policy.[9]

Operating in an improving labour market and at a time when the 16-17 population was declining, the record of the YTS in leading to employment also improved. In 1982-3, 45 per cent of YTS leavers went into employment, 37 per cent into unemployment and the balance into other training. By 1985-6, 53 per cent went to full time and 4 per cent to part time employment with 28 per cent being unemployed.[10]

When the 1986-88 leavers were followed up, 60 per cent were employed, 21 per cent unemployed and the balance either on another YTS scheme (11 per cent) or in other training.[11]

But for ethnic minority trainees, the record was less good. Three months after leaving YTS in 1985/6, 40 per cent of those of Black/African Caribbean descent were in work and 37 per cent of youngsters of Asian descent[12] in comparison with overall totals of over 50 per cent in employment. Thus, for all groups, there was obviously room for further improvement, particularly if ex-YTS trainees were feeding the stock of 18-25 year old unemployed. But equally, much progress could justly be claimed. The goal that YTS be sufficiently attractive to be preferable to unemployment was on course to being achieved.

The MSC continued to assert its view that 'the scheme should be one in which participation is voluntary, whether by the employer or by the young person'.[13] But, in fact, its non-compulsory status began to be eroded in 1983. In March of that year, YTS was designated an approved training scheme. This meant that unreasonable refusal or early leaving of a place on a scheme by an unemployed person could lead to a reduction in the Supplementary Benefit payable, at that time for a 6 week period. As will be seen later, this period was increased in 1986 to a maximum of 13 weeks and in 1988 to 26 weeks. Refusal of a place was, throughout, less of a problem than early leaving. Between December 1983 and October 1987, nearly 2,000 young people had their benefit reduced for refusing a place, but 24,000 for early leaving.[14]

As seen in Chapter 9, it was the availability of sufficient YTS places that enabled the government in 1988 to withdraw benefit rights – now Income Support – from 16 and 17 year olds. It was still claimed that YTS was not compulsory. This was true to the extent that, where other options were realistically available, such as staying on at school or finding employment, these could be chosen in preference to YTS. Young unemployed people whose families were willing and had the means to support them without other income could also opt out of YTS. But for young people from low income families, and for those who had good reason to live away from home, no such comfortable choice was available. They could seek work during the Child Benefit extension period or while on the Bridging Allowance. But if no work was to be found, then the choice was YTS, living without income or the insecurity of temporary special hardship payments. The starkness of this choice rendered YTS compulsory for them, as near as makes no odds. The scheme was now operating to facilitate one of the severest social security sanctions available.

The 18-24 year olds

This age group has always received considerable attention from the benefit and employment services. White, in his study of the long term unemployed, found that what he called 'disciplinary pressures' were commonly applied to this group, including threat of withdrawal of benefit and actual withdrawal.[15] As seen in Chapter 9, a further squeeze is applied through paying a lower rate of benefit under the new Income Support scheme to those under 26 years.

Assistance to this age group to leave unemployment took several forms. The first was a subsidy programme to encourage employers to offer low paid jobs. The Young Workers Scheme, (see Chapter 6), was phased out for 16 year olds in 1984 and withdrawn from 17 year olds in 1986 – given that YTS was now a two year programme. It was then reshaped in April 1986 as the New Workers Scheme, specifically for people under 21 years, taking up where YTS left off. It paid a grant of £15 per week to employers, for a minimum of 52 weeks, if they provided a full time job paying no more than £55 per week for a worker under 20 and £65 for a 20 year old.

This was a fairly shortlived scheme, withdrawn in January 1988, but it was reported that, between April 1986 and July 1988, 41,863 applications had been approved, a large proportion of which came from service industry employers.[16]

A longer running programme, much used by 18-24 year olds, was the Community Programme. This was a popular programme offering up to 300,000 places in 1986/7/8, though usually operating at the somewhat lower level of 250,000 to 275,000 places.[17] Originally the 18-24 age group was admitted after 6 months unemployment, while those over 25 years had to wait until 12 months of unemployment had passed.

As seen in Chapter 4, the government had operated a rather restrictive policy on the wages to be offered in the Community Programme. The average pay to be offered in the individual projects was not to exceed £67 per week in this period, a very modest increase over the rate payable in the early 1980s. At the same time, the wage to be offered was supposed to be in line with the local rate for the job. As a result, most of the jobs – 87 per cent in 1986 and 1987 – were part time. Since the part time wage was unattractive to people with dependents, around 79 per cent of those on the programme were single and 63 per cent were under 25 years.[18]

Even for those who felt they benefited from being on the programme, there were disadvantages. While the work involved was often interesting, it offered little in the way of formal training. The time on the programme was restricted to 12 months and inevitably a proportion of participants returned to unemployment at the end of the time. Figures given in March 1987 showed that while 54 per cent of former participants had had at least one job during a 10 month follow up period, only 35 per cent were in work at the end of 10 months and a further 3 per cent were in training.[19]

By 1987, the MSC were expressing concern about the 'particular disadvantage' young people under 25 were experiencing in the labour market. Many had entered the labour market and often unemployment before YTS was well developed. They lacked work experience and also basic skills and qualifications.[20] To meet this problem, a new Job Training Scheme (JTS) was introduced in early 1987, first in a few areas and later nationally. It would provide a full time job with both on and off the job training, individually planned for each participant. To encourage participation in JTS, the rules for admission to the Community Programme were altered where JTS was operating. There, after 6 months of unemployment, an 18-24 year old could be admitted to JTS, but must now be unemployed for 12 months before becoming eligible for the Community Programme.

The original goal of JTS – in March 1987 – was to expand to 200,000 trainees a year.[21] In November 1987, this was modified to 110,000 trainees, but by September 1987, only 22,000 were in training.[22] The scheme was controversial from the start. While the Community Programme had paid a wage (however limited), JTS payments were at the same rate as the individual's social security benefit (but called a training allowance) plus out of pocket expenses. The idea was to ensure that the income in training would not be lower than when on benefit, so as not to deter unemployed people with dependents – as had happened in the Community Programme.[23]

The fact that participants would be putting in a full week of both work and training for no more than their benefit rates inevitably produced comparisons with developments in the United States in a programme known as Workfare. In this scheme, recipients of Welfare

– the means tested benefit for the unemployed – were expected to do unpaid work for sufficient hours to 'work off' their weekly benefits.

The government had been showing interest in this programme. The Department of Employment commissioned a study on its possible applicability in the UK, which became available in 1987.[24] Its conclusion was that it would be feasible. It could take one million people out of long term unemployment, enhance their subsequent employability and do something to re-establish the work ethic. There would be some additional cost – in administration and training costs – but except for some possible higher allowances for special skills, these would not arise from higher benefits to the unemployed who would receive in work the same as they would have got on benefit.

The government insisted that its intention was to provide training, not work for benefits. It argued that, for the 18-24 year-old unemployed person, it was preferable to be engaged in work and training which might lead to permanent employment, than to be idle on benefit and probably frustrated by lack of opportunity, and that this was so even if the income being received was the same. Moreover, refusal of a JTS place, or early leaving from the scheme carried no penalty of loss of benefits. Nevertheless, take up remained low. New plans were needed.

Employment Training – 18-24 and 25-50 year olds

In September 1988, a new Employment Training Scheme (ET) was introduced. In order to fund it, the Community Programme, JTS, the New Workers Scheme and the Job Release Scheme were terminated, with protection for individuals already in those schemes. The new scheme would offer up to 12 months training, tailored to the needs of the individual, and with the object of achieving recognised qualifications or credits towards such qualifications. Priority for places in the scheme would be given to 18-24 year olds who had been unemployed for more than 6 but less than 12 months and to 18-50 year olds, out of work for more than 2 years. Disabled people would be admitted whatever their length of unemployment, and all other unemployed people, as well as women seeking to re-enter the labour force after child rearing would be eligible, if places were available once priority needs had been served.

The priority for 18-24 year olds was part of the government's plan to give this age group a guarantee of a training place, a place in a job club or a place on the Enterprise Allowance Scheme. (The latter two will be described later.) The emphasis on those more than 2 years out of work was an attempt to tackle the problem of discouragement among the very long term unemployed and the unwillingness of employers to take on job seekers from this group. The aim was to train 600,000 people a year, through 300,000 training places, suggesting that 12 month's worth of training would not necessarily be the norm. By March 1989, 238,000 people had entered the ET programme.[25]

The programme is too new (at the time of writing) for any worthwhile assessments to have emerged, though it has to be said that many, if not most, comments on ET are critical, just as they were in the early days of YTS, before the weaknesses of that scheme were tackled. But it is possible to comment now on the way in which ET, a training programme provided by the manpower authorities, has become entangled in the benefit system.

Ministers have stressed that ET is a voluntary programme but add that it is subject to the normal availability for work rules.[26] Refusal of a place or dropping out of the scheme would not automatically produce a benefit penalty, but it would lead to questions being raised about willingness to work. It is not unreasonable to suggest that once ET is well established, it will be drawn more routinely into the benefit sanction provisions, especially as it is classified as an approved training scheme.

But of immediate interest is the new relationship between benefits and training allowances that ET has established. JTS participants received the equivalent of their benefit entitlement as a training allowance. But they were no longer on Supplementary Benefit/Income Support. ET participants will be paid on a benefit plus basis, that is they will receive their benefit entitlement plus a premium of £10-12 per week.

Some of the participants who have been out of work for less than 12 months may have an Unemployment Benefit (UB) entitlement. This will be paid, plus the ET premium. More commonly, participants will have been receiving Income Support or UB plus Income Support. While they have this entitlement, they will continue to receive an Income Support element in the payment, so that they remain eligible for Housing Benefit, free school meals for their children and other passported benefits (i.e. benefits to which receipt of Income Support would entitle them). The object is to ensure that ET trainees will be better off than on benefits alone, though since travel costs up to £5 have to be met out of their premium, not much better off.

There are, however, additional implications to these arrangements. The benefit element of the allowance will remain subject to Income Support disregard rules. Any earnings for extra work, or as a top up from the employers, will be deducted from benefit once they exceed £5 (or in the case of couple more than 2 years as benefit, a possible £15 (see Chapter 9). If the wife of a trainee works, as with the wife of an unemployed man her wages over £5 (£15) per week will be deducted from the trainee's benefit plus. If she works more than 24 hours per week, all Income Support rights will go. If there are children she can claim Family Credit and the ET premium will still be payable to the trainee. But if there is no benefit entitlement, only the £10 ET money is payable. This applies also to anyone else without a basic Income Support entitlement, for example someone whose occupational pension, while low, exceeds Income Support limits.

Thus, on the one hand, the benefit plus ET payments can ensure access to any advantages offered by Income Support and so maintain income at a level slightly above the total income from the various means tested benefits. But on the other hand, the trainee is subject to all the disadvantages that being on Income Support involves, and most notably, to the inadequate disregard provisions described in Chapter 9.

The Restart programme – 18 years and over

The Restart programme was launched in July 1986. It was aimed at reanimating the job search activity of long term unemployed people through a personal interview and the offer of a variety of options. Initially directed to those unemployed for 12 months or more, it was later extended to persons unemployed for more than 6 months and now aims to re-interview individuals every 6 months.

Figures given for July 1986 to April 1988, during which time 3.7 million Restart interviews had taken place, indicated that less than 9 per cent had been referred directly to employment.[27] Others were referred to the Community Programme or to JTS. More recently the referrals would be to ET. For some, a one week Restart Course is recommended, in order to boost confidence and job search motivation.

Another possibility is a scheme called Jobstart. This offers a weekly allowance of £20 for 26 weeks to a long term unemployed person who accepts a job at a gross wage of under £80 pw and later £90. In the period July 1986 to March 1989, nearly 40,000 people were accepted on the scheme, and in May 1989, just under 4,000 people were on the allowance.[28] Its relative lack of popularity (in comparison with the number of unemployed people) may be attributed to the low total income which could be achieved, the fact that the subsidy lasted only 26 weeks and that it could be lost if the wage increased beyond £80 pw (or now £90) during that time.

Another choice, with an allowance attached, is the Enterprise Allowance Scheme (EAS). This offers £40 per week for twelve months to someone setting up in self-employment and is paid regardless of what the individual manages to earn. This is a useful scheme, but is most likely to be of value to newly unemployed people with some redundancy money behind them, since successful self-employment does need some financial reserves. It is a more doubtful proposition for someone who has been out of work for a long period and whose reserves are exhausted, though some do still make a success of it.[29]

Finally, there is the option to enter a Job Club. This gives unemployed people a period of access to a telephone, stationery, free postage and other aids to made an intensive job search, in the company of others in a like position. This has quite a high success rate – 60 per cent of participants obtained jobs between November 1984, when the first Job Club opened, and March 1987.[30] In January 1989, there were 1,220 Job Clubs in operation.[31]

The figures given in the House of Commons from time to time on the Restart programme do not offer a very clear idea of how useful it actually is. Asked how its success was measured, the government responded that 'the success of the programme is measured principally by reference to the number of long term unemployed people contacted, the number interviewed, and the percentage of those interviewed who are offered positive help'[32] – positive help being referral to one or other of the programmes just discussed. This covered 88 per cent of those interviewed.[33]

But Restart does have another role – as part of the network of benefit sanctions. The letter of invitation to a Restart interview contains a warning that failure to attend may affect benefits. A follow up letter contains a stronger warning. If, on investigation, there is no 'valid reason' for this second failure to attend, 'benefits are withdrawn until they agree to attend'.[34]

The interview itself is part of the process of ascertaining availability for work and this element has recently been strengthened.[35] If availability is questioned, a referral will be made to an Adjudication Officer to determine continued eligibility for benefit.

The over 50s
The over 50s are not excluded from either ET or Restart and related schemes. But, as seen, ET gives priority to those under 50 who have been out of work for more than 2 years and Restart advice tends to be focussed on the same age group.[36] The only scheme that has ever been directed specifically to the older worker – the Job Release Scheme – was closed on 31 January 1988, except for existing recipients. The reason was that the resources were to be targeted on the priority task of reducing long term unemployment, and more specifically on ET.[37]

By way of a consolation prize, in 1989 a new 50-plus Jobstart scheme was introduced on a pilot basis. It was aimed at encouraging those over 50 years who had been unemployed for more than 12 months to take low paid, part time work, as a means of re-establishing themselves in the labour market.

Controlling benefit abuse/encouraging the discouraged
These two elements of policy – controlling benefit abuse and encouraging the unemployed to maintain job search activity – have been a feature of benefit policy since Unemployed Insurance was first instituted. In times of high employment, the benefit authorities have believed that people could be got back into work and ought not to be allowed to settle down on benefit. In times of high unemployment, there is a fear that the 'idle' will take advantage of the more sympathetic environment and claim benefit without good cause, and a belief that the longer term unemployed need more rather than less encouragement to maintain job searching.

Such policies, implemented with moderation and with proper account of the state of the labour market, form a reasonable part of a total benefit policy. If, on the other hand, they are applied without the moderation required in times of high unemployment, then they are open to criticism. If to this added a suspicion that one goal of the policy is to reduce the unemployment count, a hostile reaction can be expected.

Voluntary unemployment and misconduct

The first question for a newly unemployed person is whether he or she has an entitlement, based on the contribution record, to claim Unemployment Benefit and if not, whether he/she is eligible for Income Support. As seen in Chapter 9, qualification for the insurance benefit has been made more difficult. But even if there is technically an insurance entitlement, or if not, the claimant would qualify under the means test for Income Support, there is another possible hurdle. Since 1911, a person who left the job voluntarily or was dismissed for misconduct has been subject to a possible Unemployment Benefit disqualification for up to 6 weeks. The object of the rule was to protect the insurance scheme against those who were out of work through their own fault (see Chapter 1). But if they were seeking new employment, the benefit would be restored after 6 weeks at most, and for the full period of entitlement if necessary, since they had paid the requisite contributions. Thus there was a balance between the felt need for a penalty for self-inflicted unemployment, and the recognition of the rights created by payment of contributions while in work. Rules were later developed to ensure that an individual without other income, and the family of the unemployed person, were not reduced to destitution. Means tested benefits might be claimed. This will be discussed later.

The rule was always a fruitful source of dispute. Some people do walk out of a job for no good reason and some are guilty of serious misconduct. but there may be good reasons for leaving and there are many ways in which an employer can induce an employee to leave 'voluntarily'. For those employed for too short a period to enjoy Employment Protection cover, it is not difficult to claim that an employee disobeyed a reasonable instruction or otherwise merited dismissal. An appeal could be made to a Social Security Appeal Tribunal which might restore the benefit or reduce the length of the penalty, but by the time this was done, the individual or family had probably already suffered financial difficulties.

But as long as the maximum involved was a 6 week disqualification, followed by a resumption of full benefit rights, it was tolerable. Eric Heffer (MP for Liverpool, Walton) expressed the view of his former fellow workers when he said 'The system has always been resented, but it could be lived with. We did not like it, but we could live with it'.[38]

After 75 years in which the rule had operated unchanged, the government in 1986 added a clause to the 1986 Social Security Act to extend the period to a maximum of 13 weeks and also to give the power to count the period of disqualification against the full period of Unemployment Benefit entitlement. In other words, the benefit would not just be deferred; that part of it would be lost for good. The reasons given for this were that the government did not believe that a 6 weeks suspension of benefit was a sufficient penalty for voluntary unemployment (including misconduct), and that figures showing an upward trend in the number of disqualifications for this reason suggested that the time had come to introduce a tougher deterrent. The figures given in Hansard showed a decline in disqualification for voluntary leaving in the period 1977-81, from almost 440,000 in 1977 to 246,000 in 1981, following an increase reaching 298,000 in 1985. A similar trend was evident in misconduct cases.[39] How much of this increase was due to a more stringent application of the rules, or more 'rough justice' given by a service under pressure of high unemployment numbers, was not clear.

Two years later the maximum period of possible disqualification was increased to 26 weeks with power to count this against total Unemployment Benefit entitlement. Introducing the provisions in the House of Commons, the Minister (Nicholas Scott) defined the purpose of the voluntary unemployment sanctions as, 'to discourage people from acting in a way which leaves them unnecessarily without work and a charge on the public purse'.[40] The increase from 6 to 13 weeks in the maximum length of the penalty should have led to a fall in the numbers involved but, the Minister said, 'on the contrary, the absolute number of instances where a disqualification or deduction was imposed rose',[41] at a time when claims for unemployment benefit were falling. More effective measure were therefore needed.

It might have been expected that this further step to extend the penalty period would only have been taken if the increase in the number involved was large enough to be alarming. It turned out, however, that a comparison of periods of nine months before and after the increase in the penalty to 13 weeks showed a growth in disqualifications of less than 5,000 or just under 2 per cent. Claims for Unemployment Benefits had been falling in this period, and as a proportion of all claims, disqualifications had risen from 8 to 9 per cent.[42] The figures given by the Minister did not seem to justify the drastic action being taken.

Moreover, although the 13 week period had been a maximum, leaving room for shorter periods to distinguish between serious and more marginal cases, other figures given in the Parliamentary debate showed that 75 per cent of disqualifications under the rules had been for the full 13 week period and the average length of disqualification was a little over 11 and a half weeks.[43] It was therefore reasonable to fear that the practice of imposing the maximum might be applied to the new 26 week rule. Success on application for review of the decision or on appeal was high, but this process took some time during which the claimant received no or reduced benefit.

Whether for 6, 13 or 26 weeks, the disqualification would also have an impact on Supplementary Benefit/Income Support. Before 1971, the weekly deduction made from what was then Supplementary Benefit was quite small (75 pence). In 1971 a rule was introduced requiring a 40 per cent cut in the unemployed person's benefit, but no reduction in the benefits for dependents. The Supplementary Benefits Commission were given discretion to deduct a lesser amount where there was thought to be hardship, while maintaining at least a minimum deduction. In 1983, this discretion was removed. The deduction could be reduced to 20 per cent, but only where there was someone in the family who was pregnant or seriously ill and if the joint capital was less than £100 in 1983 and £200 in 1988, when the rules were transferred to Income Support.

As the period for which disqualification applied increased, so would the difficulties experienced by families subsisting on reduced benefits. Since the level set for the means tested benefit was intended to be the minimum on which families could reasonably be expected to live, a reduction in this level, even for one member of the family, was bound to affect the living standards of the whole, including the children – innocent of any offence.

One other, more positive, move made in this period ought to be recorded. This excluded from the disqualification rules those who accepted voluntary redundancy, when a company was reducing its labour force, for example. From June 1985, these men and women could claim benefit as involuntarily unemployed.[44]

Benefit fraud

There has been a good deal of talk during the 1980s about social security fraud and abuse. It is difficult to get a clear picture of this from the evidence that is offered. To some extent this is natural, because fraud of its nature seeks to conceal its existence. But the picture is also confused by government's own attempts to prove how active it is in combatting fraud and by the presentation of suspicions, rather than actual evidence. There is also a tendency to lump together three different forms of 'abuse' – working full time or near full time while claiming to be unemployed; exceeding earnings disregard limits on a small scale without declaring it; and not meeting the availability for work rules. This section will focus on the first two of these.

Some of the concern about working while employed seems to stem from reports of the Inland Revenue on the size of the black economy. If there is a large area of this kind of work, then it seems likely that the unemployed are involved. Pahl, on the other hand, argues that the most likely offenders are not the unemployed, who are unused to operating in the sphere of informal work (apart from occasional casual jobs) but existing employed and self-employed people with particular skills which are in demand and who 'moonlighted' for cash.[45] Nevertheless, the possibility of working full time and claiming benefit could not altogether be discounted. Fraud investigation officers of the Department of Employment, therefore, undertook specific investigations of particular types of work where fraud is likely to be occurring – construction, taxi driving, despatch riders, seasonal workers in holiday areas, for example.

Reports of these fraud drives make it clear that there is a problem, but that, in relation to total unemployment, it is a small one. In May 1988, for example, it was reported that after two 'very successful fraud investigations in the West Midlands, a total of 558 claimants withdrew their benefit claims'. This represented 0.2 per cent of the total number of people unemployed and claiming benefit in the West Midlands region[46]. A further report in June 1988 said that, in the year ending 31 March 1988, some 80,088 people voluntarily withdrew their claims to unemployment benefit following a fraud investigation. 'This figure represents 1.83 per cent of the total number of people who withdrew their claims in that year'.[47]

The actual number of prosecutions for all social security fraud has fallen substantially, from just under 22,000 in 1978-79 to just over 7,000 in 1987-88. This figure had risen from a low of just under 6,000 in 1983-84.[48] The Minister (John Moore) suggested that this fall was evidence of a more humane policy,[49] but it may also represent a preference for avoiding the legal costs of prosecution and the necessity to assemble evidence which would stand up in court. A large proportion of the prosecutions are related to unemployment benefits, but even so only 3,981 people were prosecuted for fraudulent claims of these benefits from April 1988 to the end of March 1989.[50]

The incidence of the second type of fraud, undeclared earnings from casual work which exceed the limits of earnings disregards is also unknown. It might be expected to be quite high. The disregards for the majority of unemployed people are so out of touch with wage levels that they can be exceeded after only a few hours work. At the same time, declaring occasional earnings activates procedures to reduce the weekly benefit, including the seeking of evidence from the employer, and may easily lead to disruption in the flow of benefit payments. Such a situation tends to encourage people to keep their heads down and hope no-one will know they have earned some extra money to supplement their low benefits.

Discussing evidence on 'the scale of abuse and fraud', the 1988 White Paper *Training for Employment* said that the 1987 Labour Force Survey had found 190,000 benefit claimants who said they were working and claiming benefit at the same time. The White Paper commented that some of these may have been working part time and legitimately claiming reduced benefits.[51]

The low number reported, even though they are unlikely to include many whose earnings were 'illicit' may suggest that this kind of fraud is in fact lower than might be expected. The high profile given to fraud drives may be deterring small scale rule breaking, because people fear that the consequences of being found out will be out of proportion to the small additional amounts being earned. But in these cases, not only is fraud deterred, but so are efforts to work and keep in touch with the labour market an outcome which ought to be seen as counter-productive.

All this is inevitably speculative; but there does not seem to be evidence of large scale fraud involving either full time work or undeclared small earnings. Government is now more often emphasising that 'most benefit claimants are genuinely unemployed and keen to work'.[52] But while properly pursuing those claiming benefits while in full time work, it is failing to address the problems created by the low level of disregards which unnecessarily 'criminalises' those who do have small undeclared earnings and can deter others from seeking to maintain a foothold in the labour force.

Advice to unemployed claimants

Before dealing directly with the availability for work issue, reference needs to be made to services originally provided by the social security authorities and now by the Department of Employment, focused on those who had been on benefit for some time.

Unemployment Review Officers (URO) were first appointed to the National Assistance Board in 1961 and continued to be employed by the Supplementary Benefits Commission (SBC) and the DHSS. They interviewed claimants after six months on the means tested benefit. Later their role was extended to those on Unemployment Benefit without supplementation.

The SBC had around 100 UROs in the late 1970s and the Commission emphasised in its 1978 Annual Report that it was concerned that:

> The URO's task should continue to be the constructive one of diagnosing the reasons for continue or repeated unemployment, helping and encouraging unemployed people to find work, and applying sanctions only in those cases where he is satisfied that the person is neglecting opportunities of maintaining himself by working.[53]

This order of priorities was still being stated by the DHSS in 1985. Sir Geoffrey Otton, the Department head, said in evidence before the Public Accounts Committee that the job was a 'mixture of a welfare and policing role',[54] though he acknowledged that it did sometimes act as a form of pressure to go off benefit. The National Audit Office, on the other hand, reversed these priorities. It said: 'these reviews aim to establish that benefit is being paid only in genuine cases and to help those disadvantaged in employment terms to overcome their disadvantages'.[55] It also expressed doubts that the DHSS had 'given sufficient consideration to the establishment and fulfillment of objectives in this area'.[56] Some office managers in the Department apparently regarded the work as of low priority and questioned whether it served any useful purpose in a time of high unemployment.

In 1986, the task of unemployment review was transferred to the Department of Employment. The original order of priorities help first, benefit control as a sub-goal was restated at the time the decision was announced.[57] UROs were now to be called Claimant Advisers and by January 1987, there were 466 of them in post and 796 by June 1988[58].

The job of the Claimant Advisers is to provide guidance to claimants to help them move out of employment; to ensure that they are available for and actively seeking work; to advise claimants about alternative benefits to which they might be entitled; to provide advice and motivation to claimants to help them in their search for work; and to suspend benefit and refer claims to the adjudicating authorities where entitlement to benefits is in doubt.[59] More recently, greater stress is being placed on informing unemployed people about in work benefits which can be claimed in conjunction with low paid work. Among these, the key benefit for families with children is the new Family Credit scheme, introduced in April 1988.

The work of the Claimant Advisers is concentrated on those who have been out of work for more than 6 months. They take referrals from the Restart programme, following up claimants who did not attend for Restart interviews or did not act on the advice given, and taking over cases which require more detailed attention than Restart can offer. Referrals also come from within the benefit service where availability for work is in doubt or where staff think the Claimant Advisers could offer help.

Figures given in Parliament show that, in the period April 1987 to April 1988, 620,000 interviews were undertaken (some claimants having more than one interview), and 100,000 people found work or were placed in one of the special programmes. Over 56,000 were found to need a benefit other than for unemployment, for example, they were incapacitated for work. Around 26,000 were referred to adjudicating officers, presumably with queries about their entitlement to benefit, usually on grounds of non-availability for work.[60] The figures illustrate the mixture of welfare and policing that continues to operate.

In 1988, a further tier of advice and scrutiny was introduced, with the appointment of New Client Advisers. These are to give detailed interviews to all new benefit claimants. The intention is to offer more substantial advice and help in the task of seeking new employment, but also to establish availability for work, and therefore entitlement to benefit for unemployment. Advice will also be given on in work benefits and, where appropriate, on alternative income benefits.

Both the New Client Advisers and the Claimant Advisers have the potential to be very useful to the unemployed man or woman. A newly unemployed person, especially one facing unemployment for the first time, can be bewildered by the benefit system and not well practiced in the task of job hunting. Help and guidance right at the beginning of unemployment can be the key to shortening the period out of work, while ensuring that the correct benefits are paid while the search for work is undertaken. For those who have not succeeded in finding work, concentrated help after 6 months out of work can counter the discouragement and loss of confidence that the experience of unsuccessful job hunting has produced. With the development of other special measures for the unemployed, including ET, the advisers have a better range of programmes to draw on than were available to the UROs. Thus, these services can be viewed as positive policies to aid unemployed people.

But the advisers are also expected to play an active policing role, and while they do not take the final decision on the withdrawal of benefits, the evidence they offer is bound to be influential. Moreover, they are operating within parallel policies which seek to place greater stress on the issue of availability for work and which have twice increased the penalties not only for leaving work 'voluntarily', but also for remaining out of work 'voluntarily'.

Availability for work

Being available for work has always been a key condition for benefit in respect of unemployment. Until more recent changes, the operating law on this point was the 1975 Social Security Act. Under the Act, and subsequent interpretations, to be eligible for benefit for unemployment, claimants must be available for work with an employer and must not restrict their job seeking, in terms of the hours, days, pay, location or type of employment that they are willing to accept to such an exent that they effectively have no reasonable prospects of securing work within those restrictions.

There was a duty to seek work, not simply to be passively available. If work was offered, there must be 'good reasons' for rejecting it. In the early months of unemployment, the claimant need not accept work outside his/her normal field or skills level. Later, more flexibility was expected, but work below the normal rates of pay prevailing in the area need not be accepted. The claimant was also expected to follow up the advice offered, including the acceptance of an approved training place, if appropriate, and perseverance with that training. A claimant who was found to be unavailable for work or placing undue restrictions on availability might have her/his benefit withdrawn or suspended for a period of 6 weeks.

Originally, the test of availability was registration for employment was regular attendance at a Labour Exchange/Job Centre. The other tests – following up on job vacancies and not refusing a job offer unreasonably – could be applied in this context. The Unemployment Review Officers (UROs) applied further tests through the advice offered or recommendations to undertake training. The shift to self-service in the Job Centres in the 1970s weakened the process somewhat, but a more important change occurred in 1982 when the requirement to register for employment at the Job Centre was withdrawn for efficiency and cost saving reasons. Thereafter, the test for availability was applied at the Unemployment Benefit Office.

The National Audit Office looked at the Unemployment Benefit Service in 1985 and reported that the test of availability for work, in which claimants were asked if they would take any job they could do, was weak and that it was 'easy for claimants to deduce the answer required in order to qualify for benefit'.[61] Following this no further checks would be made until the claimant was seen by a URO after 6 months of unemployment, except that the same question would be posed each time the claimant signed on. The Committee of Public Accounts also commented unfavorably on the weakness of the test in 1985 and urged the DHSS to consider whether more effective tests were practicable.[62]

Action was taken on this in October 1986. A new and longer questionnaire on availability for work was introduced, and Claimant Advisers were to interview claimants whose availability was in doubt. The law itself was not changed, but it was applied more stringently. The government said that the questionnaire helped 'to identify the minority of claimants who seek to abuse the benefit system, and those people who need special advice and guidance with their efforts to find work or to claim the correct benefit'.[63] Anyone whose availability was in doubt had their benefit payments delayed or suspended until the matter was resolved. They could appeal against benefit suspension if they wished, and, in cases of hardship, apply for urgent needs payments from Supplementary Benefits. Besides the initial questionnaires and the inquiries by the Claimant Advisers, the Restart programme was also being used to check on availability. As seen earlier, failure to attend a Restart interview was seen as evidence of possible unavailability for work or unwillingness to pursue ways of getting back to work. For those who attended an interview, inquiries after April 1988 included a questionnaire partly designed to uncover non-availability. Failure to follow an agreed course of action – for example, to join a job club – could also raise doubts about willingness to work. The establishment of Employment Training added to the possible tests of availability related to refusal of a training place or leaving approved training prematurely.

In early 1989, government published figures on the number of disallowances of unemployment related benefits made by Department of Employment adjudication officers in Great Britain. Disallowances for non-availability or restricted availability rose from 39,642 in 1981 to 101,774 in 1987. Premature termination of training which led to a disallowance rose from 366 in 1981 to 6,496 in 1987. Refusal of suitable employment produced 4,779 disallowances in 1981, 1,883 in 1983 and 4,321 in 1987.[64] Thus, it seemed clear that the new procedures were having an impact. No doubt they were also having an 'incentive' effect on other unemployed people who became aware of the consequences of unavailability. These had also become more severe during the same period. Remaining unemployed voluntarily attracted the same penalties as becoming voluntarily unemployed, and (as seen earlier) these rose from a maximum of 6 weeks, through 13 weeks to 26 weeks by April 1988. Moreover, the appeal process on availability was slow, averaging 22 and a half weeks in the first three months of 1988 and although back money was payable to the 36.6 per cent of successful appellants[65], it was likely that they had undergone serious difficulties in the meantime.

But the government was still not satisfied. Unemployment was falling and available vacancies were increasing, particularly in the South East, but also elsewhere. Drawing on the 1987 Labour Force Survey, the White Paper *Training for Employment* said that it had been found that 'a substantial number of benefit claimants were not immediately available for work, or were not looking for work.[66] These included 240,000 who said they were available for work but had not looked for a job in the past four weeks. A report in 1988 on the London labour market indicated that 25 per cent of the claimants interviewed had not looked for work in the previous week, half of these had not looked for a job in the previous four weeks and 5 per cent had never looked for work at all.[67]. The government also estimated in early 1989 that there were 700,000 unfilled jobs in the economy of which 140,000 were in London.[68]

On the basis of this, changes were made in the 1989 Social Security Act to the availability for work rules. Clause 7 introduced a new requirement that claimants should demonstrate that they were actively seeking work on a week by week basis. Regulations would detail how this would operate in practice. Clause 9 modified the right to refuse employment for 'good cause'. When newly unemployed people were interviewed by a New Clients Adviser, they would be allotted a permitted period, within a maximum of 13 weeks, during which they could look for work in the field they had worked in before and at a level of pay which they had earned. Thereafter, a job could not be refused – without penalty – in other fields or at lower pay.

'Good cause' for refusing a job was to be restricted in the regulations to physical or mental stress, sincerely held religious or conscientious views, excessive travelling distances, domestic circumstances as they related to a particular job, and whether the expenses of employment, excluding child care costs, would absorb an unduly high proportion of earnings.[69] The claimant had to be willing to take not only full time permanent jobs, but temporary jobs and part time jobs of more than 25 hours a week. Those who failed to meet the requirements of these two clauses and the regulations would be subject to a benefit disallowance for a maximum of 26 weeks. Income Support, at a reduced level, would be available where hardship would otherwise occur.

There was some recognition of the difficulties faced by those who had been out of work for a long period and might be re-entering employment in an entirely new field. Where claimants had been out of work for a long period they could, after a period of not less than 6 but not more than 12 weeks, leave a job which they found to be quite unsuited to them, without incurring a penalty for voluntary unemployment. This provision would only be available once in any 12 month period. In the first reading of the Bill, the qualifying period of unemployment was set at 12 months, but the time of the third reading, this had been reduced to 6 months out of work.

Not surprisingly, clauses 7 and 9 were bitterly fought in Parliament and a number of points were made in the debate. In the actively seeking work requirements, government had resurrected a rule which had operated in the 1920s, and had been abolished in 1930 as wholly unsatisfactory. It ignored the fact that, in spite of the number of vacancies that were supposed to be available, there was still no work for two out of three unemployed people. To enforce job search at the level required would expose them to constant and demoralising rejection.[70] Clause 9 would push people into low paid work.[71] In work benefits were available for families with children in the shape of Family Credit and Housing Benefit, but childless people had no access to Family Credit and other benefits were limited or available only for a set period.

Particular concern was expressed about the impact of Clause 7 on people over 50 years,[72] disabled unemployed people,[73] ethnic minorities subject to discrimination,[74] unemployed people involved in voluntary work which could improve their confidence and employability[75] and those taking advantage of the 21 hour rule (see Chapter 6) to study so as to upgrade their qualifications.[76] Some assurances were offered about each of these groups, but not of a degree to inspire great confidence.

The new availability rules came into force in October 1989.

The unemployed in 1989

At the end of the depression of the 1930s, the large numbers of unemployed remaining were quite rapidly absorbed into the labour force, because of the demands created by the outbreak of war. The circumstances (happily) were unusual, but they served to demonstrate the employability of the unemployed of all age groups and both short term and long term.

But when, as now, unemployment is declining gradually, and labour demand is still limited, the position of the long term unemployed is different. They will tend to be by-passed by employers in favour of job changers, the short term unemployed and married women returning to the labour market after child rearing. The skills of the long term unemployed will be rusty, and may, in fact, no longer be in demand in a changing economy. Older unemployed people and others who experience discrimination in the job market – such as ethnic minority and disabled unemployed – will continue to find it difficult to secure employment. Given that there is a greater demand in the labour market for work skills, those who are unskilled may also find stable work hard to come by. For many within these groups, job search will continue to bring rejections, perhaps the more painful and discouraging when jobs are said to be available.

At such a time, programmes which help to maintain or restore the confidence and motivation of unemployed people, which help them to develop means of job search, and which encourage and support them in their efforts can all be seen to be highly desirable. So too are high standard training programmes for young people and for the adult unemployed.

At all times, it can be expected that social security provision for unemployment will include rules which aim to reserve benefits to those who are genuinely unemployed. It might also be expected that these rules would be used, with discrimination, as a spur to those who had become so discouraged in the search for work that they failed to take advantage of the kinds of programmes outlined above.

The question now to be addressed is whether the three streams of policy for the unemployed – the benefit provisions, the special employment measures and the programmes designed to control benefit abuse and encourage the discouraged – are each operating in a way which is appropriate to the labour market now and in the 1990s. It also has to be asked if these three kinds of policy are in a reasonable balance with one another, again in the context of the present and future labour market.

References

1. *House of Commons Hansard*, 7 November 1988, 51.
2. Ibid., 14 March 1989, 198.
3. 'Why Train School-leavers?' *Unemployment Bulletin*, Autumn 1988, pp.1-12, drawn from official data.
4. *House of Commons Hansard*, 25 October 1988, 193.
5. B.M. Deakin, and C.F. Pratten, 'Economic Effects of YTS', *Employment Gazette*, October 1987, pp.491-7.
6. *House of Commons Hansard*, 2 April 1987, 558 and 29 March 1988, 420.
7. Manpower Services Commission, *Corporate Plan 1987, 1991* MSC, Sheffield, 1987, p.19.
8. Ibid, p.20.
9. *House of Commons Hansard*, 25 January 1989, 625-6.
10. Ibid, 24 July 1987, 675-6.
11. Ibid, 2 November 1988, 665.
12. Ibid, 5 March 1987, 649.
13. MSC, *Corporate Plan 1987, 1991*, op.cit., p.19.
14. 'Why train school-leavers', op.cit., p.6.
15. Michael White, *Long Term Unemployment and Labour Markets*, PSI, London, 1983, pp.126-9.
16. *House of Commons Hansard*, 23 July 1987, 331.
17. Ibid, 27 April 1987, 22 and 3 March 1988, 705.

18. Ibid, 1 April 1987, 535.
19. Ibid, 3 March 1987, 561. Figures for Great Britain only.
20. House of Commons Committee on Public Accounts, Session 1986-87, *Adult Training Strategy: Manpower Services Commission*, HC 223, HMSO, London, 1987, p.10.
21. *House of Commons Hansard*, 3 March 1987, 720.
22. Ibid, 17 November 1987, 908.
23. Ibid, 910.
24. John Burton, *Would Workfare Work?*, Employment Research Centre, University of Buckingham, 1987.
25. *House of Commons Hansard*, 11 April 1989, 450.
26. Ibid, 25 October 1988, 154-5.
27. Ibid, 27 June 1988, 67.
28. Ibid, 23 May 1989, 506.
29. Ibid, 7 April 1987.
30. Ibid, 31 March 1987, 462.
31. Ibid, 17 January 1987, 174.
32. Ibid, 2 February 1988, 542.
33. Ibid.
34. Ibid, 17 January 1989, 188.
35. *Training for Employment*, CM 316, HMSO, London, 1988, p.30.
36. *House of Commons Hansard*, 21 July 1987, 161.
37. Ibid, 2 December 1987, 601.
38. Ibid, 1 March 1988, 845.
39. Dominic Byrne, and John Jacobs, *Disqualified from Benefit: the operation of benefit penalties*, Low Pay Unit, London, 1988 and *House of Commons Hansard*, 1 May 1985, 471.
40. *House of Commons Hansard*, 1 March 1988, 834.
41. Ibid.
42. Ibid, 836.
43. Ibid, 840.
44. DHSS *Press Release*, 'Benefit for workers taking voluntary redundancy', 24 June 1985.
45. R.E. Pahl, 'The Politics of Work', *Political Quarterly*, October/December 1985, pp.331-45.
46. *House of Commons Hansard*, 9 May 1988, 53.
47. Ibid, 20 June 1988, 402.
48. Ibid, 31 January 1989, 192 and 6 February 1989, 639.
49. Ibid, 6 February 1989, 639.

50. Ibid, 18 April 1989, 140.
51. *Training for Employment*, op.cit., pp.33-4.
52. Ibid, p.33.
53. Supplementary Benefits Commission, *Annual Report 1978*, HMSO, London, 1979, p.116.
54. House of Commons: Committee on Public Accounts, Session 1984-85, *Unemployment Benefit Service*, HC 434, HMSO, London, 1985, p.8.
55. National Audit Office, Report by the Comptroller and Auditor General, *Department of Health and Social Security, Department of Employment, Unemployment Benefit Service*, HC 374, HMSO, London, 1985, p.8.
56. Ibid, p.3.
57. DHSS *Press Release*, 'Unemployment Review', 23 July 1986.
58. *House of Commons Hansard*, 4 February 1987, 683 and 29 July 1988, 840.
59. Claimant Advisers' job description given in Dan Finn, 'Claimant Advisers', *Unemployment Bulletin*, Summer 1988, pp.6-8.
60. *House of Commons Hansard*, 29 July 1988, 840.
61. Report by the Comptroller and Auditor General, op.cit., p.2.
62. *Unemployment Benefit Service*, op.cit., p.vii.
63. *House of Commons Hansard*, 22 July 1987, 457.
64. Ibid, 10 January 1989, 575-6.
65. Ibid, 23 January 1989, 414.
66. *Training for Employment*, op.cit., p.33.
67. Cited by John Moore, Secretary of State for Social Security, *House of Commons Hansard*, 10 January 1989, 715.
68. Ibid.
69. Ibid, 26 April 1989, 1014-5.
70. Ibid, 10 January 1989, 727.
71. Ibid.
72. Ibid, 721.
73. Ibid, 26 April 1989, 975.
74. Ibid, 10 January 1989, 773.
75. Ibid, 26 April 1989, 977-8.
76. Ibid, 991.

11 Which way for the future?

It will be recalled that the Social Security White Paper of 1985, under a heading 'objectives of reform', said that, while social security could not remove the causes of poverty, 'it can and should give protection from the effects of unemployment'.[1] Unlike the Beveridge Report – to which the Green and White Papers made many references – the 1985 White Paper was not proposing a policy based on full employment and it qualified its statement of objectives accordingly. The goal was to create conditions for sustained economic growth and, in that way, to tackle unemployment. Social security must not hinder that growth 'either in the way the system affects individuals or in the burden it places on the economy generally'. Social security could not be 'ring fenced' from the requirements of the sensible management of the economy as a whole.[2]

But equally social security for the unemployed cannot be 'ring fenced' from the current and likely future state of the labour market. And this must include not only the number of people who are unemployed, whether claiming or ineligible for benefit, but also the way in which the labour market is developing. In both areas, marked changes have been taking place in recent years.

The unemployment outlook
In 1986 the Manpower Services Commission published its Corporate Plan for 1986 to 1990. In it, the Commission presented various projections of UK unemployment, excluding school leavers, for the year 1989. Of the five independent projections shown, the lowest was 2.6 million and the highest 3.4 million.[3] In the Corporate Plan for 1987 to 1991, the beginnings of a downward trend in unemployment were noted, but continued high unemployment was expected.[4] A

White Paper in 1988 presented a much more up-beat picture, recording further falls in unemployment and making no forecasts about future unemployment.[5] At the beginning of 1989, the numbers claiming benefit for employment fell below 2 million and have continued to fall slowly.[6]

By April 1989, the number of people claiming benefits for unemployment had fallen to 1.856 million.[7] Even taking into account the number of married unemployed women and 16 and 17 year olds who do not qualify for benefit, and any other factors which remove people from the benefit count without their entering employment, the record shows a significant improvement in the employment/unemployment situation. But the numbers remaining unemployed are still large enough to be classified as mass unemployment. Moreover, given the economic uncertainty which has characterised late 1988 and 1989, the future cannot be forecast with real confidence. There may be a continued decline in unemployment, or the numbers could settle at a still high plateau, or they could rise again. When the Single European Market comes about in 1992, it may have good or it may have bad effects on unemployment. All of this indicates the need for a benefit system, with its related rules, which is able to respond appropriately to high unemployment and to both declining and growing numbers of the unemployed.

Although the fall in unemployment has benefited all regions, both short and long term unemployed, and all age groups and special groups, it remains the case that some regions, some areas even within prosperous regions, and some population groups, still experience higher than average unemployment rates or longer term unemployment.[8]

Among those whose work opportunities are limited by disability, the unemployment rate has usually been more than double the average. In 1985, it was 23.4 per cent compared with an average 10.6 per cent.[9] Assuming that disabled unemployed people have shared the general decline in unemployment, as some evidence suggests,[10] the 1989 rate is still likely to be in the region of 14.5 per cent compared to an average 6.6 per cent.[11] Another group with higher than average unemployment rates is the ethnic minority population. In 1985, when the rate for white unemployment in the Labour Force Survey was 10.3 per cent, the ethnic minority rate was 20 per cent. In 1987, the figures were 10.2 per cent white and 16.4 per cent ethnic minority unemployment. But within the ethnic minority population there were wide variations in the rate in 1987, from 13 per cent for those of Indian origin, 17 per cent West Indian/Guyanese to 29 per cent Pakistani/Bangladeshi.[12]

A third group, unemployed men and women over 50 years of age do not show such a disparity in their unemployment rate. But once out of work, they experience above average long term unemployment. While the proportion of all unemployed men and women out of work for 12 months or more in April 1989 was 39 per cent, for those aged 50-54 years, the proportion was almost 60 per cent and for those aged 55-59 years, it was 68 per cent.[13]

All three groups – disabled, ethnic minority and older unemployed – experience discrimination in the labour market. While efforts must continue to overcome this aspect of the problem, the current realities point to the need for the benefit system, and its operating rules, to take account of the difficulties members of these groups can have in re-entering employment, as well as the problems of those living in areas where high unemployment persists.

A fourth group – 16-19 year olds – can expect improved prospects in the next decade. Their numbers will have fallen by over 1 million between 1983 and 1993,[14] starting with a fall in the numbers reaching compulsory school leaving age. But this does not obviate the need for better protection for the more vulnerable 16 and 17 year olds than exists at present, and it re-emphasises the importance of a comprehensive policy for this age group which is relevant both to their needs and to the demands of the labour market.

A further issue of importance to the planning of benefits for unemployment is the development of changing patterns of work in the labour market. These were identified in a study by Atkinson of the Institute of Manpower Studies, published in 1984. This sees an emerging model of work organisation, involving two groups of workers within companies – a core group and a peripheral group. The core group will be made up of full time, permanent, career employees with skills and experience specific to the firm. These must be prepared to be flexible in their employment practices and willing to undertake retraining if necessary, and in return are offered job stability, good wages and fringe benefits (sick pay, pensions etc). The peripheral group will be made up of three sub-groups; full time workers with easily replaceable skills, few career prospects and little access to training; part time women, public subsidy trainees and temporary workers; and sub-contracted workers, either individual self-employed persons or employees of firms engaged in sub-contracting. All three sub-groups will have little or no job security since the company's goal will be to achieve ready flexibility in the numbers on the payroll (directly or indirectly), in relation to the company's needs and to market demands at any one time. These groups will also tend to be excluded from fringe benefits.[15]

This pattern of work organisation in its most developed form would, the study suggests, probably be found mainly in large companies but elements of it may well be used by both medium and small employers. Hakim, in an article published in late 1987, describes the peripheral group as the 'flexible part' of the labour force, and says that it 'now constitutes a fairly sizeable one third of the workforce rather than an insignificant fringe on the edges of the labour market as so often thought.[16] Among men in work in 1986, 78 per cent were full time permanent employees and 22 per cent were 'flexible' workers. The equivalent figures for 1981 had been 74 per cent and 16 per cent respectively. Among women in employment, in 1986, 49 per cent were full time permanent employees and 51 per cent in flexible work. In 1981, the figures had been 53 and 47 per cent respectively.[17]

Around half the flexible workforce are part time workers. In 1987, 23 per cent of total employment was in part time work, in contrast with 4 per cent back in 1951.[18] The great majority of part timers are women and a large proportion of these are women with child rearing responsibilities'

For men, the principle features of flexible working are first, self-employment, including both operating a one man business and having a self-employed status within firms that undertake sub-contracts (in the construction industry for example); second is temporary work (limited contracts); and third is casual and seasonal work. Women are also involved in these types of employment, but to a lesser extent.

Hakim suggests that the 'dramatic changes in the business climate in recent years,'[19] has produced a heightened preference among employers for short term options over long term commitments in hiring practices. This is most notable among large employers (5,000+ employees), and given that large employers employ the largest proportion of the labour force, 'even a quite minor change in policy in this group can have a visible effect on the composition of the labour force'.[20]

Government is giving its encouragement to these changes in labour practices, in order to increase competitiveness in both manufacturing and service industries.[21] The changes are attractive to some workers – married women with children may welcome part time opportunities, two thirds of temporary workers in 1986 said they wanted this type of work,[22] and many self-employed people value the independence offered by this work status. But others are forced into the flexible sector through lack of alternatives, or attempt and fail to establish viable self-employment.

Moreover, whether by choice or by compulsion, the flexible or peripheral workforce raises issues for a benefit system for unemployed people which, at the time it was established (as Chapter 3 suggested), was 'primarily intended to deal with the short term employment of those normally in regular employment who need to be tided over a period of temporary difficulty'. The benefit system, since that time, has had to adapt to large scale and long term unemployment. But it has never handled long term unemployment well and it is ill equipped to operate within the labour market changes now taking place.

16 and 17 year olds

Before discussing a desirable future structure of benefits for unemployment, consideration needs to be given to a group which has, since September 1988, been virtually excluded from the benefit provisions. The employment demands and opportunities in the future were described in the White Paper *Training for Employment* as follows:

> The most striking feature about the new jobs of the future is the increase we can expect in the demand for skills and qualifications and for flexibility in their use. Many of the jobs created in the next decade or so will be open only to workers with skills and qualifications, especially at technical level and above. In many sectors of the economy there will be less need for unskilled and semi-skilled workers. Even where jobs do not demand of workers a high level of technical skills, they will certainly require greater flexibility in approach, greater breadth of experience, and greater capacity to take responsibility.[23]

Given this scenario, few would disagree with a policy for 16 and 17 year olds which sought to give them a choice between continuing in full time education, entering a good standard training scheme or taking employment, preferably with a training content. Moreover, it would be generally agreed, in principle if not in terms of the detailed provisions, that the process of shifting the pattern of choices of young people from education, work or unemployment, to education, training or work, has needed a combination of steps to make education/training attractive and pressure to move off benefits.

There are still weaknesses in the policies for 'attraction'. The proportion of 16 and 17 year olds who remain in full time education, that is, in school or non-advanced further education, has increased. For 16 year olds, there has been an increase from 35 per cent in full time education in 1974 to 45 per cent in 1987, while for 17 year olds, there has been a smaller increase, from 25 per cent to almost 32 per cent.[24] But it is not clear that young people from low income families, do have a genuine choice to remain in full time education. The failure to develop effective, nationwide arrangements to provide Education Maintenance Allowances (EMAs) and Minor Awards (for school and further education respectively) is a severe handicap to choice.

Since the 1950s, there have been a number of official committees which recommended the development of a national scheme.[25] In the late 1970s, there seemed some hope that such a scheme would finally emerge. Instead, on the limited figures available, it would appear that provision has worsened, not improved, in the 1980s, and that by 1984 a number of local authorities were making no allowances at all.[26] In 1978, as part of the move to national provisions, a Supplementary Benefit disregard for these allowances was introduced at a rate of £7.50 per week for EMAs and £9.50 for Minor Awards. But this was not uprated during the following 10 years.

From April 1988, there will be a marked improvement. No account will be taken of the maintenance allowances in Income Support, Family Credit or Housing Benefit. This could leave room for local authorities to improve their allowance schemes, though it was indicated by government that, if the allowances became so high that they constituted 'a significant alternative system for meeting the living needs of young people', the disregard rule would have to be revised.[27] But the schemes are to be left to local authority discretion and past experience suggests that the result will be uneven provision, good, bad and indifferent, across the country.[28] If young people's choices are not to be dependent on the chance of where they live, a national scheme, or national minimum standards for local schemes will have to be developed.

Young people who left school for financial reasons, or who made an unwise choice to leave but did not then find regular work, did have a second chance to improve their educational qualifications while on Supplementary Benefit under the 12 and 21 hour rules (see Chapter 6). It was estimated in early 1988 that almost one third of 16 and 17 year olds on benefit – some 30,000 of them – were engaged in part time education under these rules, while remaining available for work.[29] This option disappeared with the withdrawal of benefit rights in September 1988.

It has never been seen as appropriate that benefit policy should be geared to providing support in education and it could not be expected that this lost option would be restored, other than as a by-product of changes to mainstream benefit policy. But the ending of this route to a second chance serves to emphasise the importance of getting the main policy on education allowances right, so that young people are not forced to leave education, or be unable to return to it, because of financial barriers.

As seen in Chapter 10, a policy of improving the quality, and therefore the attractiveness, of YTS has been pursued with some success. For a substantial proportion of young people, not in education or work, YTS was the right choice, and one that was freely taken. For this group, there was no need to make drastic changes in the social security provisions, as long as the training offered was good and as long as the training allowances stayed ahead of benefit rates by a noticeable margin.

Nor was there justification, related to young people's behaviour, for effectively withdrawing the right to unemployment benefit from 17 year olds by changing the contribution rules. Those who would have qualified had demonstrated willingness to work and pay contributions, and if they were then out of work 'voluntarily', there were provisions to deal with this.

The government's principal concern was the 16-17 year old group on Supplementary Benefit as unemployed people. The unemployment rate among the under 18s had fallen from 24 per cent in 1983 to 11.5 per cent in 1988.[30] The numbers unemployed and claiming benefit had fallen also – from 204,293 in 1984 to around 92,000 at the beginning of 1988 to 74,450 by August 1988.[31] Not all of these young people spent long periods on benefit. Some were on their way to a YTS placement. Others were in and out of temporary or casual work. Typically at the time of the monthly count, only one quarter had been on benefit for more than 6 months, while the actual numbers were declining.[32]

It could, therefore, be argued that the government's strategy was working and that there were sufficient instruments available to put pressure on those well able to enter work or training. Instead the government lost patience – or seized the opportunity to do what it had long wished to do – and introduced the drastic measures described in Chapter 9.

The Minister (Nicholas Scott) said in the House of Commons in December 1988:

> The point we are trying to make in the new provisions is that, at the age of 16 or 17, young people are at the stage of transition from childhood to the young adult world. We must all be careful about the provision that we make for them.[33]

He went on to apply this to the importance of ensuring that young people did not move straight from education into dependence upon State benefits as 'a normal stage in their transfer to adult life'. Later he asserted that 'all that young people have lost as a result of the implementation of the new arrangements is the option of doing nothing at the public's expense'.[34]

For youngsters living in stable homes, with adequate family incomes, and with responsible parents to protect them and help them deal with the consequences of wrong decisions – their own and other people's –the regime introduced might just about be tolerable, though there is no information on what effects it is having.

But the safety net for those who need it is threadbare. Questioned about the Bridging Allowance, Employment Ministers asserted that 'it is not a form of income support, nor is it intended to support young people in any way over a long period of time'.[35] Asked about the reasons for setting the rate at £15, the only reply was that it is 'more than twice the level of child benefit'.[36] Asked how many young people run out of eligibility for the income available in the Child Benefit extension period, or for eligibility for the Bridging Allowance, without securing work or a YTS place, Employment Ministers have replied variously 'young people are not obliged to report what they are doing after bridging allowance ceases'[37] or that it is a matter for the local authority Careers Service to ensure a YTS place.[38]

Social Security Ministers have had to show more concern. There has been a constant flow of representations from voluntary agencies and groups such as Social Services Directors, drawing attention to weaknesses in the arrangements[39] as well as pressure in Parliament. As a consequence of this, and of the government's own monitoring, the minimum safety net provisions on offer – Income Support for particularly vulnerable groups during the Child Benefit extension period and the severe hardship provisions – have had to be extended on a number of occasions since their introduction. But in March 1989, the Minister (Nicholas Scott) acknowledged that he did not know how many young people had been left without income and what had happened to them. He said, 'I am considering whether we need to collect these figures in future'.[40]

The same Minister said in December 1988: 'it is not possible to regulate for every particular circumstance in which it would be unreasonable to refuse benefit to somebody under 18'.[41] Every effort was being made to protect the vulnerable. But it could equally be argued that the real issue is whether the provisions can be regarded as at all suitable either in relation to training or as a social security safety net.

The Employment Minister quoted earlier asserted that the Bridging Allowance was not a form of income support. But in fact both this allowance and the YTS training allowance are being used as forms of social security. What might be termed the normal use of the provisions would be the payment of Child Benefit for an extended period, followed by entry to YTS for 2 years with room for a change of YTS scheme, where the first turned out to be unsuitable, via a Bridging Allowance. Another normal usage might be entry to work on leaving school, the realisation that the job was a dead end, followed by entry to YTS, perhaps using a Bridging Allowance during the changeover period.

In both these scenarios, the provisions are being used as part of the training arrangements. The goal is to secure YTS training and the allowances help to facilitate this. But for an unknown number of young people, the allowances are operating primarily as social security. Some examples can be given. Someone a few months from their 18th birthday who loses a job and cannot find another, must seek a YTS place or be left without income. Similarly a girl who becomes pregnant, cannot maintain her YTS place but has not reached the 11th week before the expected birth, must seek a further YTS place to cover the intervening months. Young people, from among the highly vulnerable groups entitled to Income Support during the Child Benefit extension period (see Chapter 9), may find themselves unable to cope both with training and with the battle to survive on their own, and yet – unless they can find regular work – must keep reapplying for a YTS place so as to secure an income.

What may then occur, and anecdotal evidence suggests it is already happening, is that employers will decline to accept young people whom they see as unsuitable for training, or where the time available for training is so short as to make it pointless.[42] In training terms these are legitimate decisions – YTS is in these circumstances being misused – but the decisions leave the young people concerned without income.

The alternative then is to turn to the severe hardship provisions – assuming the young person concerned is aware of their existence and is able to meet the very stringent requirements for this benefit described in Chapter 9. But severe hardship payments are intended to be temporary. Pressure will continue to enter YTS or take some kind of employment, including casual work. The vulnerable young people whose needs have been recognised in the Child Benefit extension period, and perhaps for a period beyond this, are quite likely to experience periodic crises before they reach 18 years, and other young people, not originally identified as vulnerable, are running into problems and needing help.

The experience of the first year of the provisions for the 16 and 17 year olds raises grave doubts about this good sense of operating a social security safety net either as an offshoot of a training programme or as a series of reactions to acute crises. Nor is it clear what long term value it is to the country to harry vulnerable young people as they seek to work through the transition from childhood to young adulthood.

The case for making the drastic changes which were introduced in September 1988 was never a strong one. And the case for bringing 16 and 17 year olds back into mainstream policy for unemployed people is strengthened by the fact that, as the numbers of young people decline, more of them will spend time in employment and, as part of the labour force, will be entitled to be treated on a similar basis to other workers, should they become unemployed.

The next section will turn to a discussion of a possible future policy for unemployed people. In the process, attention will be drawn to the place 16 and 17 year olds might have in these arrangements.

A policy framework for unemployed people

In a market economy, unemployment is never likely to be entirely eliminated. Even in times of full employment, some people will spend time in unemployment. In 1951, when the unemployment rate was as low as 1.3 per cent, the annual average number of unemployed was 281,000 (see Table 3.1). Moreover, neither the monthly figures nor the annual averages give a full picture of those claiming unemployment benefits. In 1951, in Great Britain alone, there were 2.6 million claims including people who claimed more than once in the year. In 1987, there were 4.8 million claims, and in some years during the 1980s, the numbers rose above 5 million.[43] Thus, even if unemployment continues to fall, benefit provision will remain important, and if the labour market does develop the forecast flexibility, then more rather than fewer claims might be expected.

Government already acknowledges that 'most benefit claimants are genuinely unemployed and keen to work'.[44] The numbers of disqualifications for voluntary unemployment in 9 months in 1986/7 comprised 9 per cent of total claims for the period (see Chapter 10) – so that 91 per cent of claims were recognised as for involuntary unemployment. On the question of activity in seeking re-employment, the Minister (John Moore) said in 1989, 'the vast majority of claimants – and I stress this – do take the initiative in looking for work'.[45]

And as suggested earlier, government is actively encouraging increased flexibility in the labour market. In *Employment for the 1990s*, the extent of global competition is described and the lesson drawn from this is that:

> ...to meet competition at home and overseas, industry and commerce – since there is intense competition in services – must be increasingly alert to new opportunities, and must adapt to changing technologies, changing markets and changing tastes. This requires a high degree of commercial expertise. It also requires a more adaptable labour force, from top management to the office or shop floor.[46]

Thus the evidence points clearly to the fact that the great majority of the unemployed are 'victims' of the normal functioning of the economy, and that policies which may produce other 'victims' are seen as necessary to the health of the economy. The total numbers involved may decline, but they are likely to remain substantial.

It follows, then, that there is a continuing need for an orderly framework within which earnings interruption can be managed – a framework of appropriate benefit provisions, the right to which is based on reasonable rules which serve to include those who in justice ought to be included and exclude only those who ought, justly, to be excluded; and of supportive programmes which help unemployed people, through information, encouragement, guidance, training and the like, to return to employment as satisfactory as possible to them. Since the objective would be to establish arrangements principally for people out of work through no fault of their own and seeking to return to work, it would be reasonable to expect that the rules and their administration would be designed to minimise any invasion of the privacy and any loss of the personal dignity of unemployed people.

The basis for benefits

There are three possible bases for benefits during unemployment – means tested provision, social insurance, or tax funded benefits not subject to a means test.

A sole reliance on means tested provision, or even the heavy bias towards it that prevails at present, would not meet the requirements set out above. And provision of this type would tend to discourage rather than facilitate labour market flexibility on the part of the labour force. Means tested benefits, as currently operated, do not offer freedom from the invasion of privacy and often involve loss of personal dignity. Even if their operation could be improved, (and there are various propositions for this) there would still be disadvantages. Means tested benefits are designed to be exclusive rather than inclusive. For couples, they are based on household income, typically excluding married or co-habiting women, and for all claimants, there is a degree of uncertainty about eligibility, and particularly in borderline cases, dependent as the benefits are on whether the unemployed person's means fall above or below a particular line.

The fact that benefits may sometimes be available, and sometimes not, undermines an important element in provision for unemployment. The objective since 1911 has been to cushion the impact of the loss of regular earned income without first requiring that the claimant's resources be used up, at least to a prescribed level. Even with benefits by right, it is inevitable that the financial reserves of the individual or family will be run down as the adjustment to a much lower income takes place and commitments taken on when times were better are sorted out. But the assurance of such benefits – in contrast to the unpredictability of means tested provision – permits the necessary financial adjustments to be made in a more measured way, and if unemployment is relatively short term, can enable those concerned to recover from a spell of unemployment more rapidly.

Benefits by right fit better with the goals outlined earlier. They do not require an invasion of privacy and – if properly administered – ought not to offend against personal dignity. They have – or ought to have – the characteristics of predictability and reliability and they serve both to replace part of the lost wage income and, to some extent, to protect the economic well being of the individual or family. They are – or could be – very suited to dealing with the needs arising from the labour market of the future. But as the various 'doubts' in parentheses in this paragraph suggest, much will depend on the applicable rules.

With few exceptions, the evidence present to the 1984/5 Social Security Review was strongly in favour of unemployment provision substantially based on benefits by right. But there was less agreement on how they should be financed. Since the National Insurance scheme, which provides such benefits, is in place, it would seem to be the natural vehicle. But National Insurance has come under criticism in the last decade because it is said not to be 'genuine' insurance, because the contributions which finance it constitute a regressive tax, and because contribution conditions exclude many who, it is believed, ought to be entitled to benefits.

These arguments, however, do not constitute a particularly strong case for moving away from National Insurance. To begin with, if what is meant by the claim that National Insurance is not true insurance, is that it does not operate according to the practices of commercial insurance, then this line of argument is correct. But the scheme was established not as commercial but as social insurance, that is, a scheme in which all risks are pooled, and the State sets the contribution rate (and, in the past, any tax subvention) that it considers is required to meet the contingencies the scheme is to cover. The State also establishes the contribution rules and their relationship to benefit rights.

Moreover, there is nothing in the theoretical base of social insurance which requires a specific type of contribution, or the use of contributions rather than, for example, a social security tax. Regressive taxation, through National Insurance, is not an inherent characteristic of social insurance. Nor are contribution rules which exclude groups and individuals whose risks, logically, ought to be covered in a 'pooled risks' scheme. These are characteristics and rules which governments have chosen to impose and, equally, could choose not to impose. It would, thus, be possible to devise National Insurance rules which kept the scheme relevant to the future labour market.

Although a decision could be taken to provide for the common human risks[47] through taxation, in the same way as provision is made for education, the mechanism of a National Insurance scheme has proved to be publicly acceptable over quite a long period. Similarly, while there is no reason why such a scheme should not be financed by a social security tax, rather than by contributions, the idea of contributions has been long accepted by the public, while an apparently new tax could provoke a degree of hostility. Given that the National Insurance scheme can be reformed to meet the practical (as opposed to the semantic) objections made to it, there seems no obvious reason to abandon the advantages of public acceptability. Indeed, if it continues to be necessary to support a large number of unemployed people, then public support for the desirability of pooling the risk of unemployment and public acceptance of the mechanism by which this is done will be of great importance.

The present role of National Insurance

National Insurance was established as a pooled risks scheme with a fund financed by tripartite contributions – employer/employee/State (see Chapter 2). The government, in its 1985 Green Paper, sought to redefine the scheme from social insurance to a social compact. It approved of the fact that it was financed through contributions, in part because these were publicly acceptable and in part because it was 'right that people in work should see that they are paying for the benefits of those who are not, and are in turn establishing their own rights to these benefits when they need them'.[48] Given this explanation, the distinction between social insurance and a social compact seems a fine one. But one element of the Beveridge scheme, at least, was on the way out.

The 1989 Social Security Act abolished the State subvention to the National Insurance Fund. The Minister (John Moore) argued that it had been justified at a time when contributions were flat rate and had to be kept sufficiently low that low wage earners could afford them. To achieve this, the State supplement was essential. But since

1975, contributions have been wage related. The Minister went on to say:

> The tripartite principle is already effectively a dead letter. The rationale behind it has gone, and the supplement has been shrinking steadily as a proportion of the fund's income from about one third in 1948. It now stands at only 5 per cent. We consider that there is now no need for it at all.[49]

The contributions to the Fund were already covering all expenditure and the abolition of the supplement would, therefore according to the Minister, have no effect.

There may, of course, be a long term effect in the loss of flexibility in the National Insurance scheme. But, more immediately, it might have been expected that the fact that Fund's expenditure was being covered by contributions would have led to a strengthening or at least a maintenance of the rights of contributors. But this is not the case.

In considering this, it is important to distinguish between the numbers of unemployed on the insurance benefit at any one time and the numbers claiming during the year. In November 1987, 675,000 men and women were receiving unemployment benefit, 27 per cent of all the unemployed at that time. But during 1987, there were 4.8 million claims for UB, including second and subsequent claims by the same person.[50] Thus the benefit is in active operation to meet the needs of the short term unemployed.

The government has been emphasising the short term role of National Insurance.[51] But it has also been weakening this and other roles through the new and more demanding contribution rules. As seen in Chapter 9, one of these rules (requiring contribution conditions to be met in the two years preceding unemployment) was expected to exclude 350,000 people from the insurance benefit, all but 50,000 of whom would qualify for the means tested benefit. Other new contribution rules would also act to reduce possible UB entitlement and increase the uncertainty about income during unemployment. As the figures above suggest, some will qualify for Income Support, but others will be left without income, at least in the short term.

These rules will also have a flow on effect to the medium term unemployed (i.e. less than 12 months on benefit). Those deprived of access to up to 12 months Unemployment Benefit will join the already high proportion of unemployed people reliant on the means tested benefit. By November 1987, this proportion (if those awaiting benefit determination are excluded) had already reached around three quarters of the unemployed.[52]

A further factor undermining the ability of the National Insurance schemes to serve the unemployed is the increased stringency and more active application of the voluntary unemployment rules. These not only reduce temporarily the numbers entitled to the insurance benefit, but shorten the maximum possible duration of this benefit by a period equal to the length of the original disallowance. This can be anything up to 26 weeks. During the disallowance period, the individual may be eligible for Income Support at a reduced rate and, if still unemployed when the shortened UB entitlement runs out, will return to full dependence on Income Support earlier than would otherwise have been necessary.

National Insurance has no role at all in relation to the long term unemployed. There has been only one change of note since 1948 in relation to the duration of the benefit, and that was the extension of the maximum period of benefit from 6 to 12 months in 1966. At that time, the numbers unemployed for more than 12 months were quite modest – amounting to 48,000 in Great Britain in October 1966.[53] In spite of a huge increase in numbers of long term unemployed, peaking in 1986/7 at over 1 million, no attempt has been made to adapt the rules of the National Insurance scheme to accommodate even part of this population group. The numbers are now falling – reaching 685,000 in Great Britain and 744,000 in the UK as a whole in April 1985.[54] This may reduce the proportion of unemployed people on Income Support – or more probably stabilise it, given the other factors described above which are adding to the proportion – but long term unemployment remains a major problem and one for which no distinctive benefit policy has been developed.

The Beveridge Report, which recommended the establishment of the National Insurance scheme, has been much quoted in recent years. There is no doubt that it was a seminal report – though it is as well to remember that not all of its proposals reached the statute book, including that for an indefinite benefit by right for the unemployed. But its importance lies not so much in its precise proposals but for the standard of social protection it set, and the spirit of community, social responsibility and mutual aid it promoted in the provision for the common human risks, while still leaving room for individual endeavour. The schemes for social protection established in the 1940s have had to be adapted in the decades that followed and will need to be adapted again for the 1990s. But it would be a poor reflection on our own age if the standards this generation sets fall below those if the 1940s.

The National Insurance Scheme has stood up well to the test of time. It would be over optimistic to suggest that it can be adapted to meet the needs of *all* the unemployed. But it is quite realistic to expect it to maintain a central role in the benefit provision and to seek changes to its rules which would equip it to operate more effectively in the labour market of the present and the foreseeable future.

Maximising access to National Insurance

There has been no open review of the functioning of the National Insurance scheme, either during or since the 1984/5 Social Security Review. But government seems to be pursuing a policy of reducing access to Unemployment Benefit, without any serious attempt to offer a rationale for doing so. If, as has been argued here, National Insurance should play a more, not less, central role in the management of earnings interruption, then access to the benefits of the scheme should certainly not be reduced and ought, if feasible, to be extended.

As long as it remains compulsory for all employees, and their employers, to contribute to National Insurance and that included in that contribution is an element intended to meet the costs of unemployment, there is an assured fund for the support of unemployed people. As unemployment falls, those who re-enter employment begin to pay contributions, and as wages rise above the rate of inflation, the income of the fund grows without the need to increase the percentage rate of NI contributions. If other increases in the funds available are needed, then government could withdraw or lift the higher earnings ceiling, which limits the amount contributed by higher paid workers, or it could restore the State subvention available until 1989. Given this situation, government is in a position to set rules aimed at the maximum feasible access to Unemployment Benefit. But the word 'feasible' recognises that the scope for change is not unlimited.

It has been suggested (for example by the National Consumer Council) that the test for benefit eligibility should be a 'contact with employment' test rather than a contribution test, so as to solve the problem of people being excluded from National Insurance benefits 'by the mathematical vagaries of contribution calculations'.[55] While there is nothing in the principles underlying social insurance which would prevent such a development (provided contributions remained a universal requirement), the idea of the change seems to be based on the assumption that contribution rules cannot be altered. But there is plenty of evidence that they can, and although change so far has usually been for the worse, the contrary could equally apply.

Provision for unemployment is reasonably based on recent employment. It offers an income replacement benefit, following loss of wage income. For the majority, a contribution test offers unarguable evidence of a recent period of work as well as the dignity of claiming benefit by right of contributions made. But this points to the need to consider how those currently excluded from benefit by their inability to meet contribution tests could be brought into the scheme.

Prominent among these are married women who still exercise the Married Women's Option and those women, usually with dependent children, who do part time work at a rate of pay too low to create a requirement to pay NI contributions. The numbers of married and other women exercising the Option has fallen from over 4 million in 1978 to 1.5 million in 1986. It is estimated that by 1990-91, the numbers involved will have fallen to 750,000[56] and a further decline can be expected as older women still paying reduced contributions retire and others lose the right to do so, due to a period of absence from the labour force in excess of the minimum required for its retention. Other women may choose to switch to the payment of full contributions. This is, therefore, an exclusion problem that time will cure. Indeed, there may come a time when the numbers have fallen so low that there will be little point in continuing to impose a penalty for this hangover from the past.

Low paid part time work, on the other hand is not diminishing and, if the labour force forecasts are to be believed, will increase in the future. While there will be stable, though low paid, part time jobs, it can also be expected that many service industry jobs as well as those organised on the core/peripheral model, will be both low paid and unstable. If this is to be the future, then there is every reason to bring this part of the labour force into unemployment benefit provision which seeks to cushion wage loss while further work is sought. Since part time work gives entitlement only to part time benefits, there need not be a problem of too high a wage replacement rate unless the wages were so low as to be set at a scandalous level.

It would be possible to pay benefits without any requirement to pay contributions if wages are too low. A test of labour force attachment could be substituted. But there is already an incentive to hold (and accept) wages below the low limit for National Insurance contributions, so as to avoid their payment by both employer and employee. This incentive would be strengthened if, in spite of this, unemployment benefits were payable.

Recent moves to reduce the incentive to hold wages below the NI contribution level have involved changes in the contribution rate. It used to be the case that the full rate of contribution (9 per cent) had to be paid on the whole wage once it passed the lower earnings limit. Then, stepped contributions were introduced. In October 1989, these were abandoned and a rate of 2 per cent was set for wages below the lower limit, but payable only when the wages pass that limit. But this does not answer the problem of access to benefits for those below the contribution limit. For this purpose it could make sense to impose a nominal contribution – say 1 per cent – on very low earnings, in order to bring these employees into benefit provision This would include not only Unemployment Benefit, but also other NI benefits, and thus be a worthwhile step forward for these part time workers. Bearing in mind that it has been estimated that, in 1989, the cost of the 2 per cent payment would be 86 pence per week,[57] the lower cost of the 1 per cent contribution would be an excellent investment, at tolerable cost.

A second major group currently excluded are 16 and 17 year olds. Already in 1988 (as figures given in Chapter 10 showed), over one quarter of young people of this age group were in employment. The proportion can be expected to grow if the decline in general unemployment continues during a period when the numbers of young people are also declining. In work, they will be paying NI contributions but they have no possibility of qualifying for the insurance benefit before they are 18 years because of the changed rule which requires contribution conditions to be fulfilled in the two years preceding unemployment. It will be suggested later that this rule ought to be reversed. If this is done, then 17 year olds who have met the contribution conditions ought to qualify for benefit as members of the labour force who have met their responsibilities under a pooled

continued need to develop a well trained labour force, ted that a proportion of 16 and 17 year olds will be in ning Scheme or in equivalent schemes. These young people ought properly to be regarded as part of the labour force, though it could not be expected that they make NI contributions since they will not necessarily spend all their time in on the job training. Equally, it would not be reasonable to expect employers to make contributions in respect of trainees who spend part of their time in education.

But under the 2 year contribution rules, a young person who spends 2 years on a YTS scheme will have to work until the age of 20 before becoming eligible for an NI benefit should they become unemployed. Thus they will have been up to 4 years in the labour force – as trainees and then as employees – before they acquire any National Insurance rights. The situation adds to the case for revising the 2 year contribution requirement. But it also suggests that credit provisions should be made for YTS trainees so as to speed up their entry to full NI rights. These credits could properly be tied to completion of YTS training and be related to the length of that training. This would avoid undesirable incentives to leave training early or to prefer shorter to longer training. Moreover, it could be provided that the credits were not activated until a minimum level of contributions had been paid while in employment. Such provisions would serve to integrate young people into the rights enjoyed by others in the labour force, instead of treating them as an excluded 'rightless' group.

Provisions such as these raise another issue. It is being seen as desirable that some young people remain in full time education, gaining the intellectual development and/or specific skills required by the labour force of the future. There would be merit in giving this group access to NI credits, again tied to completion of these courses, to the length of those courses and to the payment of contributions when they enter employment. Such provisions could be important, not only in their own right so as to integrate these young people into normal workforce rights, but so as to avoid any inappropriate incentive to prefer YTS to education.

The National Insurance scheme still does best what it was first planned to do, that is, to offer a bridge between one period of long term employment and another, and especially where the duration of the unemployment is reasonably short. This aspect of its operation is not affected by the 2 year contribution requirement. Those who have had many years of unbroken employment and who, after a spell of unemployment, return to stable long term employment can meet the necessary conditions.

But securing fresh stable employment has never been assured. Even in the early 1970s, when unemployment was still relatively low (see Table 3.1), a survey of workers made redundant showed the difficulties experienced in re-acquiring stability and security in work.[58] In a future labour market when the proportion of stable jobs is declining and, conversely, the 'flexible' or 'peripheral' sector is growing, a return to long term employment will be harder still to achieve. And given that the older the worker, the more difficult it is to acquire any job (see Chapter 7), it is very likely, for this age group, that unstable employment will have to be accepted sooner or later. It can then happen that, in any subsequent periods of unemployment, men and women with substantial contribution records – perhaps of 20 or 30 years of payments – will find themselves deprived of NI rights, whereas justice would suggest that the greater the contribution made to the NI scheme, the more should be the security of benefits by right in unemployment.

The case for reversing the 2 year contribution role does not however, only rest on the older, long time, contributor. The government did not present any substantial case for the change from the existing rules, and no suggestion that these were not functioning perfectly well as a means of establishing an acceptable level of labour force attachment. It can only be assumed, therefore, that there was a desire to place greater emphasis on the means tested provision. But it has been argued here that this is not the appropriate way for the management of income interruption in the present and future labour market. If flexibility is to be the order of the day, there will be a need for the security given by established rights to benefit; and therefore for a return to the earlier rules, at the very least. An even better course of action would be to review the former rules with the object of giving the maximum reasonable consideration, after recent labour force attachment had been established, to the earlier years of contribution.

There will still be the issue of provision for men and women who become unemployed after short term employment, and perhaps find themselves experiencing periods of intermittent unemployment.

Assuming there has been no disallowance of benefit, there is a potential entitlement on first becoming unemployed of 52 weeks of benefit. If during this time, a job is secured which lasts 8 weeks or less, there will be an entitlement under the linkage rules, to the number of weeks of UB not already used up. Once the whole 52 week entitlement is used, then the old rule required that 13 weeks of employment of 16 hours a week or more be served in order to acquire new rights. But there was a certain flexibility built into this in that the weeks worked did not have to be consecutive, nor had they to be worked in any specific period. The present rules retain the 13 weeks/16 hours a week employment provision, but require this to be undertaken in the 26 weeks immediately preceding the new unemployment. Thus, at a time when greater flexibility is being urged upon the labour force, the benefit rules have been made less flexible.

It is of interest to note the relationship of these two rules with the new (1989) provisions for trying out a job for a period of not less than 6 and not more than 12 weeks, without fear of incurring the voluntary unemployment disqualification by leaving if the job proves unsuitable (see Chapter 10). Originally the minimum qualifying period of unemployment was 12 months, by which time any Unemployment Benefit rights would have expired. But after 6 months – the period finally set – there may be unused rights. A trial period of employment ended in more than 6 but less than 8 weeks could enable UB to be reclaimed under the linkage rules. But further perseverance – to the limit of 12 weeks – would carry a penalty. This disadvantage would also apply to someone who had already run out of UB rights. This is because the limit of 12 weeks to the job trial period excludes the possibility of requalifying for UB, being short by one week of the necessary period of work.

The 'trial work' provision is a useful change in the context of helping longer term unemployed people to return to work. But it would have made better sense if it had not been linked, presumably by design, with a rule which sets up a further barrier to access to Unemployment Benefit. Moreover, what will be needed in the labour market of the future – in which both short term and temporary employment is expected to increase – are rules which seek the greater integration of this part of the workforce into the National Insurance provisions for unemployment. It cannot be assumed that this group will be made up of individuals who are foot loose and fancy free or that they are all willingly working in insecure jobs. Where they have dependents and/or commitments, this part of the labour force, above all, will require the orderly framework for the management of earnings interruption referred to earlier.

There is one other labour group in the labour force which has no access to Unemployment Benefit, and that is the self-employed. These have been excluded from any right to this benefit from the outset of the National Insurance Scheme, though they are able to claim the means tested benefit, after a waiting period. There has been a substantial increase in the numbers of the self-employed, especially since 1980, and by the time of the 1987 Labour Force Survey, they constituted 1 in 8 of the labour force.[59] Forecasts about the future labour market suggest that this may increase further.

In 1980, the DHSS issued a Discussion Document about social security for the self-employed,[60] in which it raised the issue of cover for unemployment. The paper suggested that the main problem in extending Unemployment Benefit to the self-employed was that there was no employer to confirm the fact that they were out of work and the reasons for it. There was a possibility that some people could take unfair advantage of the availability of a benefit by right. It went on to suggest that if the right to Unemployment Benefit was extended – and this was seen as a feasible option – it might be necessary to impose a waiting period of up to six weeks, similar to that imposed (at that time) on those who left work voluntarily.

It is understood that the discussion exercise did not produce a large response and that there was little consensus on the most appropriate direction for change. No action was, therefore, taken on the unemployment issue or the other matters in the DHSS paper, and virtually no attention was paid to the self-employed in the Social Security Review. This outcome might have been understandable in 1980, but in light of the trends in self-employment, there is a good case for a fresh review of the position of the unemployed who were formerly self-employed. More needs to be known of the numbers of self-employed who claim Income Support, their experience of the claims process, the length of time they spend on benefit, the frequency of benefit spells and whether they return to the labour market as employed or self-employed persons. This would provide a starting point for examining whether access to the NI benefit would be helpful and, if so, what, if any, extra rules would have to be applied to self-employed claimants.

Duration of Unemployment Benefit

It needs to be said first that there is no case for reducing the current 52 week duration of Unemployment Benefit. There is (at the time of writing) no proposition on the table for such a reduction. But inevitably the government's recent emphasis on the short term role of the NI benefit and its tendency (in relation to other programmes) to refer to those out of work for 6 months or more as long term unemployed people – a term formerly used to mean 12 months or more out of work – raises the possibility that a reduction in benefit duration may be contemplated.

In April 1989, some 46 per cent of UK unemployed men and women had been out of work for between 6 and 12 months.[61] Even if the actual numbers fall, it is clear that a reduction to a 26 week duration would affect a significant proportion of the unemployed. A loss of access to the NI benefit by this group would represent a further undermining of the rights of National Insurance contributors. Moreover, a reduction of this kind would have a severe effect on unemployed married women contributors, since they would not qualify in their own right for any substitute means tested benefit.

On the opposite side of the coin, it would not really be feasible to propose any general extension in the duration of the NI benefit. While this would be justified in principle – especially in periods of high unemployment when jobs are simply not available – if there is a desire to maximise access to the NI benefit for the main body of the unemployed, then the additional costs of a general extension in duration could not easily be contemplated.

But this does not necessarily rule out selective policies for extended duration. These might simply be related to the number of years of contributions, but a more useful approach would be to base an extension – or even a right to an indefinite benefit duration – on age and the number of years in the labour force. A start might be made on men and women who were 55 years and over and who had spent at least 25 years in the labour force. And if high long term unemployment among the 50-54 year old group persists, the age might be lowered and the required years reduced to 20. Such a rule would help not only the older unemployed in general, but would assist disabled unemployed people, a significant proportion of whom are in this older age group (see Chapter 8). It could also offer greater justice to those long term unemployed married women, who are at present excluded from income replacement benefits after 52 weeks in spite of lengthy labour force attachment, before and after marriage.

This extended benefit would quite properly be made subject to availability for work rules of a reasonable nature. It would also make sense to ensure that the right could be reclaimed after periods of employment, including quite short periods, so that no hindrance or disincentive is put in the way of older unemployed people who seek to work whenever they can.

These measures will not give full protection to the older man or woman against the impact of unemployment on retirement provision. It will still be impossible during unemployment to maintain second pension contributions – to an occupational pension, to SERPS or to a personal pension. But it would reduce the necessity to use up all or most of the reserves accumulated for retirement, as would be necessary to qualify for a means tested benefit. Moreover, to the extent that employment can be secured, additional pension contributions may be possible for those who have not claimed an early pension. The proposals would also give greater protection to married women for the accumulation of credits for the NI Retirement Pension. Given the present structure of retirement provision, these various advantages offered by extended NI benefits in unemployment, are probably the best that can be hoped for.

The position of those already receiving an occupational pension would have to be considered. To the extent that they retain an entitlement to all or part of a benefit for unemployment and fulfill the rules required of unemployed people, then there is no reason to exclude them from extended rights. But a change in practice is needed for this group. The occupational pension level which triggers the reduction of Unemployment Benefit (£35) has not been uprated since 1980. This means that only a proportion of their income – the NI benefit – is inflation proofed. This is an injustice which ought to be put right.

The level of benefit

Although the changes proposed so far would increase the numbers of unemployed people with an entitlement to the NI benefit, a proportion of the unemployed would still rely on Income Support. And, as the benefits stand at present, many unemployed people would need to claim supplementation of their NI benefit from Income Support. Furthermore, the standard of living offered by both Unemployment Benefit alone and by Income Support as a supplement or as the main income, is too low to offer real protection from the effects of unemployment.

It will be recalled (from Chapter 9) that there was plenty of evidence, prior to the 1986 Social Security Act, that unemployment was the main cause of low income and that many unemployed people were subject to financial hardship, including those who were on what was then Supplementary Benefit(SB). A small but detailed study of 67 unemployed families with children in Tyne and Wear, undertaken by Bradshaw and Holmes just before the establishment of the Income Support scheme, gave further confirmation of the low standard of living of unemployed families on benefit. In a summary of their findings, the authors described the lives of these families as 'marked by the unrelieved struggle to manage, with dreary diets and drab clothing' and characterised by 'constant restriction' in almost every aspect of their activities.[62]

The authors were able to compare the income of 43 of the families with children on Supplementary Benefit with the income they would receive on the Income Support scheme then just about to be introduced. After uprating the SB to allow for increases that would have been given for inflation (had the SB scheme remained in force), they found that 20 of the families would be worse off under Income Support. Some 7 of these would be protected by the transitional payments which guaranteed no cash loss of benefit at the point of change, but these would become worse off as the transitional payments were eroded by inflation. The 20 losers were worse off by sums ranging from 10 pence to £12.20 pw, while the 23 gainers were better off by sums ranging from 20 pence to £10.92 pw. The higher end of the losses arose from the ending of various additional payments. The higher end of the gains stemmed from the improved disregards for those unemployed for more than 2 years.[63]

If the 1989 UB rates are compared with the Income Support rates, it can be seen that a single person (over 25) and a childless married couple (over 18) are marginally better off on Unemployment Benefit, though access to passport benefits such as free prescriptions will not automatically be available. But a family with children will be noticeably worse off on Unemployment Benefit. Leaving aside such items as free school means and milk – available to Income Support (IS) but not UB recipients – the principle difference lies in the availability of the Family Premium for IS recipients and the payment to them of child dependency additions (CDAs). UB families suffer a double problem in that they have no CDAs, only Child Benefit, and that benefit has been frozen for the last two years, and is about to be frozen for a third year. Recipients of Unemployment Benefit did gain an improvement in Housing Benefit in 1988 (though this was principally designed for low paid workers), but this does not alter the comparison just made. It merely removed an earlier injustice.

The evidence both of the official calculations (see Chapter 9) and of the study just quoted, indicates that there is still a problem of inadequacy of benefits for unemployed people – a problem compounded for IS recipients who are under 25 and who live away from home, by the lower rate paid to them. But in spite of this, the chances of a general increase in the rates paid to unemployed people are limited.

The long standing principle of less eligibility – now given the modern name of the unemployment trap – continues to exert a downward pressure on benefit levels. Given that much of the additional employment of the future is expected to be in lower paid jobs, government's desire to maintain work incentives through the mechanism of low benefits is likely to continue. But there might be room to improve the income of unemployed people and reduce the need to claim supplementation from Income Support, through two policy changes.

The first would involve both the restoration of child dependency additions to Unemployment Benefit, and the setting of these rates, and those for Income Support children, at a higher level than the present IS rates. Making such a change without adverse consequences would be facilitated by the structure of the Family Credit scheme. Provided the rates for children in that scheme were increased in line with those for unemployed families (and other families also in the case of Income Support), there need be no loss of work incentives as they relate to children. All of these families with children need a better income, so the upgrading of provision for children would have all round merit. If this was accompanied by the return to regular uprating of Child Benefit, it would be even better, since Child Benefit, payable to unemployed and employed alike, is a valuable weapon in overcoming the unemployment trap.

Such a policy would also reduce the need for UB families to claim Income Support. But it would not obviate it altogether. Where they are paying a mortgage, help with this is available under Income Support but not along with UB. This is unlikely to change until the Housing Benefit scheme itself is reformed so that it assists low income owner occupiers with more than their rates (or Community Charge) bill – a long overdue reform.

The second policy could help a wider range of unemployed people. This would involve a more substantial reform of the disregard rules than was undertaken by the Social Security Review (see Chapter 9).

The objectives of such a policy would be twofold, with a sub goal of improving the position of wives of unemployed men. The objectives would be:

- to enable unemployed people who are unable to find employment (of at least 24 hours per week) to keep a foothold in the labour market. In so doing they would maintain work habits and skills and would be in greater contact with opportunities for full time employment;
- to enable unemployed people to add to their income so as to raise their standard of living and perhaps accumulate modest reserves. These reserves would both assist families to stay out of debt (including debts to the Social Fund) and give them the greater confidence needed to embark on training or a direct return to full time employment;
- to free the wives of unemployed men from the most severe of the constraints on work inherent in the present disregard rules.

To take the last point first, the principle change needed here is to the rules related to Income Support. Under the Unemployment Benefit rules, the wife's disregard is separate from that of her husband. It is tied to the rate of her dependency addition, so that at £21.40 (in 1989/90) it offers reasonable scope for work. Because of the link with the dependency addition, her disregard is inflation proofed. The addition will be withdrawn in full if her earnings exceed that level, but earnings beyond that point will not affect her husband's benefit, and so will add to the family income.

It could not be hoped that disregard rules of this kind could be make available under Income Support, a means tested scheme based on household income. But if a separate set of disregard rules for husband and wife in a family on Unemployment Benefit is possible, there is no reason, in principle, why the wife's disregard should be tied so closely to her husband's in an Income Support family. A separate rate for the wife could be set, from the time of coming on benefit, at the same level as other Income Support recipients. At present this is £15 per week, but there is no provision for inflation proofing. There is a strong case for maintaining the value of this disregard for all recipients. If it was right to allow £15 earnings in 1988 (when the figure was fixed), it would surely be right to allow earnings of equivalent value in subsequent years. It would, in theory, also be appropriate to review the level every few years in relation to wages. If, for example, £15 pw enabled 6 hours of work a week at £2.50 an hour in 1988 the goal might be to maintain the right to work for at least 6 hours if wage levels rose ahead of inflation. Unfortunately the fact that benefits are linked only to prices would handicap such a policy, since the disregard could then become disproportionate to the benefit, whereas an inflation proofed disregard would simply maintain the original relationship with the benefit rate.

The present disregard for men and single women – £2 per day on Unemployment Benefit, £5 per week on Income Support for the first two years – is so far out of step with current wage levels as to be an invitation either not to attempt to work at all or to work without declaring the earnings. The rates ought, therefore, to be raised to a more realistic level and to be inflation proofed. The limits to realism in this case are set by the low level of the benefit itself, but there is room for somewhat more generous rates.

A suggestion of interest which emerged from a social security review in Australia[64] was that both the unemployed themselves and the wives of unemployed men should be permitted to accumulate their own unused earnings disregards up to a maximum and to earn up to this limit without benefit loss in casual or seasonal work. It was thought that, in the case of single women and all men, it might be necessary to limit this right to long term unemployed people. The proposal raises administrative problems, but these should not be unsoluble. Another idea, with a similar objective, was put forward by the organisation Action in 1988. This was for a yearly income allowance for unemployed people over 50 years, permitting earnings of up to £500 in the year by a single person and £750 for a married couple, without loss of benefit. It would enable the over 50s to demonstrate their abilities to employers and thus help to overcome age discrimination.[65] Another proposal by Action has been partially taken up by government in 1989. In a pilot scheme called Action Credit, former ET trainees on Income Support will be able to work up to 23 hours per week, earning up to £43 per week, without affecting their benefit. The money earned will be saved for them and paid over when they begin a job that takes them off benefit.

These, and other possible initiatives, indicate that there is a potential for a more constructive approach to disregard policies. It is worth noting that any improvement in these policies could have a useful flow on effect. It will be recalled that income of current ET trainees could be affected by the earnings of the wife of a trainee or by extra money earned (by trainees) during training. Better benefit disregard policies could reduce these discouraging effects.

Finally in this discussion of benefit levels, there are two groups who require attention. The first of these is single people aged 18-24, together with couples under 18 years. Now that the accommodation costs of those living independently are met by Housing Benefit, rather than through Board and Lodging allowances, it would be reasonable to re-introduce a distinction in Income Support for this age group between householders and non-householders, paying the former at the full adult rate. The gap between the under 25 rate and the full rate in 1989/90 is £7.50 for a single person and £13.20 for a couple under 18 years. The extra payment which a restoration of the full adult rate would bring is, therefore, not large enough to create a 'perverse incentive' to leave home, but is big enough to be of help to those who need to leave home – for work reasons and because of family circumstances – and also for those who seek to move to greater independence at an appropriate time. Such a policy would go with the grain of human development and not seek to turn back the clock to a period when remaining at home, semi-dependant on parents, was the norm for this age group, at least until marriage.

The second group – and one requiring urgent attention – is the 16 and 17 year olds. The young unemployed acquired a particularly 'villainish' status in the 1980s, but it is worth remembering that when there was full employment in the UK, there was no problem of youth unemployment, even among the age group then entitled to benefit (see Chapter 6). And it was argued earlier that the strategies adopted by the government in the mid 1980s were working, so that there was no need for the drastic action on benefits that was taken. Looking to the future, there are a number of favourable factors. The numbers of young people are declining; employment opportunities are increasing; and YTS is now offering worthwhile training. Thus, it will be possible to absorb most young unemployed people into the labour force, as employees or trainees, and if steps were taken to improve the system of education allowances, young people would have a good range of realistic choices.

All this suggests that there is no sound reason why 16 and 17 year olds should not be brought back into social security entitlement, including Income Support. They are as much in need of orderly arrangements to manage earnings interruptions as adults, and if the more vulnerable among them are to be protected, then more need of reliable provision. It need not be thought that a proposal of this kind is intended to offer carte blanche to this age group. The normal benefit controls would have to apply and, it will be suggested below that the help and advice available to young people may need strengthening. But in the 1990s, this country ought to be able both to 'manage' and to protect its young people without resorting to the kind of measures now operating.

Benefit control and special employment measures

A policy which gives unemployed people greater access to benefits by right of contributions needs to be balanced by active programmes which give them advice and help to get back to work. Such programmes are especially necessary during a period when unemployment is declining. At such a time, the benefits of an improved labour market can all too easily by-pass the long term unemployed and particularly the older and the disabled unemployed. Moreover, in a changing labour market, today's unemployed people have to be far more adaptable than their predecessors in more stable times. Career change presents many difficulties, not only in personal terms, but because it involves entering strange territory where the network of familiar contacts and kinship connections is not available. In this situation, the availability of New Client Advisers, Restart, Claimant Advisers, job clubs, Disablement Rehabilitation Officers, and for young people, Careers Officers, can all be welcomed as positive contributions to a policy for the unemployed. But there are provisos to this.

First, policy development ought to be concentrated on improving the quality and scope of the advice and help available rather than on strengthening the ability to detect non-availability for work. A decision to seek advice or a response to letters inviting attendance at an interview ought not to be turned into a high risk strategy – the risk of losing one's benefit income. Rather, it should be possible to make use of these programmes with confidence and in the expectation of receiving skilled help. It may be noted also that such an emphasis would give greater job satisfaction to staff who genuinely seek to be of assistance to unemployed people.

Second, it ought not to be the goal of these services simply to get an unemployed person off benefit and into any job, however dead end, low paid or unstable. It has always been recognised that unemployed people cannot hold out for lengthy periods for their ideal job. Moreover, the need to adapt to a changing labour market must be recognised. Unemployed people will often have to be helped to accept a career change, to try out different jobs or to undergo re-training. But to pressurise unemployed people, with threat of loss of benefit, into sub-standard and/or unstable jobs is a short sighted policy and may produce little benefit saving if the end result is more frequent unemployment. In the long run, to resettle an unemployed person in a job with decent pay and prospects or one which can realistically be seen as a step towards longer term stability, would be a more useful contribution, not only to individual well being, but to the health of the economy and to savings in social security costs - including savings on means tested benefits in retirement.

Third, if young people – 16 and 17 year olds – are to have their benefit rights restored, it may be necessary to strengthen the programmes which advise and assist this age group. This would include working in co-operation with statutory and voluntary agencies which have a specific concern for the most vulnerable of our young people. Their experience, and the personalised help they are equipped to offer, can do much to overcome the problem of assisting young people who cannot fit easily into the standard programmes, because of their special difficulties.

Fourth, the quality of the schemes to which the unemployed are referred, needs to be kept under review, and where necessary improved. The Enterprise Allowance Scheme has proved useful, but the allowance needs to be reviewed. It was set at £40 pw when the scheme was introduced in 1982 and still stands at £40 pw in 1989. It ought to be increased and then inflation proofed. The training offered under YTS has been steadily improved, but the scheme needs careful monitoring so that some employers are not permitted to misuse it. The ET scheme is still relatively young and it is clearly suffering from growing pains. High standards of training, planned appropriately for the individual trainee, need to be further developed so that the attractiveness and effectiveness of the scheme is improved and its quality kept under review. The improved child dependency additions and the changed disregard rules would upgrade the income of some trainees, but these would still be a case for paying the whole of the trainees' travelling expenses so that the full value of the addition to benefit is retained. This addition also needs inflation proofing.

Fifth, if unemployed people are to be encouraged to accept low paid work, for lack of better possibilities, then it is essential that the benefit arrangements – for Family Credit and Housing Benefit – work effectively so as to provide a smooth transition from one benefit income to another. At this level of income, any disruption in the financial arrangements can create quite serious difficulties.

Sixth, in all of these arrangements, the needs of groups who suffer from exclusion and discrimination should warrant special attention. These include members of the ethnic minority population, disabled unemployed people and the unemployed over 50 years. It is particularly important not to write off the older unemployed – who may well include members of the other two groups – or to give them such a low priority that it amounts to the same thing. It ought not to be assumed that older workers are incapable of being re-trained or of rising to new challenges. But they may need extra help to do so.

Even with policies as proposed above, there would still be a need to deal with fraudulent claims. Improved disregard rules could, in fact, reduce fraud so far as this relates to undeclared earnings, but working full time and claiming benefit might still have to be dealt with. No one questions the necessity for this, as long as genuine claimants are not harassed in the process.

Similarly there will be a need for some benefit sanctions to be available. Again this is hardly questioned. The Minister (Nicholas Scott) closing the second reading debate on what became the 1989 Social Security Act, said of the new actively seeking work provisions: 'genuine claimants have nothing to fear from our proposals'.[66] At the time of writing this chapter, it is not possible to judge how these provisions will be administered in practice. But if these regulations are taken in conjunction with the severe penalties in use for voluntary unemployment and for being found unavailable for work, then unemployed people – however genuine – are bound to approach the benefit and employment services with deep unease. At whatever point they engage with these services – and the range of possible contact points is now considerable – they must fear that they may fall foul of one or other of the rules which trigger a benefit sanction. And if they are judged wrongly, they must nevertheless suffer the consequences until an appeal tribunal hears the case and sets the matter right.

At the end of Chapter 10, it was asked whether the three streams of policy – benefit provisions, the special employment measures and benefit controls – were in reasonable balance with one another. It has to be said that the network of benefit sanctions is seriously out of balance with the other policies and is acting to undermine both the protection for the unemployed against the consequences of unemployment and the programmes designed to help and encourage unemployed people back into worthwhile jobs. Government insists that it is not seeking to harass unemployed people, only to encourage them back to work.[67] If this is so, the way ahead should be to strengthen the confidence of unemployed people in the programmes designed to encourage them, not to resort to the introduction of one punitive measure after another.

Some special concerns
The disabled unemployed

The older (50+) disabled unemployed will be assisted by the provisions for indefinite Unemployment Benefit proposed earlier, and all disabled unemployed people can benefit from the other rule changes proposed. Both YTS and ET make special provision for disabled trainees and these are useful provisions, provided they are implemented effectively. But younger (ie under 50 years), disabled unemployed people may nevertheless find themselves spending longer than average periods on Income Support, without the access to benefit additions formerly available.

The Department of Employment is undertaking a review of the policies and services supported by the Department and the Training Agency for people with disabilities.[68] The government has also promised a review of social security benefits for all disabled people. Rather than propose separate changes for the unemployed among them, as, to some extent, was done by the Social Security Review, it would be better sense to await the full review so that their needs can be considered in the context of all the needs of disabled people, and in conjunction with the findings of the employment review. The wisdom of adopting this approach is re-inforced by the necessity to consider how people move between the classification 'disabled' and that of 'unemployed', and the extent to which account should be taken of labour market opportunities when these decisions are made. Moreover, some of the benefits for disabled people generally, also serve to assist those who seek to remain in the labour market – for example the Mobility Allowance. It should be stressed, however, that proper attention needs to be given to the particular needs of disabled unemployed people in the proposed review of disability income.

The position of married women

The proposals made above would increase the access to Unemployment Benefit of older married women with a long labour market attachment, very low paid part time women and married women who can establish Unemployment Benefit rights, as well as improving the position of wives of unemployed men. This, however, still leaves a group of both short and long term unemployed married women who have no benefit rights because the means tested benefit aggregates the income of husband and wife.

It is difficult to see a solution to this short of a fundamental reform of the means tested safety net, involving the disaggregation of benefits and the allocation of individual benefit rights. In this context, married women could retain the right to claim as an unemployed person as long as they demonstrated availability for work. Such a reform is often talked about but is not on the immediate political agenda. Government is now saying that in the 1990s, there will be more need than ever to attract and retain the services of women in the labour force. Part of this process ought to be a review of means to secure greater rights to benefits in unemployment.

A service with dignity

It is worth saying again that the vast majority of the unemployed are out of work through no fault of their own, and seek only to return to stable employment as soon as possible. Becoming and being unemployed is for many a devastating experience. Both for adults who have previously worked and for young people seeking to enter the labour market, the process of job search, with its many rebuffs and disappointments, is a profoundly discouraging process.

It is all the more important, therefore, that the benefit system is not only designed to protect them against the economic consequences of unemployment, but that it is administered in a way which does not undermine their self-respect and self-confidence.

It is acknowledged that there must be rules which determine the right to benefit and rules on availability for work, on efforts at job search, on willingness to undertake training or re-training, where appropriate, and on co-operation with other efforts to facilitate a return to the labour force. Rules such as these which are clearly set out and based on reasonable requirements in relation to the current state of the labour market need not be seen as 'hostile' to the unemployed. Indeed, most unemployed people would expect such rules and find them acceptable. Equally, services which are designed to encourage and guide the unemployed, to combat the discouragement of the long term unemployed and to provide good quality training are highly desirable and welcome to the unemployed in general.

But there is a fine line between rules which are recognised to be a necessary accompaniment of benefit provision for the unemployed, and rules which operate on the assumption that unemployed people are, as a group, out 'to milk' the system. Equally, there is a line between help and encouragement for unemployed people and the harassment of people who are dependent for their daily needs and those of their families on the social security system.

Unemployment is no longer a temporary phenomenon. Some part of our society will be suffering from its effects for the rest of the century and beyond. They have a right to the support of those who are fortunate enough to be in work – just as they should show solidarity to the unemployed when they, themselves, return to work. And they also have a right to a service which respects their personal dignity and worth.

Addendum

In January 1990 (just as this study was being prepared for publication), the government issued a paper - *The Way Ahead: Benefits for Disabled People*[1] - in which it set out the results of an internal review of disability income. It was not the far reaching review that many had hoped for, but it did include some proposals of relevance to disabled unemployed people.

The paper acknowledged that higher unemployment made it more difficult for people to get jobs if their employability was reduced by disability.[2] It also noted three groups among disabled people[3] - the most severely disabled who received one of the two rates of Attendance Allowance and/or the Mobility Allowance, and might also have entitlement to the Income Support disability premium; the least severely disabled people who worked and thus had earned income; and a middle group who were less likely to be able to work and add to their income through earnings, but who did not qualify for the social security provisions for the severely disabled.

A third problem identified related to work incentives for people classified for purposes of social security as disabled and claiming the Invalidity Benfit or SDA.[4] The present therapeutic earnings rules had unsatisfactory aspects. Not everyone who wanted to work would qualify for this allowance. If they did, and if subsequently the earnings exceeded £35 pw or the individual was medically certified as capable of work, the allowance would be withdrawn. In addition, people whose earning potential was low could be worse off in work than on benefit, and unless they had dependent children, they would not qualify for Family Credit. Moreover, a failed attempt at working, if it ran beyond the eight weeks of the benefit linking rule, could mean a return to the short term benefits and a six months wait before requalifying for the higher, long term, Invalidity Benefit.

The 'substantial decline in unemployment in the last three years' had, the paper suggested, opened up new opportunities.[5] And the review of employment services for disabled people, then taking place, would strengthen the ability of those services to assist in overcoming barriers to employment.[6] For the 'middle' group on benefit, a new non-means tested Disability Allowance was to be introduced. This would be available for people who became disabled before the age of 65 years and would comprise the existing Attendance and Mobility Allowances, plus, in each case, a new lower tier of benefit worth £10 pw. This lower tier would be payable to those with day time caring needs insufficient to qualify for the present day Attendance Allowance, and mobility needs below the level required for the current Mobility Allowance. For those on Income Support, the new lower rate of Disability Allowance would qualify the recipient for the disability premium, which was itself being improved.

To improve work incentives, there were two main proposals. The first was a new benefit, a Disability Employment Credit, on the lines of Family Credit, which would supplement the earnings of single and married people without children who had qualified for one of the disability benefits.[7] Someone receiving the Invalidity Benefit or SDA before starting work and qualifying for the Disability Employment Credit would, if they again became incapable of work, be eligible immediately for the long term disability benefits they had received before. This new benefit and the related rules would be of assistance not only to those now unemployed, but also to those who might otherwise have claimed the therapeutic earnings allowance, to those working part time and those in low wage full time work.

One further change involved the withdrawal of an existing benefit.[8] Those who lost earning power as a result of an industrial injury were entitled to a Reduced Earnings Allowance from the

Industrial Injuries Scheme. On the grounds that the majority of recipients were also receiving the Invalidity Benefit, this benefit is to be abolished. In the process, it will also be withdrawn from those in work but on lower wages than before the industrial injury.

With the exception of the last, the proposed changes are likely to be of benefit to disabled people, and will improve the position of some disabled people now classified as unemployed, who qualify for the new lower Disability Allowance. But much will depend on where the lines are drawn. A stringent set of requirements for the lower Disability Allowance would reduce the possible qualifying population. This, in turn, would limit the numbers eligible for the Disability Employment Credit, whose means test rules will also be of importance. Thus, for disabled unemployed people, their social security classification will still be a crucial factor determining how they are treated. The new benefits will not be introduced until April 1992. At that point, when the rules are known, it will be possible to make a better assessment of the changes being proposed.

References

1. *Reform of Social Security: Programme for Action*, op.cit., p.2
2. Ibid.
3. Manpower Services Commission, *Corporate Plan 1986-1990*, MSC, Sheffield, 1986, p.34.
4. *Corporate Plan 1987*, 1991 op.cit., p.49.
5. *Employment for the 1990s*, CM 540, HMSO, London, 1988, pp.5-13.
6. *Employment Gazette*, June 1989.
7. Ibid, June 1989, s16.
8. *Training for Employment*, op.cit., pp.6-13.
9. *House of Commons Hansard*, 4 March 1987, 873.
10. Ibid, 7 February 1989, 960.
11. *Employment Gazette*, June 1989, s16.
12. Department of Employment, *Press Notice*, 'Preliminary results from the 1987 Labour Force Survey for Great Britain and revised employment estimates incorporating those results', London, 16 February 1988.
13. *Employment Gazette*, June 1989, S16.
14. *Employment for the 1990s*, op.cit., p.6.
15. John Atkinson, *Flexibility, Uncertainty and Manpower Management*, Institute of Manpower Studies, Brighton, 1984.

16. Catherine Hakim, 'Trends in the flexible workforce', *Employment Gazette*, November 1987, pp.549-60.
17. Ibid, p.550.
18. Ibid, p.556.
19. Ibid, p.558.
20. Ibid.
21. *Employment for the 1990s*, op.cit., pp.10-13.
22. 'Trends in the flexible workforce', op.cit., p.559.
23. *Training for Employment*, op.cit., p.19.
24. 'Education and labour market status of young people', *Employment Gazette*, September 1987, pp.459-64.
25. Steven Cooper, *The Education and Training Benefits*, PSI, London, 1985.
26. *House of Commons Hansard*, 10 April 1984, 164-8.
27. Ibid, 7 April 1987, 281-2.
28. *The Education and Training Benefits*, op.cit.
29. *House of Commons Hansard*, 13 January 1988, 312.
30. Ibid, 29 July 1988, 847.
31. *Employment Gazette*, March 1984, S34, *House of Commons Hansard*, 13 January 1988, 315 and 26 January 1989, 750.
32. Ibid, and 13 January 1988, 310.
33. Ibid, 5 December 1988, 146.
34. Ibid, 150.
35. Ibid, 7 March 1988, 41.
36. Ibid.
37. Ibid, 14 December 1988, 607.
38. Ibid, 10 November 1988, 299.
39. Ibid, 6 March 1989, 590, 24 April 1989, 752-3, for example.
40. Ibid, 6 March 1989, 589.
41. Ibid, 5 December 1988, 148.
42. NACAB, *Briefing on the Social Security Bill*, June 1989 and *House of Commons Hansard*, 5 December 1988, 145.
43. Ministry of National Insurance, *Annual Report 1951*, p.6 and *Social Security Statistics*, 1988.
44. *Training for Employment*, op.cit., p.33.
45. *House of Commons Hansard*, 10 January 1989, 715.
46. *Employment for the 1990s*, op.cit., p.10.
47. Unemployment, maternity, sickness, disability, one parenthood, retirement are the typical 'risks'.

48. *Reform of Social Security*, Vol.1. op.cit, p.40.
49. *House of Commons Hansard*, 10 January 1989, 719.
50. *Social Security Statistics 1988*, (on Unemployment Benefit).
51. See Chapter 9 and House of Commons Hansard, 1 March 1988, 870 for examples.
52. *Social Security Statistics 1988* (on Unemployment Benefit).
53. *Department of Employment Gazette*, June 1978, p.676.
54. *Employment Gazette*, June 1989, s25.
55. NCC, *Of Benefit to All*, op.cit., p.133.
56. *House of Commons Hansard*, 21 October 1988, 1029.
57. Ibid, 24 April 1989, 67.
58. W.W. Daniel, *Whatever happened to the Workers in Woolwich: A survey of redundancy in S.E.London*, PEP, London 1972.
59. Department of Employment, *Press Notice*, 16 February 1988, op.cit.
60. Department of Health and Social Security, *The Self-Employed and Social Insurance: A Discussion Document*, DHSS, London, 1980.
61. *Employment Gazette*, June 1989, s.25.
62. Jonathan Bradshaw, and Hilary Holmes, *Living on the Edge – a study of the living standards of families on benefit in Tyne and Wear*, Tyneside Child Poverty Action Group, London, 1989.
63. Ibid, pp.38-42.
64. Social Security Review, *Income Support for the Unemployed in Australia: Towards a More Active System*, Department of Social Security, Canberra, 1988, pp.122-7.
65. *An Allowance for Age – Work and the Over-50s*, Action, London, 1988.
66. *House of Commons Hansard*, 10 January 1989, 787.
67. Ibid, 26 April 1989, 995.
68. Ibid, 7 February 1989, 964.

References to Addendum
1. *The Way Ahead: Benefits for Disabled People*, Cm 917, HMSO, London 1990.
2. Ibid., p.11.
3. Ibid., p.28
4. Ibid., p.33-4.
5. Ibid., p.11.
6. Ibid., p.28-9.

7. Ibid., p.33-5.
8. Ibid., p.38.

Alphabetical list of sources

Abel-Smith, Brian and Townsend, Peter, *The Poor and the Poorest*, Bell and Son, London, 1965.

'Age and Redundancy' *Department of Employment Gazette*, September 1978, pp.1032-9.

An Allowance for Age - work and the over 50s, Action, London, 1988.

Atkinson, John, *Flexibility, Uncertainty and Manpower Management*, Institute of Manpower Studies, Brighton, 1984.

Berthoud, Richard *Evidence to the Supplementary Benefits Review*, PSI, London, 1984.

Berthoud, Richard *The Examination of Social Security*, PSI, London 1985.

Berthoud, Richard, *The Reform of Supplementary Benefit*, Working Paper A, PSI, London, 1984.

Berthoud, R., Brown, Joan C., and Cooper, S., *Poverty and the Development of Anti-Poverty Policy in the UK*, Heinemann, London, 1981.

Beveridge, Sir William, *The Unemployment Insurance Statutory Committee*, Political Pamphlet No. 1, London School of Economics, 1937.

Black, Boyd and Foster, Garry, 'The Youth Training Programme in Northern Ireland, *Employment Gazette*, April 1983 pp.153-7.

Bradshaw, Jonathan *et al*, 'The impact of unemployment on the living standards of families', *Journal of Social Policy*, 12/4 1983, pp.435-52.

Bradshaw, Jonathan and Holmes, Hilary, *Living on the Edge: A study of Living standards of families on benefit in Tyne and Wear*, Tyneside Child Poverty Action Group, London. 1989.

Brown, Joan C. *Annex VII to Chapter IV of the Commissions' Final Report to the Council on the First Programme of Pilot Schemes and Studies to Combat Poverty*, Commission of the European Communities, V/1051/81EN, Brussels, 1981.

Brown, Joan C., *Children in Social Security*, PSI, London, 1984.

Brown, Joan C., *The Disability Income System*, PSI London, 1984.

Brown, Joan C., *Low Pay and Poverty in the United Kingdom*, PSI, London, 1981.

Brown, Joan C. and Small, Stephen, *Occupational Benefits as Social Security*, PSI, London, 1985.

Bruce, Maurice (ed), *The Rise of the Welfare State: English Social Policy 1601-1971*, Weidenfeld and Nicolson, London, 1973.

Burton, John, *Would Workfare Work?*, Employment Research Centre, University of Buckingham, 1987.

Byrne, Dominic and Jacobs, John, *Disqualified from Benefit:the operation of benefit penalties*, Low Pay unit, London, 1988.

Callender, Claire 'Gender Inequality and Social Policy: women and the Redundancy Payments Scheme'. *Journal of Social Policy*, April 1985, 14(2) pp 189-213.

'Change in the compilation of the monthly unemployment statistics', *Employment Gazette*, March/April 1986, pp.107-8.

'Characteristics of the Unemployed', *Ministry of Labour Gazette*, April 1962, pp.131-7.

'Characteristics of the Unemployed, Survey Results', *Ministry of Labour Gazette*, April 1966, pp.156-7.

'Characteristics of the Unemployed: Sample Survey June 1973' *Department of Employment Gazette*, March 1974, pp.211-21.

'Characteristics of the Unemployed: Sample Survey June 1976', *Department of Employment Gazette*, June 1977, pp.559-74.

Child Poverty Action Group, 1984: *Changed Priorities Ahead: Evidence to the Review of Benefits for Children and Young People*, CPAG, London 1984.

Clark, Marjory, 'The Unemployed on Supplementary Benefit: Living Standards and Making Ends Meet on a Low Income', *Journal of Social Policy*, 7(4), 1978, pp.385-410.

Cooper, Steven, *The Education and Training Benefits*, PSI, London, 1985.

Coyle, Angela, *Work and the Family*, EOC, Manchester, 1983.

Crine, Alistair, 'Disabled and Unemployed', *Mind Out*, February 1981, pp.10-13.

Daniel, W.W., *A National Survey of the Unemployed*, PEP, London, 1974.

Daniel, W.W., *The Unemployed Flow*, PSI, London, 1981.

Daniel, W.W. and Stilgoe, Elizabeth, *The Impact of the Employment Protection Laws*, PSI, London, 1978.

Daniel, W.W., *Whatever happened to the working in Woolwich? A survey of redundancy in S.E. London*, PEP, London, 1972.

Deacon, Alan, *In Search of the Scrounger*, Bell and Sons, London, 1976.

Deakin, B.M. and Pratten, C.F., 'Economic Effects of YTS', *Employment Gazette*, October 1987, pp.491-7.

Department of Employment, *New Earnings Survey* 1970-84, HMSO, London,

Department of Employment, *Women and Work: A statistical survey*, HMSO, London, 1974.

Department of Employment and Productivity, *British Labour Statistics, Historical Abstract 1886-1968*, HMSO, London, 1971.

Department of Finance, *Digest of Statistics Northern Ireland*, 1957-1981 (two a year) HMSO, Belfast.

Department of Finance, *Social and Economic Trends in Northern Ireland 1978 and 1980*, HMSO, Belfast.

Department of Health and Social Security, *Annual Reports* 1968-1977, HMSO, London.

Department of Health and Social Security, *The Impact of the Reformed Structure of Income - Related Benefits*, DHSS, London, October 1987.

Department of Health and Social Security, *The Self Employed and Social Insurance: a Discussion Document*, DHSS, London, 1980.

Department of Health and Social Security, *Social Assistance: A Review of the Supplementary Benefits Scheme in Great Britain*, DHSS, London, 1978.

Department of Health and Social Security, *Social Security Statistics*, 1972-88, HMSO, London.

Department of Health and Social Security, *Supplementary Benefits Handbook 1984*, HMSO, London, 1984.

Department of Health and Social Security, *Unemployment Benefit Summary Statistics November, 1984*, DHSS, London, 1985.

Department of Social Services and Registrar General Northern Ireland, *The Northern Ireland Census 1981*, HMSO, Belfast, 1983.

Devlin, Paddy, *Yes we have no Bananas: Outdoor Relief in Belfast 1920-39*, Blackstaff Press, Belfast, 1981.

Dilnot, A.W., Kay, J.A. and Morris, C.N., *The Reform of Social Security*, Clarendon Press, Oxford, 1984.

Dilnot, A.W. and Kell, M., 'Male unemployment and women's work', *Fiscal Studies*, Vol 8(3), August 1987, pp.1-16.

Disability Alliance, *Invalid Procedures? A study of the control system for Invalidity Benefit*, London, 1983.

Disability Alliance, *A very high priority? The impact on people with disabilities of government policies since the last election*, London, 1980.

Ditch, John, *Hard Terms: Unemployment and Supplementary Benefits in Northern Ireland*, National Consumer Council, London, 1984.

'Duration of Unemployment and Age of Unemployed', *Department of Employment Gazette*, September 1971, p.830.

Elks, Laurie, *The Wage Stop*, Poverty Pamphlet 17, CPAG, London, 1974.

Employment for the 1990s, Cm 540, HMSO, London, 1988.

Evason, Eileen, *On the Edge: a study of poverty and long-term unemployment in Northern Ireland*, CPAG, London, 1985.

Equal Opportunities Commission, *Women and Men in Britain: A Statistical Profile*, EOC, Manchester, 1986.

Finn Dan, 'Claimant Advisers', *Unemployment Bulletin*, Summer 1988, pp.6-8.

Foot, Michael, *Aneurin Bevan 1897-1945*, Paladin, London, 1975.

'Forecasts of the future working population', *Ministry of Labour Gazette*, September 1962, p.346.

General Household Survey 1985, HMSO, London, 1987.

Gilbert, Bentley, B., *The Evolution of National Insurance in Great Britain*, Michael Joseph, London, 1966.

Gilbert, Bentley, B., *British Social Policy 1914-1939*, Batsford, London, 1970.

Glendinning, Caroline and Millar, Jane, *Women and Poverty in Britain*, Wheatsheaf Books, Brighton, 1987.

Gordon, Paul and Newnham, Anne, *Passport to Benefits? Racism in Social Security*, CPAG, London, 1985.

Harris, Jose, *William Beveridge: A biography*, Clarendon Press, Oxford, 1977.

Hakim, Catherine, 'Trends in the flexible workforce', *Employment Gazette*, November 1987, pp.549-60.

Help with Board and Lodging Charges for People on Low Incomes: Proposals for Change. A Consultation Document from DHSS, DHSS, London, 1986.

House of Commons, Committee on Public Accounts, Session 1986-7, *Adult Training Strategy: Manpower Services Commission*, HE223, HMSO, London, 1987.

House of Commons, Committee on Public Accounts, Session 1984-85, *Unemployment Benefit Services*, HC 434, HMSO, London, 1985.

House of Commons Hansard.

House of Commons Social Services Committee, Session 1981-82, *Age of Retirement*, Vol.1 *Report*; Vol.II *Minutes of Evidence and Appendices*, HC 26-1 and 26-II, HMSO, London, 1982.

'How many self-employed?', *Employment Gazette*, February 1983.

Hughes, P.R. and Hutchinson, Gillian, 'Changing characteristics of male unemployment flows 1972-81', *Employment Gazette*, September 1986, pp.365-8.

'An increase in earlier retirement for men', *Employment Gazette*, April 1980, pp.366-9.

Institute of Directors, *The Welfare State(1) submission to the Review of Benefits for Children and Young People*, London, 1984.

'The Job Release Scheme', *Department of Employment Gazette*, April 1978, pp.442-3 and 425.

Jordan, David, *A New Employment Programme for Disabled People*, Disability Alliance/Low Pay Unit, London, 1979.

Kohler,Peter A.and Zacher,Hans F.,(eds) *The Evolution of Social Insurance 1881-1981*, Studies of Germany, France, Great Britain, Austria and Switzerland, Frances Pinter, London, 1982.

Levy, Hermann, *Back To Work? The Case of the Partially Disabled Worker*, Fabian Society, London, 1941.

Lonsdale, Susan and Walker, Alan, *A Right to Work: Disability and Employment*, Disability Alliance/Low Pay Unit, London, 1984.

Makeham, Peter, 'The anatomy of youth unemployment', *Employment Gazette*, March 1950, pp.234-6.

Maki, Dennis and Spindler, Z.A., 'The Effect of Unemployment Compensation on the rate of Unemployment in Great Britain', *Oxford Economic Papers*, November 1975, pp.440-54.

Manpower Services Commission, *Annual Reports*, 1976-84, MSC, London.

MSC Manpower Review 1982, Manpower Services Commission, London, 1982.

Manpower Services Commission, *Corporate Plan 1986-1990*, MSC, London, 1986.

Manpower Services Commission, *Corporate Plan 1987,1991*, MSC, Sheffield, 1987.

Manpower Services Commission, *Developing Employment and Training Services for Disabled People*, MSC, London, 1978.

Manpower Services Commission, *Employment Rehabilitation:A review of the Manpower Services Commission's Employment Rehabilitation Services*, MSC, London, 1981.

Manpower Services Commission, *Manpower Review 1980*, MSC, London, 1980.

Manpower Services Commission, *Manpower Review 1982*, MSC, London, 1982.

Manpower Services Commission, *A New Training Initiative:A Consultative Document*, MSC, London, May 1981.

Manpower Services Commission, *A New Training Initiative:A Programme for Action*, Cmd 8455, HMSO, London, 1981.

Manpower Services Commission, *The Quota Scheme for the Employment of Disabled People:A Discussion Document*, MSC, London, 1979.

Manpower Services Commission, *Review and Plan 1977*, MSC, London, 1977.

Manpower Services Commission, *Review of Assistance for Disabled People: A report to the Commission*, MSC, London, 1982.

Manpower Services Commission, *Review of the first year of special programmes*, MSC, London, 1979.

Manpower Services Commission, *Review of the Quota Scheme for the Employment of Disabled People: A Report*, MSC, London, 1981.

Manpower Services Commission, *Review of Services for the Unemployed*, MSC, London, 1980.

Manpower Services Commission, *Towards a Comprehensive Manpower Policy*, MSC, London, 1976.

Manpower Services Commission, *Youth Task Group Report*, MSC, London, 1982.

McLaughlin, Eithne et al., *Work and Welfare Benefits*, Avebury, Aldershot, 1989.

Martin, Jean and Roberts, Ceridwen, *Women and Employment: A lifetime perspective*, Department of Employment/OPCS, HMSO, London, 1984.

Ministry of Labour, *Report on an Investigation into the Employment and Insurance History of a Sample of Persons Insured against Unemployment in Great Britain*, HMSO, London, 1927.

Ministry of National Insurance, *Annual Reports 1944-1952*, HMSO, London.

Ministry of Pensions and National Insurance, *Annual Reports 1953-1965*, HMSO, London.

Ministry of Pensions and National Insurance, *Benefits for very short spells of Unemployment or Sickness: Report of the National Insurance Advisory Committee*, Cmd 9609, HMSO, London, 1955.

Ministry of Social Security, *Annual Reports 1966-67*, HMSO, London (includes Reports of the Supplementary Benefits Commission).

Ministry of Social Security, *The Administration of the Wage Stop*, HMSO, London, 1967.

Moylan, Sue and Davies, Bob, 'The Disadvantages of the Unemployed', *Employment Gazette*, August 1980, pp.830-2.

Moylan, S. et al, *For Richer For Poorer? DHSS Cohort Study of Unemployed Men*, HMSO, London, 1984.

Mukherjee, Santosh, *Through no Fault of their own*, PEP/Macdonald, London, 1973.

National Audit Office, *Report by the Comptroller and Auditor General: Department of Health and Social Security, Department of Employment: Unemployment Benefit Service* HC 374, HMSO, London, 1985.

The National Assistance Board, *Annual Reports 1948-1965*, HMSO, London.

National Consumer Council, *The long term unemployed still at the bottom of the heap*, NCC, London, 1985.

National Consumer Council, *Of Benefit to All*, NCC, London, 1984.

National Union of Teachers, *Reform of Social Security*, London, 1985.

Nickell, S.J., 'The Effect of Unemployment and Related Benefits on the Duration of Unemployment', *The Economic Journal*, March 1979, pp.34-49.

Northern Ireland Assembly, *Report: Green Paper on the Reform of Social Security*, HMSO, Belfast, 1985.

Northern Ireland Social Security Statistics 1983-1987, DHSS, HMSO, Belfast.

Pahl, R.S., 'The Politics of Work', *Political Quarterly*, October/December 1985, pp.331-45.

Parker, S.R. et al, *Effect of the Redundancy Payment Act*, OPCS/HMSO, London, 1971.

'Payment of benefits to unemployed people', *Employment Gazette*, April 1981, pp,.197-203.

Peevor, R. et al, *From YOP to YTS: Meeting the special needs of the disabled*, MSC, London, 1983.

Pelican, John, *Studying on the Dole*, Youthaid, London, 1983.

Phelps, Brown, E.H., *The Growth of British Industrial Relations*, MacMillan, London, 1965.

Piachaud, David, *Children and Poverty*, Poverty Research Series No. 9, CPAG, London, 1981.

Reform of Social Security Vol. I, Cmnd 9517, HMSO, London, 1985.

Reform of Social Security: Programme for Change Vol. II, Cmnd 9518, HMSO, London, 1985.

Reform of Social Security: Background Papers Vol. III, Cmnd 9519, HMSO, London, 1985.

Reform of Social Security: Technical Annex, HMSO, London, 1985.

Reform of Social Security: Programme for Action, Cmnd 9691, HMSO, London, 1985.

Report of the Committee on Abuse of Social Security Benefits (the Fisher Report), Cmnd 5228, HMSO, London, 1973.

Report of the Inter-departmental Committee on Rehabilitation and Resettlement of Disabled Persons (the Tomlinson Report), Cmd 6415, HMSO, London, 1943.

Report from the Select Committee of the House of Lords on Unemployment, 142, HMSO, London, 1982.

Reports of the Social Security Advisory Committee, 1981, 1982/83, 1984, 1985, 1986/87, 1988, HMSO, London.

Report of the Unemployment Insurance Committee (the Blanesburgh Report), 2 volumes, HMSO, London, 1927.

Robson, William, *Social Security*, Fabian Society/George Allen and Unwin, London, 1943.

Royal Commission on Unemployment Insurance: Final Report, HMSO, London, 1932.

Sawyer, M.C.I., 'The Effect of Unemployment Compensation on the Rate of Unemployment in Great Britain', *Oxford Economic Papers*, March 1979, pp.135-46.

Smith, Catherine, T., *Redundancy Policies: A survey of current practice in 350 companies*, British Institute of Management, London, 1974.

Smith, David J., 'How unemployment makes the poor poorer', Police Studies, July 1980, pp.20-6.

Social Insurance and Allied Services (the Beveridge Report), Cmd 6404, HMSO, London, 1942.

Social Insurance and Allied Services: Memorandum from Organisations, Appendix G to Report by Sir William Beveridge, Cmd 6405, HMSO, London, 1942.

Social Insurance Part I, Cmd 6550, HMSO, London, 1944.

Social Security for all the People: An alternative to the New Poor Law, Society of Civil and Public Servants, London, 1985.

Social Security Review, *Income Support for the Unemployed in Australia: Towards a More Active System*, Department of Social Security, Canberra, 1988.

Solomos, John, 'Problems, but whose problems: the social construction of black youth unemployment and State polices, *Journal of Social Policy*, 14/4, October 1985, pp.527-54.

St John-Brooks, Caroline, 'Working for their benefit', *New Society*, 30 January 1987, p.22.

Supplementary Benefits Commission (Great Britain), *Annual Reports 1975-79*, HMSO, London.

Supplementary Benefits Commission (Northern Ireland), *Annual Reports 1974-79*, HMSO, Belfast.

Swain, Graham, 'YTS - Then what', *Youth in Society*, February 1985, pp.15-17.

Tomlinson, J.D., 'Women as 'Anomalies': The Anomalies Regulations of 1931, their Background and Implications', *Public Administration*, Vol. 62, Winter 1984, pp.423-37.

Training for employment (White Paper), Cm 316, HMSO, London, 1988.

Unemployment Assistance Board, *Annual Reports*, 1935 Cmd 5177; 1936 Cmd 5526; 1937 Cmd 5752; 1938 Cmd 6021, HMSO, London.

'Unemployment estimates from the Labour Force Survey compared with the monthly count', *Employment Gazette*, October 1955, pp.393-6.

'Unemployment figures: the claimant count and the Labour Force Survey', *Employment Gazette*, October 1986, pp.417-22.

'Unemployment Flows - New Statistics', *Employment Gazette*, August 1973, pp.301-7.

'Unemployment Flows: Northern Ireland', *Employment Gazette*, December 1984, pp.550-3.

University of York, *Living Standards of Unemployed Families: Characteristics of the Employed and Unemployed in the Family Finances Survey*, DHSS 117-9/82, University of York, Department of Social Administration and Social Work, Social Policy Research Unit, 1982.

University of York, *Standards of Unemployment Families: Incomes*, DHSS 110/6/82, University of York, Department of Social Administration and Social Work, Social Policy Research Unit, 1982.

Unqualified, Untrained and Unemployed: Report of a Working Party Set up by the National Youth Employment Council, Department of Employment/HMSO, London, 1974.

'The Unregistered Unemployed in Great Britain', *Department of Employment Gazette*, December 1976, pp.1331-6.

The Way Ahead: Benefits for Disabled People, Cm 917, HMSO, London, 1990.

Wells, William, *The Relative Pay and Employment of Young People*, Department of Employment, London, 1983.

White, Michael, *Long Term Unemployment and Labour Markets*, PSI, London, 1983.

White, Michael and McRae, Susan, *Young Adults and Long Term Unemployed*, PSI, London, 1989.

'Why train school-leavers?', *Unemployment Bulletin*, Autumn 1988, pp.1-12.

Woolton, G., *The Official History of the British Legion*, MacDonald and Evans Ltd, London, 1956.